General Editor

W. MONTGOMERY WATT

¶ Forthcoming titles in this series will include the following

*Islamic Spain*

*Islam in Africa south of the Sahara*

*Islamic Art*

*Islamic India*

*Islamic History*

*Ottoman History*

*Islam in China*

'. . . admirably produced . . . a special word is due in praise of the recently inaugurated Edinburgh *Islamic Surveys*. . . .'

Already published

*Islamic Philosophy and Theology*

¶ Henri Laoust, Collège de France, Paris, in *Middle East Journal*, ' Ce petit ouvrage clair, précis, fort bien documenté et agréable à lire, est plein de qualités . . . plein de finesse et d'intelligence. . . . Nous ne manquerons pas de le recommander vivement à nos étudiants.'

¶ S. D. Goitein, University of Pennsylvania, in *Muslim World*, October 1963, ' a really excellent survey . . . the writer speaks with authority and from closest contact with the subjects treated. The carefully selected bibliographies and the detailed index help much to enhance the value of the book, which augurs well for the series of *Islamic Surveys*.'

*A History of Islamic Law*

'This able survey of the genesis and growth of the law . . . will be of interest to students of Islam, lawyers, and those concerned with the practical application of Islamic law.' *British Book News*.

ISLAMIC SURVEYS 3

# *COUNSELS IN CONTEMPORARY ISLAM*

KENNETH CRAGG

*EDINBURGH*
*at the University Press*

EDINBURGH UNIVERSITY PRESS
1 George Square, Edinburgh 8
*North American Agent*
Aldine Publishing Co, 64 East Van Buren Street, Chicago 5
*Australian and New Zealand Agent*
Hodder & Stoughton Ltd, 429 Kent Street, Sydney
425 Little Collins Street, Melbourne
41 Shortland Street, Auckland



PRINTED BY R. & R. CLARK, LTD. EDINBURGH

# FOREWORD

In 1939 the prospect of a war which would involve many Asian nations made men in positions of responsibility in Britain suddenly aware of the meagre number of our experts in Asian languages and cultures. The Scarbrough Commission was set up, and its report led to a great expansion of Oriental and African studies in Britain after the war. In the third decade after 1939 events are making clear to ever-widening circles of readers the need for something more than a superficial knowledge of non-European cultures. In particular the blossoming into independence of numerous African states, many of which are largely Muslim or have a Muslim head of state, emphasises the growing political importance of the Islamic world, and, as a result, the desirability of extending and deepening the understanding and appreciation of this great segment of mankind. Since history counts for much among Muslims, and what happened in 632 or 656 may still be a live issue, a journalistic familiarity with present conditions is not enough; there must also be some awareness of how the past has moulded the present.

This series of "Islamic surveys" is designed to give the educated reader something more than can be found in the usual popular books. Each work undertakes to survey a special part of the field, and to show the present stage of scholarship here. Where there is a clear picture this will be given; but where there are gaps, obscurities and differences of opinion, these will also be indicated. Full and annotated bibliographies will afford guidance to those who want to pursue their studies further. There will also be some account of the nature and extent of the source material.

While the series is addressed in the first place to the educated reader, with little or no previous knowledge of the subject, its character is such that it should be of value also to university students and others whose interest is of a more professional kind.

The transliteration of Arabic words is essentially that of the second edition of *The Encyclopaedia of Islam* (London, 1960, continuing) with three modifications. Two of these are normal with most British Arabists, namely, *q* for *ḳ*, and *j* for *dj*. The third is something of a novelty. It is the replacement of the ligature used to show when two consonants are to be sounded together by an apostrophe to show when they are to be sounded separately. This means that *dh*, *gh*, *kh*, *sh*, *th* (and in non-Arabic words *ch* and *ẓh*) are to be sounded together; where there is an apostrophe, as in *ad'ham*, they are to be sounded separately. The apostrophe in this usage represents no sound, but, since it only occurs between two consonants (of which the second is *h*), it cannot be confused with the apostrophe representing the glottal stop (*ḥamẓa*), which never occurs between two consonants.

In the case of Indian names, where a man has written a book in English (or been written about), the aim has been to keep the form of the name used on the title-page. An exact transliteration has usually been given in brackets after the first instance, but sometimes it has been enough to add diacritical marks to the name. Unfortunately some names occur in several different forms, and in these cases the most recent practice has generally been followed, with a bias towards a simplified version of the system just described. It is hoped the inevitable inconsistencies will not cause undue pain to any purist.

W. Montgomery Watt
GENERAL EDITOR

# CONTENTS

# PREFACE

"A PEOPLE in the middle" is how the Qur'ān in an oft-quoted passage describes the community of Islam. Modern Western usage has unwittingly confirmed it by referring characteristically to Islamic heartlands as "the Middle East". But the Qur'ān's intention in the phrase, enigmatic as it is, should be seen as wider and richer than the geographical. Muslim moralists sometimes read in it the vocation of their communities to ethical moderation and modest enjoyment which avoid the excesses of the profligate and the abstemious. Mystical writers take the sense further and see in *terra Islamica* "a land where things are for ever bearing witness to ideas and ideas to things; where things and ideas, alternately and simultaneously, are exalted and humiliated", in a "constant shift from act to essence, from abstract to concrete".[1] Orthodox theologians are sure that "middle-ness" points to the duty of trusteeship and mediation by which the faith from God passes over into the unbelieving hearts of men by the fidelity of its due custodians. More pragmatic historians may simply agree that Islam late in its fourteenth century is between the times, heir to a large and tenacious past, and set towards a future of radical change.

The chapters that follow are a brief review of certain aspects of this equation in Islam today between past and present, between apprehension and confidence, between the stuff of events and the dictates of the spirit. With the companion books in this series of

[1] J. Berque: *The Arabs*, Eng. trans., London, 1964, p. 283.

Islamic Surveys it is no more than an abridgement of a vast and complex theme and, for that reason, wide open to criticism for omissions and silences. Experts in the field will appreciate how much is left un-noticed. But the lay reader may find the small scale of the map a serviceable introduction to the business in hand. Only the Arab East, Turkey, Pakistan and Indian Islam are included. Persian, Indonesian, African and European or Soviet Islam are not discussed. The title has been deliberately intended and should be understood strictly as it stands. Anything more ambitious at the head of these pages would be pretentious.

The General Editor has written in the Foreword of the impulse in events of Western history to a surer knowledge of the faiths and cultures of the rest of the world. That need, freely admitted, is best fulfilled as a motive in a genuine effort to learn Islam, not as *our* "Eastern" problem, but from within its own ethos grappling with the encounter from the other side. Only so shall we hear it authentically in its own counsel chamber.

This is the sort of book which could only be viable as one of a series. Its range can perhaps be poetically distilled into the component elements of the English, or rather the Greek, word "character", which began life as a mark or impression engraved or stamped into some receptive material like wax or clay. The marks hardened, literally and metaphorically, into letters and signs, and so, in turn, into types and then, onwards, into people representing or portraying types, into "characters" and *dramatis personae*, and thus, again, into the qualities and natures of people themselves, into "character" as the sum total of a man's being. What follows is about all these—the impact of events, the receptivity of history, the hardening of attitudes, the postures of leaders and mentors, the roles of guardian and innovator, and under all the abiding stuff and genius of a household of faith, "a people in the middle". We are looking, as it were, for the autograph of a religion. But when we ask for it we know what a large thing and a fleeting moment it embodies.

KENNETH CRAGG, CANTERBURY, 1965

## ACKNOWLEDGEMENTS

THE Edinburgh University Press is grateful to the following publishers for permission to quote copyright material. To Collins for a quotation from *Letters from a Traveller*, (Teilhard de Chardin); to Oxford University Press for quotations from *Civilization on Trial*, (Toynbee) and *A Sleep of Prisoners*, (Fry); to the University of Oklahoma Press for a quotation from *Turkey in my Time*, (Yalman); to the University of Chicago Press for a quotation from *Modern Trends in Islam*, (Gibb); to the Hogarth Press for a quotation from a poem by William Plomer; to Djambatan N.V. for a quotation from *'Urubah and Religion*; and to the Editor of *The Middle East Journal* for a quotation from an article by Phillips Talbot.

أَمْرُهُمْ شُورَىٰ بَيْنَهُمْ

*Their affairs are by counsel among them*

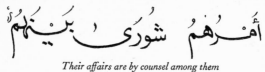

CHAPTER I

# CHARTING THE DEBATE

A STRANGER to the Qur'ān might be forgiven if he found its chapter-headings a rather daunting and puzzling array: "The Blood Clots", "The Spider", "The Constellations", "Ṭā Hā", "The Chambers" and the rest. But Sura 42, with the title "Counsel", might attract him as promising a more obvious and illuminating theme. If he pursued its invitation he would at length reach the title word in verse 38, in the midst of a description of the loyal Muslim. There, between the two most characteristic injunctions of Islam about "performing the prayer and paying the alms", he would read that Muslims "conduct their affairs by mutual consultation" (*shūrā*).

The allusion is somewhat enigmatic and commentators are not unanimous about its precise significance. Some take it strongly as a Divine decree enjoining the duty of "democratic" discussion in all matters; others as possibly relating to a pattern of family or tribal concert in things social and economic affecting the well-being and orderliness of the community. For the rest of the passage goes on to require the avoidance of all heinous and degrading sins, and moderation in acts of retaliation, with the extolling of forgiveness. Organs of public opinion which might give form and force to *shūrā*, or counsel, will concern us later. Of Islam as an entity shaped, in measure, by self-direction there can be no doubt. It is the range and quality of its counsels through the crowded years of this twentieth century with which this book is concerned.

How circumstances in that time have conspired to evoke and exert the will to self-expression and provide the themes of debate! So unprecedented have the issues been that counsel itself, in its criteria and authority, has become a central topic of discussion, making an intriguing equation between what defines the community and what constitutes it. The *shūrā* of Sura 42.38 may derive, etymologically, from the action of extracting honey from a row of hives—a prosaic picture indeed for the vigorous and sometimes passionate business of eliciting and recruiting the opinions and verdicts of pundits and populace over wide-ranging matters of Islamic fulfilment and destiny. That there is both sweetness and sting in the activity the zest and controversy of current apology plainly indicate. The parallel might even extend to the curative industry of the bees, which Sura 16 celebrates as being among God's signs of mercy. At all events, human counsel spreads its reckonings far and wide, is clearly a collective pursuit and tends to gather its forces into recognisable schools, or hives, of adherence for the tasting of the systematisers and the sampling of readers. Numbers, accumulation and mystery belong alike to the extraction of honey and the formation of a communal mind. But here the suggestiveness of a word metaphor must stay. For it is in fact no more than a lexicographer's idea and in any case makes no allowance for the unpredictability of real life as men know it in this time.

"What a colossal world it is for a religion to assimilate",[1] as Teilhard de Chardin remarked in his *Letters from a Traveller*. Islam, of course, as a supreme theism, is faced with precisely the same issues now stirring the depths of Christian theology. It is called, no less, to the virtues he exemplified of gallant commitment to the discipline of devotion on the one hand and the rigours of scientific integrity on the other. The universe in its vastness is one for the mosque and for the church. What de Chardin observes about Sinai is true for Muḥammad's Mount Ḥirā'. On ship in the Suez Canal he wrote:

> "I would have liked to land on those rocky slopes (Sinai), not only to test them with my hammer, but also to learn whether I too could hear the voice of the burning bush. . . . But has not the moment passed when God speaks in the desert . . .?"[2]

The scientific recession in the sense of God, the vacancies that allegedly call for a religionless humanity—these press upon Islam no less than on the faith of the Incarnation. The Qur'ān, with its splendid insistence on nature as a realm of Divine "signs", is squarely confronted by the contemporary temptation to find in it no more than observable phenomena and natural law. Islam is one with the Christian Gospel in its answer to the question: What is *given* in nature? Merely data for science, or reverent dominion for man? It is therefore involved in the identical battle for the due sanctification of things and in a common paradox of the secular and the holy. Though it disallows the Christian clues of the Incarnation and the Cross, Islam has the same vocation to be an "open" religion, having business with all doubt because it has need of all truth, and in this way vindicating its ringing Quranic conviction that God "has not created the world in jest". (Sura 21.16; and 44.38.) The seriousness of Islam, which many have noted as characterising even demeanour and temper in some quarters, means that it can properly abandon or decline no issue pertaining to the integrity of theism. Its intolerance of idolatry and blasphemy should mean a perpetual alertness to the casual suspensions of belief and adoration so characteristic of the present scene. In other words, to be alive to the cosmos without fear and without reserve is the ultimate condition of all other counsels.

But cosmology, and cosmonauts, do nothing to ameliorate the problems terrestrial. Of these Islam has its generous share. We must take stock, as it were, of the counsel-chamber of circumstance in which its decisions are taken. This, in turn, means some brief synopsis or assessment of the main lines of Islamic self-consciousness. We may then be in a position to estimate the topics and trends of the great debate.

It may be useful to broach this by way of illustration from the recent experience of a different religio-cultural system, namely, India. Speaking to Chancellor Adenauer of Germany, Madame Vijayalakshmi Pandit is reported to have said that the Chinese aggression on India's northern borders had called in question the spiritual bases of Indian policies and compelled a search for a new "metaphysic" of power. For this reason there are those who see the intrusion of China into the Indian mind as a major turning-point in the latter's history. National solidarity has been sustained but with a new element of "realism" in the face of a major physical threat to "the soul of India" requiring a physical defence which in fact imperils ancient ideas and present social objectives. If one may leave aside the issues of Kashmir, this represents a new dimension in the experience of the Hindu mind in modern times. It is plainly different from the quality of the struggle that terminated the British Raj, while that Raj itself for long years had carried the responsibility of external defence. So there is a fundamental crisis of spirit in the Indian mind born of the current issues of power as these are determined by the postures of China.[3]

It is illuminating to reflect on this and to note the contrasted case of contemporary Islam. That world also has passed dramatically out of the era of tutelage in which the external preservation of whole stretches of it was in the care of foreign force—British power in the sub-continent, in Muslim Africa, in Malaya; British influence and treaty power in the Gulf, in Egypt and the Sudan and variously elsewhere; Dutch power in the East Indies; French authority in North Africa and other French territories. All these, and other Islamic areas like Turkey and Iran which in nineteenth-century terms were in charge of their own securities, have come upon an independent existence in which it is now their own business to determine themselves in the national and political arena. There is no place here to retell the swift tale of these emancipations in our generation, with emerging new, or old, Muslim nations on every hand. The inner logic of one of them, Pakistan, will be traced in the next chapter. In sum, they constitute a great new actuality of Islamic existence in every way comparable to the Indian sense of Indian self-reliance which China alerted to deep self-examination in 1962. Two further points must immediately be made. The one is that Islamic self-awareness in this period is quite differently constituted from the Indian in respect of the themes of power: the other is that its confrontations, with the peculiar exception of Israel, have been internal and domestic. Contemporary Islam has suffered no external challenge as drastic as the Chinese to India, but its instincts and mentality have been no less tested by the evils of poverty, suffering and society, with no less radical summons to self-assessment.

From the very beginnings of Islam there has always existed a vigorous approval of the necessities of power. Unlike the Indian mind in its apotheosis in Mahatma Gandhi, Islamic thought, since the precedents of the Prophet himself, has regarded physical means as indispensable to religious ends. There has been from the outset a conjunction of creed and state, of faith and polity. This, of course, is evident in the career of Muḥammad, in the nature of the *Hijra* (the migration from Mecca to Medina) and in the form of the Caliphate. *Fitna* in the Qur'ān means in the early days of prophetic exposure the tribulations of the faithful: after Muslim political success it becomes the sedition by which the enemies of the faith in power conspire against it. This is the clearest measure of the truth that Islam finds full justification in the alliance of necessary, protective, effective force. Its strength and genius lie in its complete freedom from inhibition about the use and validity of physical action furthering religious community. India's experience from China would require and occasion no Islamic metaphysical re-appraisals.

This characteristic affinity with power on the part of Islam means that the events of the last few decades have to be seen not simply as the recession of Western empire but the recovery of Islamic patterns. There is in them not simply a negative quality of imperial retreat but the positive restoration of a true destiny after a strange and dismal aberration. We quite fail to see the clue to contemporary Islam if we miss this fact. Islam under the British, or the French, or the Dutch, was an incomprehensible eventuality, quite inexplicable by any recognisable Islamic criteria. How should the people of the final faith pass under tutelage to the rulers of another? The finality of Islam should mean the finality of the Islamic. Here, of course, lay the misery and dismay of Indian Islam in the nadir of its fortunes after the Mutiny, a calamity of spirit from which it was only rescued by the sound sense and spirit of Syed Ahmad Khan (Sayyid Aḥmad Khān). He it was who insisted that *Dār al-Islām*[4] could and should be seen in Islam under British government, since mosques were open, the fast of *Ramaḍān* kept and pilgrimage allowed, even if by the full criteria of statehood Islam was wanting.

By this vigorous logic he enabled his fellow-Muslims to ride out their painful perplexity at a history gone awry. Some aspects of this question will recur below. What is immediately important is that the dilemma is almost everywhere now at an end. Once more, authentically and indisputably, Muslims have Muslim rule and power belongs with Islam.

It is, of course, no longer unitary power, no more caliphal, no more pan-Islamic. It is fractured into numerous nations. But it is power Islamically wielded, which is what power should be, at least where Muslims are involved. So by this most proper of tokens, Islam has recovered a true self-possession. This is the first, and last, consideration for all estimate of its current counsels. They are counsels with executive opportunities, at least as far as the political admits: subject to the imponderables which beset us all, or the vagaries of economic or technological contingence, they are operative counsels. The lease of power to the states of Islam is a lease of life to her ideologies.

Our other claim is that the major issues awaiting the Islamic determination of Muslim states have been inward and domestic. Israel is seen, of course, as an abiding threat to the security, and certainly the spiritual composure, of the Arab world. But Zionism apart, the occupations of the Muslim mind within the new nationalisms have been internal. Yet they tax its resources as urgently as the Chinese presence at India's northern gateways. There are the inner problems of power itself, its disposition within the state, its roots in the popular will and its responsibility to public opinion and Islamic ideology. It is significant that in most Muslim states since independence there have been crises of constitution making and breaking in the search or struggle for effective power. Within the issues of power and its exercise are the sharp problems of poverty and the ever-growing pressures of population. Muslim peoples are among the most desperate areas of the world in this regard, where some 10 to 15 per cent of the populace suffer from malnutrition of a chronic kind and about 50 per cent from deficient diet inadequate for vitality. They belong with that society of frustration where the population density, outpacing all economic development, seems to mean a bitter exchange of eventual adult starvation for the earlier infant mortality.

This fundamental burden is only sharpened by the contrast of Western opulence which persistently penetrates into Eastern awareness through the ubiquitous presence of films, radio and the press. Marx's prophecy of the increasing inequality of the classes, internally within capitalism, capitalism itself has found a tactic to prevent. But it is being unexpectedly fulfilled in terms of external and national disparities. The world, in fact, is manifesting ever widening divergencies of wealth and poverty. This tragic truth of our time is, moreover, blatant and unconcealed. There are no more any seclusions or privacies of wretchedness: the poor know themselves poor with the sort of disquiet, unknown to most of their forebears, which comes from glimpsing the affluence they are denied.

Nor are the provoking vistas of wealth entirely Westward and outward. Technology has its local Midas touch, more especially in the oil of the Middle East. Where soil seems all too often an equation in poverty, oil, in an ever more avidly mobile world, is a sort of liquid gold. Having in mind the massive revenues accruing from it in the lands of Islamic genesis what becomes of the Qur'ān's anxiety about usury? And how penetrating are their consequences, dispersed in fact or in potential through the entire region, despite the strange inequalities of the providence in geology.

"That broker . . .
That daily vow-break, he that wins all . . .
That smooth faced gentleman, tickling 'commodity'.
Commodity, the bias of the world . . .
And why rail I on this commodity
But for because he hath not wooed me yet?
Since kings break faith upon commodity,
Gain be my lord, for I will worship thee."[5]

And with the power to get wealth or to feel an envy at its getting by another, go the steady, subtle pressures of the activism, the human self-sufficiency, the neglect of the dimensions of the spirit and the claims of the "ideal". Secularity weighs heavily upon the world of Islam, the more so for the devastating speed of contemporary changes and the onset of revolutions, material, industrial, nuclear, which in their Western matrix spread themselves rather less feverishly among the generations. In some places today the single father-son sequence marks a transition from the economic or social patterns of an Abrahamic antiquity to those of the tanker jetty and television. Where the older generation asks suspiciously: "How shall we know it's us without our past?"[6] the younger, coming generation answers ardently: "How shall we be ourselves without this present?" And there, in personal disquiets and ambitions, is the brunt of what Arnold Toynbee called "our non-contemporary world". What do dogma and creed, mosque and sermon, make of it?

This is the world, beneath the stars, as well as beyond them, which "religion must assimilate". The reader must turn elsewhere for the detailed history of the developments to which our counsels and counsellors here are Islam's reaction and response. It is clearly impossible to comprehend in this limited span the diverse and tumultuous events which have belonged with

Islam in this century, from Morocco to Indonesia, from Ankara to Zanzibar. Unless a survey is to become a dull catalogue it must be content with selection. If we ignore the Masjumi or Djakarta, or the Ismāʿīlī in Bombay, or seem to neglect the Wahhābī and the Sanūsī, and have no space for Shīʿī complexities and the claims of the Bahāʾī, our plea must be an alibi of exposition. We are occupied elsewhere in the wide panorama. Selection of course may be wise or unwise, but at least in this context it is inescapable. The aim is to take the measure, or feel the pulse, of Islamic responsibility to Islam, against the background of its current history. The key-notes of that history are opportunity through political self-reliance, diversity in new national and separate statehoods, recovery thereby of a basic condition in fragmented form, perplexity in face of bewildering and proliferating questions of human life and death, and a strange paradox of elation and disenchantment, of aspiration and illusion.

It follows that the counsels we must explore are in part strident, in part timid, sometimes sanguine, often competitive, on occasion naïve, but always invoking loyalty and Islamic fulfilment. They are by no means only verbal and vocal: they take shape in institutions, policies, societies, brotherhoods and parties. Yet in this writer's view, with the encouragement of Sura 42.38, "counsels" seems the preferable word. For what we have to investigate can be too easily obscured if we see it solidified into "movements", "schools" or even "trends". All these may be said to exist, in some sense. But it remains part of the complexity of our whole concern, that they tend to disappoint the tidy organiser and frustrate the neat expositor, by failing to supply the continuities he demands or by breaking away from his analytical scheme into unpredictable vagaries and contradictions of their own. So many pioneers, as we must see, have in fact failed to achieve sustained and identifiable following and the whole story has many loose ends and *non sequiturs*, as do the counsels themselves. Passion, exuberance, expectation, recrimination, brood over all and, given the pace and thrust of contemporary change, no diagnosis at this point can be more than an interim report. The very tolerance of ambiguity which many apologists exhibit complicates the tasks of their reviewer. How is the careful analyst to react to the position stated, with fair approval, by Isma'il Ragi al-Faruqi?

> "The Islamist is fully entitled to make . . . such use (of the concept of Islam) as he pleases, unfettered by the kind of ambiguities which beset any nationalist. . . . The concept of Islam easily lends itself to distension so as to enable the Islamist to outdo all opponents by welcoming every new value discovered, as already included within Islam."

He goes on to cite what he calls the "classical representatives of this position" in the Muslim Brotherhood.

> "Its classic expression is a word of advice given by al-Murshid al-'Āmm (the supreme guide) Ḥasan al-Bannā, to a group of young followers: 'If the communists', he reportedly said, 'argue with you saying: 'Our principles are humane, tolerant, assisting the poor and weak, realizing equality among men, social, economic and political justice,' then answer: 'So be it: our principles do more than include yours. You can boast of no principle we cannot match or excel!' This same idea is found in almost every book or pamphlet associated with the movement."[7]

The same instinct to claim as Islamic whatever is praiseworthy characterises more than the Ikhwān al-Muslimūn. Dr. Faruqi himself sees "Islam" as "the transcendental ideal values themselves".[8] From this it follows that we must add to the general difficulties of our survey arising from place, time, circumstance and diversity, a further element of ambiguity, or even confusion and pretension, in the very understanding of what it is that counsellors have under discussion.

> "Islam, being a normative realm of value, is dissociable from any reality that is identified with it. Islam is not the Muslims' social system, nor the Muslims' theological, aesthetic or other system, but that which all these strive to realise.... Any criticism, therefore, directed to that reality cannot ever discredit Islam."[9]

One might be tempted to conclude that if any report from outside about those "systems" of Muslims proves bewildering this fact will be the surest indication of its fidelity.

For observable purposes, Islam in the end must be what Muslims say it is, only we need first to identify the Muslim. Any circularity implicit here is inseparable from the nature of all faith and practice. There must always be in the end an interdependence between belief and believers, between religion and the religious, between dogma and community. But that inter-relation will be itself a primary theme of debate and controversy. Dictionaries, in the end, come from lexicographers, however much language is woven on the loom of speech and society. The counsels, as the Qur'ān observes, are "among them" and must therefore include credentials as well as claims. This underlying theme of authority, the "Who is he?" within the "What says he?" must be in mind throughout.

By the same token the institutional, historic and documentary "authorities" of Islam are squarely set in the centre of the counsels we must review. Even the superficial questions have a way of becoming fundamental, and the peripheral central. In its ideological self-sufficiency under active process and searching obligations, contemporary Islam is set in more crucial relation to its Prophet, its Qur'ān, its *Sharī'a* and its Tradition, than at any other point in its fourteen centuries. It will be necessary in what follows to keep each of these in mind as denominators of concern. Apology must be studied, not only in relation to names and pioneers, schools and disciples, but also in respect of its verdicts and ventures *vis-à-vis* Quranic status and content, prophetic biography and communal heritage. We must try to assess the present position in Islamic reception of the Qur'ān and in the significance of the prophet-figure. No attempt can here be made to describe or analyse legal changes. But it will be imperative to consider the counsels that go with them and, in particular, the bearing of religious sanction on social behaviour. We probably do not need to be warned that there are pitfalls innumerable in trying to assess a scene that holds both President Habib Bourguiba and Syed Abul-'Ala Mawdudi (Sayyid Abū-l-'Alā' al-Mawdūdī) or the current bitter debate about the minimum marriage age in Pakistan.[10] It is in such issues that the ultimates take controversial, concrete shape. There, with apologies to Isma'il al-Faruqi, Islam, for partisans if not for philosophers, is ardently, even defiantly, "associated" with certain "establishments", conservative or liberal, Zealot or Herodian,[11] for which men contend and politicians campaign.

Suitably chastened by these tokens of our formidable business, how may we plot its course? It seems reasonable to begin with "Counsel for Pakistan" as being the most evident single institutional expression of the mind of Islam. It has the merit of being decisive in its character and, set in its whole context, there is no more definitive event in the history of Islam. The creation of Pakistan is a cumulative verdict about Islam, on the part of a large contemporary segment of it, taken in circumstances of elemental quality. It has the further merit of focussing, in its special form, the general, pervasive theme of nation, state and faith which belongs to all Islam today. From this chapter of counsel, it will be natural to proceed to two major figures, the one of Arab, the other of Indo-Pakistani, Islamic interpretation, and from a study of their intellectual leadership and their main pre-occupations to pass to other exchanges and positions, leading towards some judgement on the status of recurrent themes and reflections in prospect.

CHAPTER 2

# COUNSEL FOR PAKISTAN

"WHEN the Hindu stretched out his hand for the sceptre the Muslim cried out for Pakistan."[1] Though shortening the perspective by a dramatic licence, this is a memorable statement of the truth. When Indian independence became a near reality, Islam took counsel with its inner logic, and with the inflexibility of Muhammad Ali Jinnah (Muḥammad 'Alī Jinnāḥ) opted for separate statehood. The story is an index to the Muslim mind, and as such needs to be carefully sifted, with the pros and cons of a crowded scene, and factors both of absurdity and inevitability which belonged with it. Hardly less instructive is the aftermath of the state's creation in the decade and a half of subsequent endeavour and confusion.

First as demand, and then as actuality, Pakistan embodies the Muslim assurance that Islam is a religio-political unity, unique, separate, distinctive, demanding and deserving survival by continental disruption. It stands as an instrument of the Islamic sense of identity and as the price of its continuity. It constitutes a kind of active apologia, which both provokes and enforces a host of apologetic words, and a measure of the degree to which Islam sees itself as *sui generis*. It should be seen as the twentieth-century version of Islamic order, combining immediate opportunism with age-long and ultimate factors. Its progress from idea to fact is a complex of forces not easy to reduce without risk of injustice to their brief essentials.

The sense of a long and splendid past has always haunted the Muslim outlook in India. The glories of Akbar and Aurangzib bequeathed a tradition of power and dominance. The dissolution of that heritage and the slow deterioration of Muslim fortunes produced the crisis of the Indian Mutiny. SYED AHMAD KHAN (1817–98) emerged from that nadir of fortune as a clear figure with a virile leadership, aimed at lifting the Muslim spirit from sullenness and lethargy and from the rigid conservatism of such movements, of Wahhābī sympathy, which in the late eighteenth and early nineteenth centuries had been articulate in the Indian Muslim scene. These were the Farā'idī and the Ahl-i-Ḥadīth, mainly centred in Bengal and Bihar, whose spiritual children in more recent times have been the Ahl-i- Qur'ān and the Kharksars. Their traditionalism Ahmad Khan set out to counter. Against mountainous prejudices he strove to "reconcile" his fellow-Muslims to the British Raj and the Western ethos as consistent with *Dār al-Islām*. Fear of secularity he insisted should not exclude a proper welcome for science and technology. He aimed to adjust Islam intellectually to the West and politically to British presence.

This called for the promotion of friendly relations and mutual interpretation. It also presupposed an openhearted attitude towards Hindus and the ideal of a united India. Ahmad Khan's revision in old age of some of his attitudes should not be allowed to obscure the essential dissonance of the later Pakistan notion with the main lesson of his career, though it should be kept in mind that in his day Hindu-Muslim susceptibilities were still far from the test of a "transfer of power". It was of course the slow fitful advent of that climax which precipitated the incompatible realities.

Yet Ahmad Khan's achievement and its great symbol in the Aligarh College must be given their true proportions. In his *Essays on the Life of Mohammed* we hear in early form the oft repeated counsel about discrimination over the real and the traditional Islam.

> "I hope every lover of the truth will candidly and impartially investigate the truth of Islam and make a just and accurate distinction between its real principles and those . . . that are solely the productions of those persons whom we designate as learned men, divines, doctors and lawyers."[2]

The clue for him to such discrimination between the essence and the accretion lies in his philosophy of nature. Hence the epithet *nechari* sometimes associated with his school. Writing in his enterprising Commentary on the Bible, he averred:

> "We acknowledge that Nature is the work of God and Revelation is His Word: that no discrepancy should ever occur between them forasmuch as both proceed from the same source."[3]

Considering that he wrote in 1862, it is his progressive will we should emphasise rather than what might be reprehensible at a later point, namely, his easy assertion that all progress in knowledge will conveniently confirm the Qur'ān or that, if it seems not to do so, the fault, dear Brutus, is in ourselves and our stupidity.

But the present bearing of this intellectual stance lies in his assurance that Islam must get on terms with the future, and not pine or sulk in the *Dār al-Ḥarb* version of British India,[4] as if by the cult of self-pity and a curse on the fates the day could be won. Yet, precisely as this galvanising of Muslims proceeded, the ultimate, further issue deepened, namely, the form of Muslim–Hindu relationship. Clearly they were natural allies in the pursuit of political independence, yet their instinctive repulsions, religious, social, personal, even culinary, made for the paradox of co-activity in mutual avoidance. And to make the situation triangular there was the over-all fact of British government. Should common political action expect or evolve cultural unity?—a question with a growing import as popular representation was by stages conceded. The Congress had been founded in 1885, the Muslim League in 1906—the year of separate electorates.

During the three decades from that date until the "conversion" of Jinnah to "Pakistan" in 1939 (or thereabouts: some would say 1938), there was a real prospect of all-India Hindu–Muslim unity. In retrospect the hope may have some aspects of a mirage, but it was solid enough in many minds. On what were the "federal" Muslims relying and why did their policy finally collapse under the pressure of the "Pakistan" alternative? It is a narrative indispensable to any measure of the Islamic self-definition implicit in partition.

Externally Indian Muslims sought security and insurance in the pan-Islamic dream. The Khilafatist movement, led by the brothers Shawkat and Muḥammad ʿAlī, hoped—as the event proved against all the logic of Arab nationalism—for a revival of the Caliphate during the twenties. For a reactivated Ottoman power they had petitioned the Allies at Versailles. They had been concerned also, in part, for the Muslim custody of the twin sanctuaries of Mecca and Medina, which the establishment by Ibn Saʿūd of his hegemony in the Hijaz decided unilaterally. With this, and the force of Arab national feeling calling for independence, and most of all the new political philosophy of Muṣṭafā Kemāl Atatürk liquidating "Ottomanism" from within Turkey, the Khilafatists found themselves abandoned by events, though in 1931 Muḥammad ʿAlī's burial within the Ḥaram ash-Sharīf in Jerusalem symbolised the deep pan-Islamic mission of his life.

The end of Khilafatism left Indian Islam emotionally adrift and bereft of its main psychological assurance (from world Islam), from within which it could contemplate with equanimity a political unity of action with Hindus. Out of this "vacuum" grew the temptation to fall back upon aggressive communalism and in turn to the argument that the "independent" form of communalism is the two nation theory, with partition as its goal. Yet the temptation found stubborn rejection in many quarters *in the name of Islam*. Mawlana Abul-Kalam Azad (Mawlānā Abū-l-Kalām Āzād), its main antagonist, will be studied in a later chapter. But he had many allies through the thirties including the redoubtable Jinnah himself, who had joined the Muslim League in 1913 only on the strict condition that it did not imply any disloyalty to the idea and cause of united India. In 1919 he gave evidence before the Joint Select Committee that he wished to see an end, as early as possible, to all distinction in politics between Hindus and Muslims,[5] and this attitude he sustained into the late thirties. Muḥammad ʿAlī was equally explicit:

> "In India we shall have something better than an America, because we shall not only have a United States, but we shall have United Faiths."[6]

He denied that temporal power was a necessity for Islamic existence which was "a spiritual force never dependent on temporal dominance. . . ."[7] Muhammad Iqbal (see Chapter 4) was in his equivocal way also a "federal" Muslim, with his poetic repudiation of the supposed cleavage over idolatry between the two religions:

> "And if the Brahmin, preacher, biddeth us
> Bow down to idols, furrow not thy brow.

Our God Himself who shaped an idol fair
Bade Cherubim before an idol bow."[8]

"An infidel before his idol with wakeful heart
Is better than the religious man asleep in his
mosque."[9]

Both Iqbal and Jinnah in 1931 accepted the principle of All-India Federation. At the Round Table Conference in 1931–3, there was the following exchange with Yūsuf ʿAlī and Muhammad Zafrullah Khan (the latter subsequently, and briefly, Foreign Minister of Pakistan):

"Quest. 9598 'Will they tell me whether there is a scheme for Federation of (Muslim) Provinces under the name of "Pakistan"?'
Ans. 9598 A. Yusuf Ali: 'As far as I know it is only a student's scheme: no responsible people have put it forward.'
Quest. 9599 'What is Pakistan?'
Ans. 9599 Zafrullah Khan: 'So far as we have considered it we have considered it chimerical and impracticable.' "[10]

They were referring to one Raḥmat ʿAlī, who, apparently, had first thought of the name, Pakistan, country of the pure (*pak*), formed of the initial letters of Punjab, Afghan, Kashmir and Sind, with "i" supplied and "tan" added, these being the (western) states he visualised within it. But he rallied his Cambridge followers to the notion, as to an obscure, indeed, a hopeless, cause.

Yet the "extreme" notion came to pass within fifteen more years and there are few more total and rapid reversals in history. Iqbal had made a proposal at

Allahabad in 1930, in a somewhat casual way, about four north-western provinces having administrative unity and seems to have believed that Muslim nationalism might need territorial sanction. Yet it ran entirely counter to much of his philosophy. The really decisive advocacy, as well as the epitome of the causation, belongs with a quite different biography, that of Jinnah. Poets might rhyme and pamphleteers (like Raḥmat ʿAlī with his bitter tirades against "Indianism") might rant, but the real task was a politician's.

Jinnah saw the inherent inevitabilities, the hard underlying alienations, and the fact that independence would precipitate irreversible destiny. It had then better be safe and inalienable. So he espoused the student's chimera. His adherence to the Pakistan concept brought just the element of calculating ambition, astute statecraft, powerful logic and insistent diplomacy which the cause demanded and circumstances approved. Muslims anyway held the whip hand, as Gandhi himself perceived:

> "If the vast majority of Muslims regard themselves as a separate nation, having nothing in common with Hindus and others, no power on earth can compel them to think otherwise."[11]

Jinnah knew this too, and setting himself in the van of a policy which could attain power and dismember a continent, he took up the still large business of convincing "the vast majority of Muslims" as to their proper separateness and its need for territorial, political and national sanction. In succeeding, he made himself irresistible.

The Quaid-i-Azam (Qā'id-i-Aʿẓam), as Jinnah came to be known, remains one of the most enigmatic figures in twentieth-century Islam, and yet for all that somehow representative. The most ardent advocate of

Islamic statehood was not a noticeably religious man. He was content to gather a wide range of Muslim sentiment behind the policy for Pakistan, while deliberately evading the definition of the Islamic state he demanded. This may have been politically shrewd but it was spiritually barren, and brought many confusions subsequently home to roost. He had found the one form of Muslim crusade capable of rousing and rallying the masses. Yet he moved among them without being of them. He was an aristocrat become demagogue. English in manner, dress and outlook, he learned Urdu only late in life. Irrational fervour in the crowd was for him no more than a negotiating asset. Yet he asserted over the population an almost mystical authority once the die was cast. His speeches make excellent study in the tactics of political psychology: of Islamic thought and theology they are almost totally free. They concentrate with most effective skill on the achievement of a given purpose, but raise no final issues. Direct references to the Prophet are rare in the extreme: even the *'Īd* speeches turn the fast to political profit. It is indeed remarkable that the supreme architect of Pakistan, whose leadership has become a national symbol, should in personal outlook and public appeal have been so little concerned with the deeper aspects of religion in the life of men and states. Future historians may well pause to wonder that the protagonist of Pakistan succeeded with so scant an Islam in the spirit. Islam for him was the Muslim League in pursuit of separate statehood.

As late as 1937, the Muslim League commanded only $4\frac{1}{2}$ per cent of the Muslim electorates. By 1946 every seat in the Central Assembly was held by their members. Jinnah's aim had been to stand adamant on the "two nations" theory and to insist that there was no other Muslim party, or viewpoint. Only the League could speak and negotiate for Muslims. The Congress could not but resist that claim unless they were to jettison all hope of unity. Jinnah traded on that refusal, to reject in turn the constitutional and other safeguards which Congress was anxious to guarantee. While certain excesses of the Hindu Mahasabha played into his hands, the crucial factor was his own evasiveness, which enabled him both to frustrate agreement and yet induce a situation in which deterioration would "justify" a stiffer handling. Negotiations became manœuvres.

The Rubicon was reached in March 1940, with the Lahore Resolution, enunciating independent statehood for predominantly Muslim areas and invoking something like the old "hostage" theory of minority security. The Cripps proposals in 1942 conceded a provincial right of non-accession and this, virtually, recognised partition. The post-war Cabinet Mission brought plans for a loose federation which the Congress rejected on points of detail. Jinnah accepted them as having "the substance of Pakistan". He revoked the acceptance when the Viceroy found himself unable to commit the Interim Government to the (accepting) Muslim League. From these sorry if successful tactics came the final decision for British withdrawal and a Congress acceptance of partition.

It is plain that the idea of Pakistan was, logically, absurd. It was created, on a plea for self-determination on behalf of some 24 per cent of all India (that is the Muslims), while itself enclosing from Hindu India a non-Muslim minority of 40 per cent. Thus it does greater violence to its own principle than does the India from which it seceded, and in doing so

> "in the thousands of square miles where Hindus, Sikhs and Muslims lived in closest intermingling, unofficial warfare routed ten million people from their homes and brought about sharp economic

> distress, disintegration of the social fabric and the near downfall of the new governments."[12]

It was a sanguinary climax, on behalf of a state in two halves, partitioning both the Punjab and Bengal, with no historical frontiers, and racially no more homogeneous than a united India. The Hindu–Muslim distinction runs through the whole of the land, so that Pakistan could only partially and tragically fulfil its own doctrine of the "two nations". In its insistent separatism it violated some of the finest features of its own Islam.

It is necessary to set down these hard facts that the quality of the counsel for Pakistan may be weighed. There are, of course, potent Muslim answers to these paradoxes of its genesis. It may be argued that it could not avoid violating its own principle in achieving a major Islamic consolidation. Its existence may serve even those it must exclude, though in the sequel the fact of Pakistan has been as much embarrassment as sustenance for Indian Islam. Logic, we agree, is not all. As for the thousand-mile gap between West and East Pakistan, this may be seen as a liability shouldered rather than a folly perpetrated. Hindus and Muslims may be inextricable in their Indian cohabitation, yet Pakistan be seen as a feasible and proper safeguard for the Muslim identity.

Nevertheless Islam by Pakistan is saying without possibility of denial (though Indian Islam must go on denying it or succumb) that Islam can only be itself as a political expression. This verdict is, of course, its original instinct, its definitive history. Yet there seemed in the eyes of many, and in their honest yearnings, a chance for brotherly concord and multi-religious unity of statehood, which Pakistani Islam rejected harshly and with peremptory finality. That decision stands:

history now contains it: it constitutes the most eloquent delineation of Islam from within Islam in our time. As an article of faith, said the Qā'id-i-A'ẓam, Pakistan is "a matter of life and death".[13] He was right: there was death in the counsel as well as life.

And the strange fact is that so little about ultimate Islam went into its official "apology". Of this, as we have seen, Jinnah himself was incapable by temperament. Its advocacy took little or no account of the implication, so clear to its opponents, that Islam proclaimed hereby its inability to subsist, or persist, except in terms of political authority, its reluctance to risk minority status and throw the whole weight of its prosperity on its spiritual resources, its moral durability, its inward quality of doctrine and discipline. Yet it indirectly condemned Islam in truncated India to just these dimensions of survival. Among the questions that persist are: Were there no forces that could have dispelled the fear complexes? Why did the Jinnah policy triumph within Islam so completely? Was it "emotional" satisfaction that carried the day or economic factors? Was religious vitality within federalism impossible to Islam? If so, what are the implications about its essence? Or is the whole story no more than Western, imperialist machination? Why is it that apologia for Pakistan in the years of its creation showed so little awareness of the issues in the decision so ardently applauded?

This last query is given point not only, as we have seen, by the speeches of Jinnah himself, but also by numerous writers. Rahmat Ali, of course, remains in the limbo of vapourings against "Indianism". For him, Hinduism is the root of all evil. In apocalyptic language, he trumpets the Millet. No doubt the kindest thing is to ignore him. F. K. Khān Durrānī, in *The Meaning of Pakistan*, presents what might be called in general an

Iqbal case. He urges that "Islamic nationalism is basically different from the nationalism of other peoples".[14] It is a *Weltanschauung*, or way of life, democratic not theocratic, in which men "shall be free from oppression, injustice and exploitation, free from selfish greeds, covetousness, fear of poverty . . . this ideal state of their imagination. . . ."[15] Ziauddin Suleri, another writer, in his *Whither Pakistan?*, similarly insists on Islamic nationalism as having a quality unique to itself, spiritual and not territorial.

> "Our solutions of all problems must be Islamic. What they will finally be is for the leaders of thought to outline, discuss and fashion, but here the assertion that needs to be made is that the Muslim comprehension of the universe is unique."[16]

This assurance that the "nationalism" in Pakistan is somehow different, seems to imply that there is an underlying feeling of compromise about it, which writers sense only to scout. This is observable in Iqbal himself with his inherent ambiguity as to whether or not Islam needs nationalism. There hangs over all a sort of assumption that somehow the justification of Pakistan will come in the sequel. This silence of awaited vindication meant a sad abeyance of critical examination while the action was under way. In truth, the creation of Pakistan merely postponed the religious crisis and in the meantime so pre-occupied emotions and energies with the unexamined and activist panacea as to imperil with atrophy the sinews of the soul.[17] An identical diagnosis confronts the honest student of Arab Islam in the same context. Political action does duty for theological responsibility.

A further feature pointing to the same conclusion is the generally quiescent opposition of the religious leadership to the Pakistan idea. We have seen Jinnah's distance from the mullahs. References to the Qur'ān in his speeches are as infrequent as black sheep in an English meadow. His was in fact, in Keith Callard's phrase, "a secular campaign to create a state based on religion".[18] Religious leadership from within the mosques and law schools, from Deoband and Qadian, and from the *Jamā'at-i-Islāmī*, dissatisfied with the Jinnah campaign, suspicious of the nebulous Islamic state, and divided about the issues associated with theocracy, seems to have travelled in a dissident drift of reserve, consternation or vociferation, towards the climax of partition. The Aḥmadiyya, of course, found themselves involved by it in a major physical relocation of their centre. But this, depending as it does on partition lines not partition policy, must not be taken as the original or essential ground of their antagonism. Yet these forces in Islam seem quite to have failed to mount or sustain a deep, creative controversy within the Muslim community as its effective leadership carried it into its most crucial decision. Their part of the expectant justification would seem to have been the indulgence of a dream of opportunity, under statehood, which left them supine or only querulous in the face of immediate obligations.

Or was it that they were apprehensive of some of the implications of the philosophy used, for example, by Mawlana Azad, in under-girding Hindu–Muslim unity? His view of the transcendental oneness of all faiths, as distinct from the compromises of their faithful, could well alarm or bewilder the conservative mind. But at least it was corroborated by unmistakable "religious" feeling and devotion which ought to have been reassuring to the fearful. It was, after all, Azad, not Jinnah, who toiled in and out of prison over a monumental *Tarjumān al-Qur'ān* (to be discussed anon) and whose *Tadhkira* has no counterpart in Jinnah. Nor were

Azad's thoughts on the theology of multi-religious co-operation in independence by any means the only Islamic possibility in that direction. Yet somehow the great debate that might have done justice to the price and cruciality of Pakistan never really happened. For Azad, Jinnah and the partitioners had only partisan diatribe and political accusation. Pakistan emerged from the welter of circumstance and propaganda, and a multitude of words, without its ultimate *raison d'être* ever receiving the quality of conscious and spiritual determination which its magnitude deserved. There was, we may say, a strange elusiveness of quality in the shaping of a climax that is undeniably conclusive.

There are, of course, many extenuating factors. Hindu–Muslim relations were perpetually open to strain and abuse through the third fact of the triangle—the British Raj. The genesis of Pakistan has even been credited to the Foreign Office. "Divide and rule!"—fact, or legend, or both—served as belief, or slogan, to excite, or justify, estrangement, suspicion and ill-will, so complicating all questions, including the question of its own truth. There were also the wide divergencies in educational background and temperament of the Muslim League leaders and the mullah types. The intelligentsia and the ulema (*'ulāmā'*) have all too little in common, both in training and instinct. "Secular" politicians meant by the appeal to Islam very different things to those the "religious" custodians had in mind. There is consequent, crippling ambiguity, about the meaning of the state for faith and the fulfilment of the faith through statehood, of such proportions as to seem insuperable and to admit only of manœuvre, intrigue, partisanship, of politics without the vision, and with all the vexation, of religious relation. And with all these pressures and liabilities are the desperate economic and social consequences of partition itself. The historian, therefore, concerned to do justice to the crisis of history constituted by the genesis of Pakistan, must beware of any easy abstraction from reality. Yet at the heart of that reality, patiently and compassionately assessed, stands this fundamental decision. Pakistan, as concept, policy and fact, must be seen as the surest Muslim index to Islam in our time, doing for its contemporary definition what the Hijra did in the seventh century.

The sequel in the sixteen years of its existence bears out its central significance and extends the issues it left in expectant ambiguity. The successful establishment of a state in the name, and for the sake, of Islam thrust into prominence the whole ideal of "the Islamic State". All the implicit questions as to its meaning, content and sanctions, acquired both the urgency and inherent frustration of practical politics. These were focussed, naturally, into the writing of a constitution which would embody the meaning and ensure the vindication that statehood had assumed. There must be an appeal to "Basic Principles" as a guide to constitutional provisions. These in turn involved the theme of "repugnancy" to the Holy Qur'ān and Islam and the further problem as to how and by whom such repugnancy was to be identified. If the appeal of a general Islamic democracy did not suffice, should there be some other instrument of authority by which assurance of due Islamicity could be obtained? How would this relate to the sovereignty of the people? In these and vexing other ways Pakistan has been wrestling with the translation of its will to statehood for Islam into a state with the will of Islam. The justifications anticipated become the anticipations to be justified and on this course the ship of state still moves through uncharted waters and strong cross-currents.

It is not our intention here to assess the whole process of Pakistani constitutional debate, promulgation, suspension and present status, except to suggest that the sequel confirms the analysis. Some of the aspects involved will recur elsewhere. Since Pakistan made faith and creed decisive in the determination of nationhood it incurred a sort of "existential" obligation to resolve the baffling equation of Islam and state, and to do so in the midst of the intrusive perplexities of the twentieth century. And thus far, whether in the final draft of a constitution, or in the issue of its military suspension, it can hardly be said that the fundamental problem has been solved. Yet, for all its bewildering quality, the emergence of Pakistan in the name of Islam remains. And, whether in the strong piety of the devout or the cynicism of the man of affairs, that invocation remains as the first of political realities. It could hardly be otherwise if Pakistan is not to undo itself.

CHAPTER 3

# MUḤAMMAD ʿABDUH, ARAB PIONEER, AND TWO SUCCESSORS

"SEEK ye first the political kingdom and all other things shall be added unto you." So runs the now familiar misquotation made in his autobiography by President Nkrumah of Ghana.[1] It might well be taken as the precept inspiring Pakistan, with its conviction of first survival and then salvation, by statehood. It is in fact the universal counsel of contemporary Asia and Africa, intent upon the eviction of Western imperialism by clues derived from its own nature. The twentieth-century Arab world is no exception. Our study of the Islamic mind in the index of Arab affairs must have the political in constant view. It is the ever-present denominator in all else, the framework, if it is not at times the eclipse, of the religious and the intellectual. This is precisely the lesson the fact of Pakistan is calculated to enforce. But in studying the Arab scene there are important differences of quality and circumstance.

There is, of course, no partition theme, except, for peculiar reasons, in the case of Palestine.[2] Nor is there in the Arab world any precise equivalent to the British Raj of India. The French, it is true, occupied Algeria in 1830 and Tunisia in 1881, while the British took over Egypt in 1882 after the failure of ʿUrābī Pasha's régime. But until or apart from these events, it was with an Islamic power, the Ottoman Empire, that early Arab aspirations after nineteenth-century liberation had to contend. Great stimulus had come from the Napoleonic invasion with its retinue of cannons and archaeologists. First in the military sphere, and later in milder sciences, the advantages of European imitation had come home to the alert, and the fashion of study in Paris had been set by engineers and generals. So the precedents were soldierly. The greatest of them was the success of Muḥammad ʿAlī and his son Ibrāhīm in establishing in 1809 a régime in Egypt, and in the fourth decade of the century in Syria also. British intervention in the interests of Ottoman continuity led to the termination of Ibrāhīm's authority in Syria in 1840. But his father's was confirmed in Egypt, with complete internal autonomy. It was his successors, in either their lavishness or incompetence, who provoked the British intervention, after having endowed the country with the new significance of a Suez Canal.

The fact that, prior to this climax, Arab nationalism struggled, in its first great upsurge, with an Islamic power and had the near example of a successful achievement, gave it a quality other than that of post-Mutiny Islam in India. When in the twentieth century it came to its second great phase after the disappointments of the Mandates issuing from the First World War, there were dimensions of frustration and bitterness not paralleled in the sub-continent. Arab nationalism, for obvious reasons, had also a different attitude from the Khilafatists to the Ottoman power, both before and after the termination of the Caliphate in 1924. But, within these contrasts, runs the same essential story of Islamic renewal and reinvigoration moving in and with the vicissitudes of political struggle. The same questions are implicit—the role of nation and state in Islam, the tensions of assimilation and exclusion over against modernity, and the issue of a true Islam disserved by false Muslims, with much controversy to define the one and convict the other. The most celebrated name in the nineteenth-century chapter of Arab Muslim thought is that of MUḤAMMAD ʽABDUH (1849–1905), scholar, mufti and "Fabian" reformer.

The fundamental conviction of his career was that Islamic response to the inroads and pressures of Europe, both political and intellectual, must be by educative action rather than revolt.[3] This decision is the more deliberate in that it represents a clear revision of the instinct, and impetus, of his great mentor and master, JAMĀL-AD-DĪN AL-AFGHĀNĪ (1839–97). In a restless career, and with notable vigour and versatility, Jamāl-ad-Dīn strove to galvanise Muslims into strong pan-Islamic fervour and action. Unity under the Caliph he believed to be the clue to destiny and fulfilment. For a brief spell he was influential in Afghanistan: he travelled widely in Egypt, India, Europe, Persia and Syria, had a hand in the Persian Revolution and finally died in Constantinople. He exerted a powerful influence over numerous young disciples, of whom ʽAbduh was the most remarkable. At the moment when Jamāl-ad-Dīn came like a comet into ʽAbduh's world, the latter's thought was dominated by two factors, the one a sense of futility and disquiet about his scholastic experiences in Al-Az'har, the other a fond attraction for the emotions and sanctities of Ṣūfī practice, according to the Shādhilī Order to which he had been introduced by an uncle.

The impact of Jamāl-ad-Dīn weaned him, in large part, from both, though the Ṣūfī strain in his make-up remained as an underlying quality sustaining a deep personal piety which was not the least of his remembered legacies. A new activism came into his temper and a recovered hold on both the significance of Islamic theology, which Al-Az'har had sorely jeopardised, and on the urgency and feasibility of action. With Jamāl-ad-Dīn he took up political journalism and was exiled with him, in 1882, to Syria and later France and North Africa, returning to Egypt in 1888. His sojourn outside his native country widened his vision and matured his judgement. During it he edited the short lived *Al-ʿUrwa al-Wuthqā*, journal of a secret society of the same (Quranic) name and one of the more notable of a spate of publications emanating from the new lease of life given to Arabic letters by Lebanese and Syrian writers.[4] Its aims were Islamic solidarity and Arab renewal.

Even at this stage, however, his concerns about education were prominent and he sent a report on the subject to Constantinople after an inspection of schools in Syria. He was convinced that it would be folly for the new effendi class to assimilate only the externals of Western life, ape its luxuries or acquire merely its military and administrative skills. New standards of Islamic scholarship must reckon effectively with the implications of European thought. Events anyway were later to make Jamāl-ad-Dīn's pan-Islamic hopes an anachronism. Meanwhile ʿAbduh's bent for teaching inclined him to the Fabian approach, for which he was well placed after his return to Egypt, where he threw himself vigorously into theological teaching, and the study of the *Sharīʿa*.

One of his ventures, however, was to translate from its original Persian to Arabic, Jamāl-ad-Dīn al-Afghānī's sole, sustained philosophical work, *Ar-Radd ʿalā'd-Dahriyyīn*, "The Refutation of the Materialists", which deserves some notice as the first major product of Arab Muslim counsel. It was sharply antagonistic to the mood of Syed Ahmad Khan, whose enamoured attitudes towards Western culture and his political "co-operativeness" Jamāl-ad-Dīn al-Afghānī rejected. He dismissed the *nechari* notion of Islam according to nature, though he claimed nevertheless that its revealed status was also eminently rational. Islam for him was true not because of a conformity with nature, but by dint of Divine revelation. Nationalism, a European thing, he condemned as incompatible with Islam and destructive of true religion.[5] His antipathy to things European chimed with a robust dismissal of the odd beliefs of Christianity about an Incarnation and the suffering of God, notions which plainly had no ground of reason or good sense. This note of antipathy for the faith of the Christian Church is a recurrent measure of the articulate assurance of Islam. Like all later apologists, Jamāl-ad-Dīn inveighed against *taqlīd*, or traditionalism, and called for a "religious party claiming the right to investigate the sources of religious belief for themselves and to demand the proof of those beliefs".[6] This plea for apology as in some sense a proper function of modern religion and part of the self-help without which God Himself will not ameliorate the condition of His people (Sura 13.12), is reiterated and developed by most subsequent reformers. It raises strenuous debate about the whole nature of intellectual initiative and its authority, to be reviewed in Chapter 5 below. In this same context we hear first with Jamāl-ad-Dīn the refrain of all later writers that all is well with pure Islam: the basic evil is impure Muslims. There is perfection in the faith itself, rightly understood, if only it were rightly practised. The discrepancy, its source, implications and correction, are the whole chorus of our counsellors.

ʿAbduh, for his part, was assured of the efficacy of wise, vigorous and sustained education. Its qualities he set himself both to exemplify and to foster. He sought for constructive changes in the curriculum and organisation of Al-Az'har, by which the self-respect of the shaikhs could be improved and the conditions of students reformed. Of no less importance was the force of his own example, in lectures, later published by

Rashīd Riḍā, under the title *Risālat at-Tawhīd*,[7] and other theological ventures. Ṭāhā Ḥusayn, in *Al-Ayyām*,[8] is one witness to the influence these exerted, though also, sadly, to the cynicism by which much of his esteem was abandoned after his demise. During the last six years of his life he held office as Grand Mufti of Egypt and brought to his duties brave and imaginative qualities of enterprise which served as a liberating force, familiarising men with new notions of a flexible kind of loyalty and of the proper adaptability of law. He was both meticulous and tireless in his discharge of public duty. He would certainly have approved the initial slogan of the new régime in Egypt in 1952: Unity, Discipline and Work.

His leadership inevitably incurred the sharp and even malicious opposition of reactionary or ignorant elements. As far back as 1877 his own graduation had been impeded by intrigue. Hostility and inertia in his way took toll of his physique and were perhaps in part the cause of his death at the relatively early age of fifty-six. Had he survived into the immediate post-war period and the time of his friend Zaghlūl Pāshā's ministry, to guide those more formative years of Egyptian history, the contemporary situation would certainly have been the richer. For he had no successor of comparable stature, versatility or courage to consolidate and extend his achievement or exploit the gains of his pioneer battle with obscurantism and prejudice.

His essential thesis was that a true Islam, freed from un-Islamic accretions, was perfectly reconcilable with modern thought and conditions. Islam needed the recovery of its primitive self: delinquent allegiance was its chief foe. The twin theme, the excellence of Islam and the reproach of Muslims, echoes through his works. To demonstrate the one and redeem the other was the task of his war upon *taqlīd*. Passive acceptance of interpretations based on blind authority, he insisted, had distorted Quranic meaning and perverted Muslim thought. Proper initiative and indepence of mind have been vitiated by such slavishness and the positive relationship of Quranic truth to scientific ideas concealed. The whole stance of the Qur'ān, he argued in his Commentary, intended rational liberty of exegesis and condemned blind, authoritarian habits of credence. Indeed, once *taqlīd* was eliminated the Qur'ān "would rend the veils of error" and "science would follow it, since science is its true friend and associate. . . ."[9]

'Abduh doubtless stood in too pioneer a relation to the whole question of what might happen to this assurance of instinctive affinity between faith and reason, if men took his invitation to rational independence too seriously. *Taqlīd* was still immensely strong and the problem then was more of arousing than satisfying a readiness to think. Or perhaps we should rather say that in 'Abduh's time men could hardly be persuaded to take science and reason adequately before they had learned to take them hospitably, and that the larger problem, accordingly, belonged to his successors. Meanwhile, with him, dogmas held to be inviolate co-existed with freedoms commended as entire, and did so with confident assurance and admirable individual pertinacity.

*Risālat at-Tawḥīd* contains the most accessible statement of his positive theology. Though its introduction is somewhat scholastic, it is essentially a popular work and represents 'Abduh's didactic style at its best. It presents dogma in the spirit of his whole mission and stands squarely on the heritage of Islamic orthodoxy. He insists firmly on the fact and necessity of revelation for the knowledge of God. The competence of reason is strictly confined to the areas of nature and the "scientific" and has no metaphysical writ. He castigates certain medieval Muslim thinkers who ventured into a rational theology or theodicy.

> "To reflect on the essence of the Creator . . . is forbidden to the human intellect because of the severance of all relation between the two existences."

Holding God and creaturehood firmly apart, he continues:

> "It is futile and harmful (to rationalise about the being of God): futile because it is an endeavour to comprehend the incomprehensible: harmful because it leads to confusion of belief, for it is the definition of what it is not permissible to define and the limitation of what it is not proper to limit."[10]

Thus the basic affirmations of Islam, the unity of God, Muḥammad's prophethood, the uncreatedness of the Qur'ān, the obligation to the "five pillars" (basic duties), the Divine Names and the like, must be accepted as facts of life and of Divine declaration. Where insistent questions intrude, such as the interaction of Divine and human will in Providence, or the significance of the Names of God, or the relation of the Qur'ān's eternity to its temporal incidence, and incidents—these must be foreclosed as inappropriate. There is, of course, wide precedent both in and out of Islam for this position, particularly in the disclaimer of any rational competence in the understanding of God's nature. But it remains questionable whether so round an attack upon *taqlīd* can consistently belong with an exclusion of any epistemological enquiries about the nature and circumstance of revelation. It also throws some doubt upon the source, if not the content, of 'Abduh's rejection of Christian theology which has often claimed for faith about the Trinity just this appeal to the ineffable and the illimitable. It would seem that the plea of mystery and supra-rational transcendence cannot rightly discriminate between occasions of its making, unless it is ready in some sense to return to discursive reason, or take refuge in authoritarian insulations which can mean and convey nothing to "outsiders" and leave their "insiders" with no consistent or honest escape into reason anywhere. But this is to anticipate a focus of ʿAbduh's problem which his time and place could hardly be expected to incur, as long as the pre-requisites had still to be achieved.

Having taken his stand upon the fact of Islam, ʿAbduh was free to welcome an apprehending role to reason in the recipience of the dogmatically "given".

> "The summons of Islam to reflection in regard to created things was not in any way limited or conditioned: because of the knowledge that every sound speculation leads to a belief in God as He is described in the Qur'ān. . . ."[11]

The harmony between soundly used reason and revealed theology is assured. The exegetical corollary of this is that rational meanings in the Quranic text must be preferred to traditional ones. The acknowledgement of Muḥammad as a true Prophet means that what appears illogical in its context must be interpreted rationally without it, or left to God and His knowledge. There must be reverent loyalty to the intention of the text and a conserving of its moral purposes. This duty of living interpretation belongs to each generation and must not be arbitrarily finalised in any one of them. The present generation, in particular, must rise to its proper vocation, since it stood in a new time when science was opening fresh dimensions of nature and life, which should predispose men to religious faith.

ʿAbduh made some efforts, in the columns of the

journal *Al-Manār* to find in Quranic verses anticipations of modern technical discoveries in medicine, biology and geology. He set in this an unfortunate precedent which with later apologists became an obsession. Nevertheless his general concept of religion and science educating each other in reverence and accuracy, and complementing the truths of their respective realms, was both far-sighted and dispassionate—both virtues in a day when religious traditionalism was at once so timid and so assertive.

Another feature of ʿAbduh's counsel about Islam is worthy of note, both for itself and for its recurrence in later writers. It is the thesis that Islam is the culmination of a development or evolution in religion. Each succeeding "faith", he argues in *Risālat at-Tawḥīd*, is suited to the needs of humanity in its time. As mankind matures, the miraculous element can diminish and onerous asceticism be outgrown. Islam marks a culmination: it is the religious ideal realised and thus it can rely on reason without miracle and safely allow the body its full rights. That Islam is the final term of religious development is the meaning of the belief that Muḥammad is the seal of the prophets. Discrepancy between this ideal and the actual is explained by the fact of decadent Muslims. He emphasises that the aim of Islamic prophecy is religious. Hence it should not be forced into "scientific" interpretations to displace what reason should attain or undertake. As for prophetic miracle it must be seen as within the prerogative of God for revelatory ends, but final vindication must always lie in results. Among these he included the *iʿjāz*, or matchlessness, of the Qur'ān and Muḥammad's illiterate inspiration. Arabic eloquence is the Qur'ān's evidence of Divine composition. It yields, with the *Ḥadīth* or Traditions, the categorical guidance in what relates to worship (*ʿibāda*), whereas the principles governing men's relations with men and the patterns of their societies (*mu'āmala*), are, so to speak, only the general charter, leaving the bye-laws to be written by men. For the rest, 'Abduh believed strongly in the *umma*, or nation community, as the form of the Islamic polity, though after the period of active association with Jamāl-ad-Dīn he bent his main energies to the intellectual and doctrinal tasks, aiming to ensure both a progressing and conserving Islam.

As a pioneer, his achievement was remarkable, the work of a vigorous and courageous mind. But there were elements of assertion, and even evasion, in his argument which persisted in his followers. He was too ready to claim both modernity and orthodoxy at once, too prone to miss the implications for what he defended of what he conceded, too ready to assume that reason would go dogma's way. His account of an Islam, in which the rational and the revealed, science and faith, are in harmonious amity, needed much more radical examination than he gave it. It would be quite false to question, as Margoliouth did, his intellectual integrity, or, with Lord Cromer, his genuine faith in Islam.[12] What he failed to do, and what any thinker at that juncture might have come short of, was to measure and to shoulder the full range of responsibility implicit in his aims. Nevertheless

> ". . . more than any other single man he gave modern Egyptian thought a centre of gravity and created, in place of a mass of disconnected writings, a literature inspired by definite ideas of progress within an Islamic framework."[13]

The inner irresolution of Muḥammad 'Abduh's modernism is more apparent still in the work of two of his disciples who must suffice here as some measure of his immediate legacy. There are, of course, other names presenting themselves in another context, having emotional or biographical links with the leadership of ʿAbduh. But Rashīd Riḍā, (1865–1935), his devoted editor and biographer, and Muṣṭafā ʿAbd-ar-Rāziq (1885–1947) serve usefully to illustrate the dilemma of a conservatism of mind that is anxious to keep step with modernity and is at the same time "fearful for the ark of God". That ultimate area of immunity, the uncriticised core, within ʿAbduh's progressive dogmatism was their main pre-occupation.

The movement of time must be constantly in view, for it brought increasing intimidation, or at least apprehension, to the cautious, and steadily slackening rein to the secularisers. The latter, as with Atatürk, might suppress the citadel of dogma altogether as the cohesive centre of reaction. Or, more likely, they would call on all fronts, political, judicial and cultural, for progressive changes, leaving Islamic doctrine in itself either to reverent neglect or to a merely pragmatic function which saw its intellectual problems as largely an academic business that need not disturb its useful social significance. Secularists, at any rate avowed ones, were few in the early years of the twentieth century. In any event, these attitudes could only dismay sincere representatives of the counsels of ʿAbduh.

These were ready to abandon the medieval accretions, the embarrassing outworks, the subtleties of the schoolmen, the excesses of the Ṣūfīs. All these could and should be purged away and Islam disencumbered of their embarrassing associations. But this only left the ultimate sanctities of the Qur'ān and the basic elements of Islam all the more crucial. Thus, for the partial reassurance of the ulema alarmed by the thought of the things abandoned, and for the better defence of the front against Western secularity, the moderate reformers sought for political ideas, legal reforms and educational programmes which could assure Islamic continuity as they saw it. For a time Rashīd Riḍā was enamoured of the pan-Islamic counsels of Jamāl-ad-Dīn al-Afghānī, but time itself was to eliminate the Caliphate. Where Jinnah reached for "Pakistan", Arab thinkers and leaders, presented with their actual or potential *ummas* by the demise of the Ottoman Empire and other external developments, had perforce to debate in more immediate terms. For Rashīd Riḍā and Muṣṭafā 'Abd-ar-Rāziq it was, in the main, a more fundamental conservatism than might have been expected to issue from 'Abduh's influence.

Muḥammad Rashīd Riḍā claimed descent from the Prophet. He came from Tripoli (Lebanon, then in Syria). Like his great mentor, there were Ṣūfī strains in his upbringing, while *Al-'Urwa al-Wuthqā* served to kindle his ardour for renewal. He went to Egypt and became a close disciple of 'Abduh, and after his death devoted himself to the perpetuation of his influence through the editing of his writings. He developed 'Abduh's Quranic Commentary, merging with it his own exegesis in a sort of posthumous partnership. Rashīd Riḍā remains our main source for knowledge of the genius and career of 'Abduh, and his own achievement after 1905 is interpretative rather than original. Aside from the barren campaign over the Caliphate in the early nineteen-twenties, his activities, like those of 'Abduh, were for the most part educational and literary.

His point of departure was a careful conservatism. The Al-Az'har journal (*Majallat al-Az'har*) in an obituary notice acclaimed him as a great scholar whose name would be immortal in Arab history, for a defence of Islam against heresy unparalleled in modern times.[14] He asserted the infallibility of Muḥammad.[15] "Unyielding adherence", concludes C. C. Adams, "in the most orthodox sense, to the Qur'ān, the Sunnah and the Divine law, was fundamental to his whole manner of thinking."[16]

His chief mouthpiece was *Al-Manār*, the journal which he founded and led for thirty-seven years (1898–1935). With the pen of a crusading fervour, he discoursed on Islamic polity, society, dogma and law, castigated apathy, *taqlīd* and saint-worship, promoted general education and the mutual interpretation of the world segments of Islam. He saw diversities in the schools of law as generating trivial partisanships and hindering true godliness. He welcomed Western techniques without testing their premises and inculcated Islamic practice shorn of accretions and compromises. He stood resolutely on a double front against ultra-conservative obscurantism and intrusive secularity. Like ʿAbduh, he invoked the decadence of Muslims to vindicate the ideal quality of Islam. Its difficulties lay in its extraneous features.

His position on the canons of Quranic exegesis is illuminating for his whole outlook. In the *Al-Manār* Commentary (for which ʿAbduh's notes reached only to Sura 4.125), he strove to eliminate the old-style, controversy-ridden comment on the commentators, which made Quranic margins so tedious, and to reflect the contemporary situation, that the wise Qur'ān might be the lively guide of each age. He decried the mentality that had made a virtue of the very disjointedness of the Qur'ān and endeavoured to trace the connections of thought within the suras and verses. Yet throughout there was a firm insistence on its infallible authority in every particular. In all matters of fact (as distinct from allegory or interpretation), it must be taken as what it says, without cavil or hesitation. If proven scientific "findings" seem to collide with Quranic statements of fact, the collision is only with their apparent sense.

Nor can historical or "scientific" issues be rightly escaped by invoking "religious" significance.

He is ready, however, to allow to each Muslim the right to understand the Qur'ān and the Sunna without dictation from an intermediary. But each Muslim needs perforce to consult the competent authorities, since exegesis requires expert, even obscure, skills which he lacks. That there are crucial ambiguities in this allowance and proviso is immediately evident.

For his part, Rashīd Riḍā moved unmistakably towards a sharper conservatism as he aged. This may be partly explained by the disappointment of his Caliphate policy and by the emergence of Ibn-Saʿūd in whom he came to see the best promise of Muslim unification. Hence his later interest in Wahhābism[17] and the common cause he could find with it against pietistic superstitions and Western inroads alike. Two years before his death he published *Al-Waḥy al-Muḥammadī*,[18] a summary of which measures his mediation of ʿAbduh thirty years on. The first edition was translated into Urdu and Chinese and much of the presentation has non-Muslim and Western persuasion in mind.

"The Qur'ān", he says, "cannot but be the truth of God." Revelation to Muḥammad is wholly supernatural, the casting of words into the heart of the Prophet, not the welling up of thoughts within him.[19] He dismisses discussion of the uncreatedness, or otherwise, of the Qur'ān, as purely speculative and curious.[20] A large section of the book is devoted to the theme of the Qur'ān's *iʿjāz*, the self-evidencing miracle of its inspiration, "a wonder unlike all other wonders". All who seek human welfare and are capable of independent thought must accept Islam.

> "There is in the world no general, perfect, sound and reliable religion except Islam . . . it is the religion of

truth and peace, of justice and right, giving its truth to every nation and every individual."[21]

Almost fifty pages at the end are given to quotations of eulogy. The whole import of the book may be distilled into its simple declaration:

"It is your business to believe what God and the prophets have found good either to establish or deny, without addition or subtraction, without comparison and without comment, and it is not your business to sit in judgement on the ultimate mystery of God's essence and attributes, nor on the details of His addressing the prophets . . ."[22]

Rashīd Riḍā's steady drift towards this position of assertive conservatism is the long range formulation of ʿAbduh's legacy in the perplexing circumstances of three succeeding decades.

Muṣṭafā ʿAbd-ar-Rāziq's work shows a similar character. Son of a leading associate of ʿAbduh, he shared the master's moderate reformism, travelled in Europe after graduation in 1909 at Al-Az'har, and adopted a liberal welcome to the revival of Arabic letters and to educational reform. In 1925 he published a study of Muḥammad ʿAbduh.[23] In the year before his death he became Shaykh-al-Az'har, in succession to Muṣṭafā al-Marāghī. His cultured mind and graciousness of personality did much to temper the severity of Az'har mentality and politics. Of his dignity, ability and tact there is no doubt. But in the intellectual formulations he left behind, notably *Tamhīd li-Tārīkh al-Falsafa al-Islāmiyya* (1944) "A General Introduction to the History of Islamic Philosophy", and *Ad-Dīn wa-l-Waḥy wa-l-Islām* (1945) "Religion, Revelation and Islam", he shows a marked reluctance for the exactions of full apology. "Scrutiny and controversy in belief lead", he fears, to "the abandonment of religion."[24] The second work relies on quotations and is too slight to be of positive significance, with an excessive concentration on mere terminological definition. Religion is, for him, the system of beliefs and practices relating to the things accounted holy by a nation, or *umma*, which is a unity. *Umma* is inseparable from *dīn*. There is meticulous, but arid, discussion on *waḥy*, or revelation. His analysis of the receptive side of revelation is summed up in the analogy of the mirror: the Prophet's soul was to the mediate or immediate celestial communication as a mirror is to what confronts it. *Islām* is faith where faith should be. The discussion throughout moves only within the limits of authorities, texts and linguistic definition. No light is therefore thrown on the existential stakes of contemporary theology. Islam is immutably all that it was finalised in the Qur'ān to be, both as to doctrine and precept. Muṣṭafā ʿAbd-ar-Rāziq, despite the lapse of years, is no closer to an ultimate grappling with the implications of ʿAbduh's welcome to modernity and adherence to orthodoxy than ʿAbduh was himself. There is a sort of abeyance of fundamental issues, in a theology that has not sensed, still less surmounted, its destiny.

These two figures must complete the discussion here of what ʿAbduh came to mean. That his influence had other consequences will be apparent later. But in the *Al-Manār* school and in Muṣṭafā ʿAbd-ar-Rāziq lies the commentary of the next generation on his Islamic intent. Though its spokesmen were leaders of integrity, energy and fervour, they perpetuated, with less excuse, the master's inconclusiveness, while external events went on apace.

CHAPTER 4

# MUḤAMMAD IQBĀL AND HIS PRECURSORS

"WHY ask of Razi what the Book denotes?
Behold its best interpreter am I.
Muslims! I have a word within my heart
More radiant than the soul of Gabriel."[1]

In the poems of Iqbal we are at a far cry from the cautious circumspection of ʿAbduh and his closest disciples. The place and the time are different: it is Indian not Arab Islam and when ʿAbduh died Iqbal was not yet thirty. Verse has replaced commentary and instead of the ponderous tones of *Al-Manār* we have the wings of song. Yet at least in their centrality to Arab and to Indian counsels on Islam, Muḥammad ʿAbduh and Muhammad Iqbal share a similar stature, as the figures to whom debate in either sphere returns. In retrospect they stand out as the personalities that became the main pre-occupation of discipleship or controversy. There, however, the single likeness ends. For Iqbal, as befits his flights of word and notion, has received a far more enthusiastic adulation than ever rewarded the steady probity and scholarship of ʿAbduh. The choice with which they leave us lies between a painstaking theology in prose and flights of philosophic poetry irresponsibly dynamic, and with this contrast the indefinable diversity of Cairo and Lahore.

A chapter on Iqbal, however, might with a sound imagination start out from Aligarh. Here, in 1877,

SYED AHMAD KHAN founded his famous Anglo-Muhammadan College, which in 1920 became the Muslim University of Aligarh. Its intellectual vicissitudes, which we have no time to trace in detail, provide an intriguing commentary on Islamic counsels. For a university is always a sensitive point of communal self-awareness and intellectual decision, not least when it specifically embodies a policy for revival. Ahmad Khan saw Aligarh as the Oxford-Cambridge of Islamic society in the sub-continent and the spearhead of his ambition for a religious leadership hospitable to Western patterns and alive Islamically to the modern world.

> "All good things spiritual and worldly, which should be found in man, have been bestowed by the Almighty on Europe, and especially on England"[2]

he wrote in 1869 during his visit to England. These blessings he meant to graft on the stock of Islam by his educational enterprise at Aligarh.

The venture certainly succeeded in lifting Urdu letters and literature into a new authority. It bred a new self-assurance in Muslim communities, which contributed to the claim by 1906 of separate electorates. Its graduates, in the words of K. M. Panikkar, became "an intellectual general staff for the work of Muslim integration".[3] Yet its very successes underlined its theological dilemma. What place should dogma take? How should a new intellectual *élite* tackle the ultimate issues of belief, beyond the practical, tactical, battles for communal vitality and expression?

To these final questions, Aligarh returned no clear answer and by its silence illustrated the theological truancy of modernism. Ahmad Khan himself laid down no detailed theological curriculum.[4] He seems to have assumed that Western ethos, properly communicated, would somehow induce the right solution. He certainly recruited outstanding English scholars. But the Aligarh graduate was liable to emerge with no theological home, his high ethics posed in an intellectual void and his hospitality to science in essential dichotomy with a separate, or a corroded, Islam of the soul. By 1920 the temper of the College was largely secular. One student, Muhammad Ali, the Khilafatist, reflected:

> "The Qur'ān remained practically a closed book to us and the traditions of the Prophet were no more than a name. . . . Of theology in the sense of dogmatics and dialectics, there was no trace in any textbook."[5]

When the political movement gathered force Aligarh's Anglophile outlook was an embarrassment. Some of its graduates, like Muhammad Ali, had to find their Quranic kinships of heart in the stern disciplines of imprisonment. By the time of the "Pakistan" concept, Aligarh, with its theological abeyance of thought, became a relatively uncritical accessory to the fact.[6] Liberal secularism gave way to politico-religious fervour. Both belonged with failure to find an adequate, or even an approximate, re-orientation of Islamic theology to cope with the modernity Ahmad Khan had greeted and its own interior obligations towards it.

This issue, focussed in institutional terms at Aligarh, is the context within which the emergence of Iqbal is to be set. He and his predecessors are handling, in one way or another, the intellectual aspects of this same equation, against the background of the political developments already measured in Chapter 2. The first of them for this exposition is AMEER ALI, more exactly Sayyid Amīr 'Alī (1849–1928).

He was the author of one of the most familiar works of Muslim apology: *The Spirit of Islam.*[7] The first

Indian to be appointed to the Privy Council, he had a long, distinguished career. Not content, as some, merely to assert that Islam is not illiberal or unscientific, he turns the tables and claims that Islam and progress are synonymous. In a most assured *tour de force* he harmonises the mosque and modernity, and in so doing involves himself in highly novel interpretations of basic Islamic terms and concepts which at least have the merit of bringing issues, however extravagantly, into the light of day. No author prior to him has so thoroughly necessitated the query: Is Islam so? And thus he is a great provoker of the themes of *ijtihād*. He is enthusiastic, resilient and confident, with an Achilles heel, perhaps, but none the less a knight in shining armour.

He begins, like ʿAbduh, with the *bête noire* of *taqlīd*, the fixities of obscurantism and blind authority. Literalism and barren orthodoxy make for a false Islam. The true Islam of Muḥammad is the quintessence of human wisdom, a religion admirably suited to human nature, practical, readily identifiable as the very stuff of historical progress and scientific culture. Disagreement with this verdict, he implies, must be either malicious or obtuse. A somewhat extensive passage may serve here to give the best picture of his case and temper.

> "The Muslims of the present day have ignored the spirit in a hopeless love of the letter . . . they have made themselves the slaves of opportunism and outward observance. It was natural that in their reverence and admiration for the Teacher, his early disciples should stereotype his ordinary mode of life, crystallise the passing incidents of a chequered career, imprint on the heart orders, rules and regulations enunciated for the common exigencies of the day of an infant society. But to suppose that the

greatest reformer the world has ever produced, the greatest upholder of the sovereignty of reason, the man who proclaimed that the universe was governed and guided by law and order and that the law of nature meant progressive development, ever contemplated that even these injunctions, which were called forth by the passing necessities of a semi-civilised people, should become immutable to the end of the world, is doing an injustice to the Prophet of Islam.

No one had a keener perception than he of the necessities of this world of progress, with its ever changing social and moral phenomena, nor of the likelihood that the revelations vouchsafed to him might not meet all possible contingencies. . . . The great Teacher . . . conceived that a time would come when the accidental and temporary regulations would have to be differentiated from the permanent and general . . .

The blight which has fallen on Muslim nations is not due to the teachings of the Master. No religion contained greater promise of development, no faith was purer, or more in conformity with the progressive demands of humanity.

The present stagnation is principally due to the notion which has fixed itself on the minds of the generality of Muslims that the right to the exercise of private judgement ceased with the early legists, that its exercise in modern times is sinful and that a Muslim in order to be regarded as an orthodox follower of Muḥammad should belong to one or other of the schools established by the schoolmen of Islam and abandon his judgement absolutely to the interpretations of men who lived in the 9th century and could have no conception of the necessities of the 20th. . . . The Prophet has consecrated reason as the highest and noblest function of the human intellect. Our schoolmen and their servile followers have made its exercise a sin and a crime. . . . Before there can be a renovation of religious life, the mind must first escape from the bondage which centuries of literal interpretation and the doctrine of conformity have imposed upon it."[8]

The "stride" of this argument is impressive. The appeal to changed times is eloquently stated. What is not clear is the extent of Islamic sources covered by a phrase like "rules and regulations . . . for the day . . . of an infant society". Some of the maxims and precepts of the lawyers are no doubt meant. But these amplify and extend the original Quranic injunctions and the copious Traditions. Elsewhere Ameer Ali holds firmly to the latter as "that faithful chronicler of the past".[9] He was by no means willing to relinquish Tradition as a whole. The crucial issue, however, is the place of the Qur'ān itself in this temporal equation. That it holds within itself deep, abiding, universal truths such as Ameer Ali claims, no one would rightly deny. But it also contains elements equally part of particular, and past, time, as the scholastic, legal precepts that are said to have lain as an incubus on Muslim life and effort. Ameer Ali does not face the full theological implications of his own criteria.

Another feature of his attitude to the Qur'ān is worthy of note, namely, his seemingly different concept of the relation between revelation and its expression in the Prophet's inspiration. The frequent phrases about "the great Teacher", "the Master", "the mind of this remarkable Teacher in its intellectualism . . . essentially modern", have a different ring from the traditional understanding of the illiterate Prophet, who, as Rashīd Riḍā has it, received revelation by the casting of words, not the welling of thoughts, in his heart. Ameer Ali, of course, notes the illiteracy of the Prophet and once refers to the miracle of the Qur'ān's eloquence in those terms, though he does not, apparently, mention the preserved tablet of the heavenly Qur'ān.[10] But he continually speaks of the contents of the Qur'ān as deriving from Muḥammad's genius or wisdom or sagacity, involving, that is, the fullness of his mental powers not, as orthodoxy holds, their abeyance and supersession by Divine mediation of truth both in word and meaning.

Ameer Ali speaks of Muḥammad "directing that during the prayers the Muslim should turn his face towards Mecca".[11] Of the pilgrimage, he writes: "Here again the wisdom of the inspired lawgiver shines forth",[12] while other Quranic injunctions are spoken of as what "Muḥammad prescribed".[13] More surprising still, he characterises the early Meccan passages descriptive of Paradise in these terms:

> "Probably in the infancy of his religious consciousness, Muḥammad himself believed in some or other of the traditions which floated around him. But with the wider awakening of the soul, a deeper communion with the Creator of the universe, thoughts which bore a material aspect at first became spiritualised. The mind of the teacher progressed."[14]

This may well be an intelligent conclusion. What matters here is that it points towards a very different understanding of the nature of revelation and of the influence of Muḥammad's context on the content of the Qur'ān. If this were developed, the Qur'ān need not thereby be less revelatory but it would clearly be differently so. These remain, however, as no more than hints in *The Spirit of Islam*. Radically pursued they would sustain a revolutionary account of the eternal–temporal mystery in revelation and introduce into exegesis a much freer appeal to the significance of Quranic time.

If in this way Ameer Ali was feeling towards a new theology, it was perhaps more by way of enthusiasm than deliberation. His general account of the Prophet's career is the story of "the great Pioneer of Rationalism", who

> "concentrated into a focus all the fragmentary and broken lights which had ever fallen on the heart of man. . . . The Recluse of Hira, the unlettered Philosopher born among a nation of unyielding idolaters, impressed ineffaceably the unity of God and the equality of man upon the minds of the nations who once heard his voice. . . . His persistent and unvarying appeal to reason and to the ethical faculty of mankind, his rejection of miracles, his thoroughly democratic conceptions of Divine government, the universality of his religious ideals, his simple humanity—all serve to differentiate him from his predecessors, all affiliate him with the modern world."[15]

Elsewhere, perhaps speaking out of his Shīʿite background, he finds a perpetual presence of Muḥammad with his community:

> "The immanence of the Master's spirit during the devotions establishes the harmony between the soul of man and the Divine essence."[16]

*The Spirit of Islam* needs to be read for its fullness, its exuberance, its sweep of confidence to be appreciated. The course of things has come a long way from the dejection which was Ahmad Khan's main pre-occupation for Indian Islam. The assurance takes new and yet more novel form in Iqbal. The very idea of "the spirit" of Islam brings a certain new fluidity of mind. But by the same token the questions multiply.

S. Khuda Bukhsh (Khudā Bakhsh) (d. 1931) represents a still more venturesome liberalism than Ameer Ali. Reared in a home of deep piety and wide erudition, he moved with ease in Western scholarship also, and achieved a degree of candour and detachment in his assessments of Islam which give his writings unusual objectivity and dispassionateness. It is odd, though, that he spent his time putting German books into English rather than into Urdu or Bengali. There was something aristocratic about his learning. He was Professor of Islamic History in the University of Calcutta, but did little to popularise the scholarship he possessed and wrote almost entirely in English.

He was one of the earliest thinkers to claim a right to use the Qur'ān, so to speak, idealistically, whether or not the interpretation was, by historical criteria, "fictitious". Referring to the scholarly necessity of liberating Islam from "the fetters of authority" and "the dead hand of past ages", he wrote:

> "Concession to the demands of the time being admitted, these concessions are justified by appeals to the Qur'ān and the Traditions of the Prophet. Whether the appeal be real or illusory, the fact of the appeal is one more instance of the utility of legal fiction in the history of human development."[17]

People, in other words, must be Quranically persuaded even if a sense is read into the Qur'ān in doing so, which canons of strict exegesis would not admit. We shall find Iqbal, in his poetic manner, adopting just this practice without so clearly stating the nature of his procedure. Khuda Bukhsh is ready to reckon with blemishes in the life of the Prophet, taken, however, in the stride of a great achievement and an unmistakable sincerity. Islam was not, he insisted against Ameer Ali, just "a passion for righteousness": it was the "five pillars" of traditional practice.[18] Nevertheless religions in their diversity had one universal ethical intent. *Taqlīd* must be repudiated and suppressed. Law must be separated from religion.

> "Islam, stripped of its theology, is a perfectly simple religion. Its cardinal principle is belief in One God and belief in Muḥammad as His Apostle. The rest is mere accretion, superficiality. The Qur'ān, rightly understood and interpreted, is a spiritual guide containing counsels and putting forward ideals to be followed by the faithful, rather than a *corpus juris civilis* to be accepted for all time."[19]

This view would prevail only as leadership tackled the vexing problems of ignorance, lethargy and prejudice. But Khuda Bukhsh himself had little of the controversial reformer in his character. He approved the vitalism of Iqbal but could not readily imitate it.[20] Until almost the end of his life he staunchly held with Hindu-Muslim unity and applauded the Khilafatist vision. "Indian solidarity could be mightily single, splendidly whole." But in the last entry in his volume of studies he came round decisively to the view that Muslim survival necessitated their working out their own salvation.[21]

Ameer Ali and Khuda Bukhsh have something of a kindred spirit in ʿAbdallāh Yūsuf ʿAlī (1872–1953) at least in respect of the approach to the Qur'an. In his extensive translation and commentary,[22] he tends to discount the historical factor and the traditional exegesis by invoking general, sometimes mystical, significance, which, he claims, is of enduring relevance when the historical is superseded. On this basis a "spiritualising" interpretation is offered, which leaves aside grammatical or idiomatic considerations, and asks: What wisdom can we extract from this for our present day?[23] In discussing the familiar distinction in Sura 3.7 between the *muḥkamāt* and the *mutashābihāt*, the categorical and the allegorical, he observes on the Qur'ān:

> "It is very fascinating . . . to exercise our ingenuity about its inner meaning, but it refers to such profound spiritual matters that human language is inadequate to it, and though people of wisdom get some light from it, no one should be dogmatic, as the final meaning is known to God alone."[24]

This "ingenuity" is one of the salient aspects of Iqbal. Yusuf Ali resembles him also in the poesy he uses to distil the sense of each sura. His glosses on the text have not, of course, found favour in all quarters and his habit of ecstatic interpolation alarms the cautious. There have been numerous critics to decry his principles.[25] Nor have the conservatives been reassured by his account of pilgrimage as a chance to exchange spiritual experience, or constituted by a "pious contemplation of noble personalities". He sits loosely by the canonical forms of fasting and prayer. The former is self-denial, the latter the offering up of will to God, to which he adds:

> "There are *also* [sic] canonical prayers in which we associate with our fellow men and women in *some* form so that our spiritual strivings may be in common and may yield its influence in a sort of collective service."[26]

However, the exemplar *par excellence* of this pattern of appeal to "the spirit of Islam", its vitalism and its Quranic susceptibility to ingenuity of interpretation is

MUḤAMMAD IQBĀL (1876–1938), the most outstanding, and exasperating, figure in twentieth-century Islam in the sub-continent. The poet trumpeter of a renewed Islam, his work has suffered from the fact that his admirers have turned it into channels after their own hearts. This fate his looseness of thought invited. It is now sanctified by his having become the centre of a cult, whose anniversary is celebrated throughout Pakistan, with poems, eulogies and articles, as patron saint of the republic.

By birth a Punjabi, he wrote his poems in Persian and Urdu and his main philosophical work in English. After studies in the Punjab, Cambridge and Munich, he devoted himself, like so many of his predecessors, to the war against *taqlīd* and to the resurrection of Asian Islam from lethargy and tradition. He was not by nature a politician. His weapon was poetry. It is true that from 1925 to 1928 he was a member of the Punjab Legislature and that in 1931, presiding at Allahabad over the Muslim League Conference, he made the suggestion that the four north-western provinces should be consolidated into a single state. But the idea was not repeated at the Round Table Conference that followed and about the same time he had written that "Islam is non-territorial in character".[27]

His poems even in translation convey an impression of extraordinary vitality and sustained emotional power. There can be no doubt of the force of personality and conviction which informs them. And the medium was probably well chosen since the very form of poetry absolves the writer from necessities of logic, consistency or argumentation. He could be dynamic, vehement, outrageous, satirical, suggestive, passionate, trenchant and allusive, by turns, without the obligations of consistency or justification to which prose is bound. He turned his fire on Western materialism and mullah-ignorance with equal zeal. But the tumult of his verse carried him into the kind of assertions and denials which in any other context would have given pause, or scandal, to any normal Muslim. He called on his readers to exalt their ego so high that God Himself would consult them before determining their destiny.[28] His militancy somehow made his wildness permissible. Loose ends were no embarrassment: they were rather a point of pride. A poet could assert the perfection of Islamic "theocracy" without facing its contemporary feasibility, or inveigh against an iniquitous capitalism without offering any scheme of operable socialism. Universalism and communalism, Islamic dynamism and Islamic finality, mysticism arraigned and mystics extolled, all jostled together in his stanzas.

"That I may lead home the wanderer
And imbue the idle looker-on with restless
  impatience,
And advance hotly on a new quest
And become known as the champion of a
  new spirit."[29]

was an ambition which inner contradictions need not deter or discredit.

His most famous poem *Asrār-i-Khūdī*, "The Secrets of the Self", sees all life as consisting in finite egos, associated in a growing universe proceeding from chaos to cosmos. The progress of creation requires the intensifying of individuality. Senses and intellect are instruments for the assimilation of obstacles by which the self approximates to God. What fortifies and promotes personality is good, what weakens it is bad. The ego's movement has three stages: obedience to the law, self-control, Divine vicegerency. The biography of Muḥammad is taken as a lesson in this assimilative movement, and the early heroic history of Islam has the same meaning. When the Qur'ān (as in 23.14) speaks of God being *aḥsanu-l-khāliqīn*, "the best of creators", this is what it means, for clearly men are creators, in this sense, also.

The poem reproves modern science for its imprisonment in phenomena and his fellow-Muslims for their being its dupes. Islamic *tawḥīd* as "unity" really means this Nietzschean unity of ego with super-ego. To this Muslims must return. The very flame of life is desire and intellect is its child. "Save thyself by the affirmation of thyself", he cries. Self-abnegation is a ruse of subject races, set down in the fable of the sheep who went among the tigers proclaiming himself the apostle of God to call them to civilised life. The tigers duly embrace the sheep's religion and take to a diet of fodder. Iqbal, in this section, even allows the sheep to use Quranic quotation to achieve the deception and subjugation of the tigers.

According to *The Tulip of Sinai*, the self is its own revealed law, the desire, that is, to give itself in growth. Obedience thereto is more valid than to Sinai. Yet it certainly makes for an Islam quite unlike the one the centuries have recognised. The very theism of Islam, in any traditional form, is jeopardised by these poems if they are to be taken seriously. But no doubt to be "serious", in that sense of suspicion or scandal, would be also to be obtuse. Poetry is elusive, given to extravagance, on the wing. If Muḥammad's religion is a flash of the creative fire, it may still go on defining its own directions with the same pristine energy.

His *Lectures on the Reconstruction of Religious Thought in Islam* carry an unfortunate title. They are in no way a survey of Islamic modernism. "*A* reconstruction" is all, at best, they could claim to be. Many Muslim critics would describe them as a Muslim's ventures in religious speculation, with reservations even about that. They are too English in their address and assumptions ever to be a potent force popularly within the Islamic setting. But as a construction into which Islam is somehow built they represent the most ambitious and inventive adaptation of dogma attempted by a Muslim. The Quranic and other ventures of Ameer Ali and Yusuf Ali are left far behind by the fertile imagination of Iqbal.

The main sources of his thought are Bergson, Nietzsche, McTaggart and Freud. His aim is to reconstruct an Islamic philosophy of religion with due reference to contemporary developments. He distinguishes sharply between empirical scientific knowledge and the knowledge born of religious "experience". Any conflict between these arises from misconception. This methodological distinction does duty for an entire apologetic over against science. Religious reality, though not altogether its interpretation, is outside the rational. It is rooted in prophetic relation of self and not-self. The Quranic principle of *tawḥīd* he equates with the perfect ego. "He does not beget and is not begotten" means the immunity from reproduction which characterises God as eternally complete. Creation, therefore, cannot be seen as any objectifying, historical deed by which God makes what is other than Himself. It is rather

> "... the creative activity of the ultimate Ego, in whom deed and thought are identical functions as ego unities. The world in all its details, from the mechanical movement of what we call the atom of matter to the free movement of thought in the human ego, is the self-revelation of the great I AM ..."[30]

Leaving certain corollaries of this to "the future theologians of Islam", he explains that "nature is to the

Divine self as character is to the human self". It is the systematic mode of behaviour and as such "organic to the ultimate self". He eludes the question whether the world is therefore necessary to the being of God, by saying that it is "abstract speculation" for which the Qur'ān has no love, while continuing ambiguously to assert that the world is the organic of God the ultimate. Problems of providence, destiny, foreknowledge, prayer, all of course vital to Muslims, abound in this theism of pantheism. Evil is seen, on its physical side, as part of the discipline by which free spirits are defined. In the moral sense, evil is the consciousness begotten of the emergence, by the fall, from a state of primitive appetite into a selfhood capable of doubt and rebellion. The "risk" implicit in this choice allowed to finite egos is part of the onward creative realisation of destiny. Iqbal's doctrine of man relies heavily on Sura 17.85: "Say, the soul proceeds from the *amr* of my Lord", which he interprets as meaning the Divine ego in its energy as the directive force of personal life. Immortality means belonging to the significance of the universe, co-existing, though finite, with the infinite, on condition of an ever-growing ego-vitality. At death there is a kind of "stock-taking" of the past achievements and future potential of the self. Body is only necessary to mortal environment. Heaven and Hell in the Qur'ān mean this advancing or decaying egoism: they are states of ego-building, or ego-dissolving.

Prophecy reaches its finality in Islam by "discovering the need of its own abolition". By its termination in Muḥammad, men are liberated into a sole reliance on inner experience, which means the end of authoritarian religion externally imposed. This prepares us for radical revision of the "five pillars" in Islam. Iqbal's reinterpretation of *Ṣalāt* (worship) must here suffice to indicate the lines on which he takes the others. He sees it as a spiritual awareness of reality, a process of assimilation, more intense than thought, by which "the little island of personality suddenly discovers its situation in a larger whole of life".[31] The relation of prayer to the Divine will is that it makes man a sort of second creator, through the growing nearness of his will to the Divine. He attaches great importance to the pattern and postures of congregational prayer because of the solidarity and "sacramental" aspiration they embody. But he insists that the reality must transcend and criticise, as his poems frequently do, all forms and traditions.

As for polity, the state, nation and *umma*, these must be seen in the context of the ego-realisation he teaches. Iqbal regards Islamic political order as the means whereby, in practice, corporate ego-attainment can be translated into forms of space and time. It is perhaps here that we must find the source of the ambivalence in his attitude to "Pakistan". On the one hand he insisted that Islam had been from the beginning a civil society, for which the spiritual could only be achieved in statehood. Yet states are by nature territorial in location and exclusive in their collective veneration of the past and their communal self-interests. These features, not least territoriality, are alien to essential Islam. He seems to have imagined, or hoped, on the analogy of the state's evaporation in Marxism, that nationalism in Islam would be a temporary expedient, indispensable indeed as a means to liberation, but destined to be later itself transcended. On this basis he was able to approve a Muslim partitioning of India and yet deplore how "the race idea . . . working in modern Islam with greater force than ever" might "ultimately wipe off the broad human outlook which Muslim people . . . imbibed from their religion".[32]

This issue, in any event, was part of that crisis of

self-emancipation which he knew to be proceeding. The sharpness of its exterior problems was the measure of its interior demands. The impact of his life and spirit it is hard to assess with any final assurance. That he succeeded in galvanising Islam in India into new vigour and exciting its spirit to fresh horizons there is no doubt. He had a disconcerting way of turning the tables on the timid and giving a new fluidity to their securities. Thus the finality of the Prophet ought he said to make for the most emancipated people on earth. It is possible to validate some of his apparently wildest claims from Islamic precedents somewhere in history or literature.[33] Certainly in Quranic exegesis he pioneered new perspectives and liberties of which the end is not yet. The "legend" he has become cannot be belied, for it is itself the approval of his counsel. In some measure what Muslims have taken him to be must authenticate what he has taken Islam to mean.

Yet there remain some serious reservations in the mind of the detached outsider who tries to look with impartial scholarship not only on the thought of Iqbal but on the discernible content of centuries of Islam. If one says: "Islam is truly *x*", one may well be right and the liberty for the claim must be assured. But there must be an equal freedom for the claim that history disowns *x*, or that the criteria that establish it are unauthentic. This may be illustrated at the sensitive point of Iqbal and the Qur'ān. "Call upon me and I will answer thee" (Sura 40.60) he takes to refer to that confrontation within which sense experience yields the presence of other minds. The alternation of day and night (31.29) becomes the theory (A. N. Whitehead) of "process". The Qur'ān and Bergson are unanimous that "every moment in the life of Reality is original, giving birth to what is absolutely novel and unforeseeable".[34] The basic term *Rabb*, or "Lord", is interpreted to mean the principle of creative evolution, "nurturing" (*murabbin*) emergent life and history. The etymology is dubious, or at least debatable.

What is alarming in all this is not the instinct to seek Quranic ground for modern thought. This enterprise has its own proprieties as part of a living theology. The menace lies in the total unconcern about primary meanings. The question is not raised as to what these verses meant to the men of Mecca and Medina in Muḥammad's time. Their hortatory, religious, original connotations are ignored. The Qur'ān emerges from Iqbal's hands as a kind of *Space, Time and Deity* treatise of a twentieth-century philosopher. It is odd indeed to find him reproving other cruder readers for importing their views into the sacred text "at the expense of its plain meaning".[35]

Yet this very audacity and uninhibited quality of mind have the great merit of posing inescapably the central problem of self-definition, namely, that of defining the definers! If Iqbal is an unacceptable interpreter, what is acceptable interpretation? And why? We must isolate from the great, and continuing, debate the controversies about its own procedures.

CHAPTER 5

# CONSENSUS AND COMMUNITY

"To live", runs the proverb, "is to outlive." Change is seen as the necessary circumstance of continuity. Life must outgrow its own past. Yet the living entity within the flux of change must be somehow recognisably continuous. Otherwise, to what does the change belong? The very notion of change itself dissolves away unless there is that beyond and through it whereby it can be measured. So in turn "to outlive is to live".

This perpetual equation is one which writers both inside and outside Islam seemed long reluctant to relate to the faith and law of the Qur'ān. Lord Cromer's curious remark that "Islam reformed is Islam no longer"[1] is one that, for all its obtuseness, would have been echoed by numerous shaykhs and mosque preachers of that time. The very prominence of *taqlīd*, as the tough and tenacious villain of the later Muslim centuries in the verdicts of apologists, proves this sustained aversion to change, this devotion to steadfast conformism of mind, that cling to the Islamic story well into this century.

But changes, in battalions, have been besieging this will to immunity, so making development itself a sharp issue within the spirit and theology of Muslims. The outward scene dictates the inward stress: the core of all exterior changes is the interior reckoning with change. This theme has already arisen urgently in the pretensions of Iqbal. It is there, soberly, in the moderate liberations pioneered by Muḥammad 'Abduh and broods over the apprehensive cautions of Rashīd Riḍā. It follows us, in later chapters, where pressures of the secular-state ideal urge it to venturesome lengths, or sectarian rigorism carries it into broils in the market-place. It is imperative, therefore, to set down the main outlines of the debate about authority and the status of *ijmā'* (consensus) and its instrument *ijtihād* (initiative) as principles and organs of Islamic development.

"Agreement of communal counsels shaped by the competent" might suffice as a broad definition of these dual terms. Or we might more loosely speak of "Muslims shaping Islam", which, in fact, they have always been doing, however true the retort be that it is, rather, Islam which shapes Muslims. Believers are without doubt moulded by doctrines and their institutions. But conversely, no doctrine can be finally insulated from what its adherents take it to be. That elusive thing "public opinion" is a sort of counsel of the population. Even dogmas have to co-exist with it. But how is it rightly, or actually, formed and embodied? By what means is living and outliving ordered in Islam? The answer involves the assessment of *ijmā'* and *ijtihād*, and has to do with community in consensus.

There is one preliminary consideration which may first be explored. It is that the loss of the Caliphate in 1924 threw a greater onus on community and at the time engendered a real, if indefinable, feeling of loss. The institution had endured, after all, from the immediate hours of the Prophet's death and through all its fortunes had been taken as a *sine qua non* of Islamic life and order. When the Turks terminated, first the Imamate, and then the Caliphate, bewilderment, indeed a sense of outrage, took hold of Muslims everywhere. The religious efficacy of the duties and ritual of Islam were understood to depend upon the existence of the Caliphate, who was head of the faithful.[2] The

Khilafatist movement, until its sad disillusionments at the hands of Arab nationalism and Turkish secularity, was a passionate and intelligent expression of deep Islamic convictions. Nor was the caliphal symbol less than sacrosanct to the mind of Arab Islam. Even when events were rapidly running against him, Rashīd Riḍā, writing in 1922,[3] insisted that the religious functions of the Caliphate were vital. He saw that a resuscitated Ottoman Caliphate would expose a vital Islamic institution to possible Western domination. But he countered this danger with a proposal for the temporary vesting of the office in some Muslim state, while a college of Muslim electors from all Islam should confer on an elected holder, whose rulings would have final authority. For Islam can in no way dispense with what the office means, even if under modern conditions Islamic statehood must take it over. He is ready to write off the imperial but reserves the essential. Islam, he insists, is not a theocracy and every Muslim has the right of interpretation of the Qur'ān. But this presupposes the competences which cannot be ensured except under the Caliphate.[4]

This was the general view. Its persistence and vigour serve to measure the regrets and perplexities which arose when caliphal "resurrection" proved impracticable.[5] Another measure can be found in the explosion of anger which greeted the contrary thesis about the Caliphate when it was propounded by 'Alī 'Abd-ar-Rāziq in 1925. Since this was, in its time, one of the most courageous of contemporary counsels, and since yesterday's radicalism has a way of becoming today's assumption, it calls for some paragraphs of exposition here.

'ALĪ 'ABD-AR-RĀZIQ (b. 1888), a younger brother of Muṣṭafā, published his *Islām wa-Uṣūl al-Ḥukm*, "Islam and the Principles of Government", the year after the abolition of the Caliphate so that it was a *post facto* discussion. But in bold and confident style, it refuted the whole notion of the indispensability of the Caliph to Islam, and in so doing enunciated quite novel theories about the nature of Islam itself and of Muḥammad's mission. The author at once set aside as useless the proposals of Rashīd Riḍā and of Al-Az'har university about a new caliphate. The Turkish *coup de grâce* to the institution had not created a problem: it had exposed a fact. Islam never really needed and never, essentially, had a caliphate. Its alleged foundations in the Qur'ān he said were unsound, and those in *ijmā'* had never been unanimous.

> "We have no need of this Caliphate either for the affairs of our religion or for the affairs of our secular life. . . . The Caliphate was and continues to be a discredit to Islam and to Muslims, a source of evil and corruption to both our religion and our everyday life."[6]

How then had so "fundamental" an entity gathered its false status? Simply because the Prophet's demise naturally left a great gap which called loudly for a symbolic authority to fill it. Then a purely pragmatic measure had come to be endowed with a pseudo-sanctity. Admitting that there were some unascertainable details of Muḥammad's administration and practice, 'Alī 'Abd-ar-Rāziq claimed it was broadly true that he had never intended the Caliphate. He was never essentially—and this was the author's boldest stroke—a head of state. The Prophet had no political pretensions.[7] Hierarchical status could not rightly be derived from him. The name or idea of "statehood" should not be identified with the sort of personal, prophetic ascendancy which Muḥammad indisputably exercised over his followers. The Qur'ān itself forbade such a belief.[8] Prophetic conquests were by prophetic speech and this authority was non-recurring.

So the whole idea of succession (the root meaning of *khalīfa*, "caliph") goes by the board. Muḥammad's mission being spiritual it was unique and inalienable. Moreover, it led to a universal religion which no *Arab* hegemony could monopolise or express.[9] So, for the mistaken and now blessedly defunct Caliphate, Muslims must substitute a spiritual loyalty. A fixed form of political autocracy, and with it external, perpetual codes of law and behaviour, must go.

This would indeed be liberation.

> "Nothing in religion prevents Muslims from following the lead of other nations in sciences, in society, in politics, or from overthrowing that antiquated system under which they have been subdued and humiliated, or from building their principles of sovereignty and their system of government on the most modern lines that human minds have approved."[10]

Muḥammad never had in view the regulation for all time of civil affairs. Islam is concerned with relations between God and man. As for civil laws they must come from the wisdom and experience of men in society. They are "too light a matter for God to undertake its management, save through the minds with which He has endowed us".[11]

These views were something of a *tour de force* and aroused bitter debate and controversy.[12] The writer would have been on surer ground both in Qur'ān and Tradition if he had frankly conceded that Muḥammad did in fact unite faith and rule, belief and state, but that this was a necessity of that time and place, which can now be revised. He preferred to adopt the line we have reviewed and so incurred larger liabilities. His discussion of *jihād* (holy war) in particular is evasive and he makes more than his case will sustain of the admitted irreplaceability of Muḥammad himself. He certainly disqualifies centuries of Islamic belief.

What matters here, however, more than the merits or otherwise of his argument, is the degree to which it opens up the whole frontier of Muslim mind with daily life. The resentment with which conservatism greeted it is some test of the nervousness it inspired. The Caliphate anyway had gone (though contemporaries did not know from month to month how irrevocably). If this was a real, and brutal, ratiocination of its demise, then truly the fearful might say: "We see not our signs". The upshot, whether in fact or theory, is to throw all the greater weight of responsibility upon the community in the decisions of belief and action. This brings us back, anxiously or ardently, as the mood dictates, to consensus and its controversial tasks.

*Ijmāʿ*, of course, presupposes the antecedent realities which have fashioned the community that yields it. These are the Qur'ān and the Practice or *Sunna* based on the Tradition (*ḥadīth*) of the Prophet. These are always regarded as primary sources which may not be overruled by any consensus. Repugnancy to them, as the Pakistani constitutional debates expressed the matter, *ipso facto* invalidates any opinion. But loyalty to the Qur'ān is, at least in some areas, difficult to define categorically. The appeal to it is of necessity compassed about with much complexity—a fact apparent enough already from the previous chapters. Moreover, the corpus of Tradition is voluminous and intricate. In its actual history stands a long pattern of sifting and testing, with the consequent suspicion of the spurious and the obsolete. It is difficult for many minds to see Traditions now immune from this "tradition" about themselves, the more so as times lengthen and the circumstantial context differs so radically.

These dubieties in the receiving and interpreting of the documentary sources, whether within or without *waḥy* (revelatory action), become in turn further problems for consensus to assess.

Nevertheless, it defers to these prior authorities in status. The Qur'ān is *Al-Furqān*, the criterion, *Hudā*, guidance from the Lord of the worlds, and also *Adh-Dhikr*, that which must always be in mind and mention when direction is sought and cited. Its contents have paramount authority. Yet it is silent on numerous themes: its contents are by no means conterminous with the dimensions of modern life. Nor do the complementary sources of Tradition, for all their plenteousness, suffice for guidance. They have yielded, in the early centuries, a vast store of precedents, which legal acumen and contention have elaborated into the dicta of the Schools. But other sources of authority, other means of direction, are still required beyond that *Sunna*, or beaten path, and beyond what even the most resourceful extension of prophetic precedent can afford.

*Qiyās*, or analogy, was here invoked. By dint of it explicit provision of Qur'ān or *Sunna* could be enlarged by argument extending the "intention" of the directive to parallel situations which it could be arguably understood to include, though failing specifically to state them. Thus the provision that property rights be not restored too early to wards and orphans (while they may still be exploited by the ruthless) would seem to provide an analogy whereby girls should not be subject too early to husbands, i.e. there should be a minimum marriage age. For who would deny that rights in the self are more sacred even than rights in property? (Or would some so deny?) If so, then one provision analogically includes the other.[13] But *qiyās* is a severely limited "enlarger" and the most pressing problems are unlikely to offer analogous elements.

It is at this point that the dependable community enters as a source of direction and the principle *vox populi, vox Dei* may be invoked—always in its Islamic limits. The Prophet is said in Tradition to have assured posterity that his people would never agree on an error. Individualism breeds heresy (the name for it in Islam is "innovation", *bid'a*) and a prominent group of theological adventurers are called "the separatists" (the Mu'tazilites). But communal convergence of mind is likely to be orthodox. So it is that the appeal to *ijmā'* can result in law having the same status as that promulgated by revelation itself. The indefectible community thus supplements the definitive documents in loyalty to authority.

But how does a communal mind emerge? Over what time and through what dispersion is it established? How long does one wait for it to become authentic and what are the organs to pronounce it so? These questions, not all of which admit of simple or unchanging answer, take us to *ijtihād*, the recognised means whereby consensus is attained. The word has to do with effort, diligence, venture and enterprise. By these the *mujtahid*, or initiator (in the Sunnite sense of the word), achieves or proposes a view or a verdict whereby a public mind may be directed and evoked. The qualifications, however, requisite to this function are traditionally very exacting and far beyond the reach of the average Muslim—Arabic expertise in grammar and parsing, the minutiae of Quranic exegesis and knowledge of the science of Tradition, and the like.

It is also circumscribed in other ways. The initiating bent cannot freely break into liberating crusade, if the criteria of the Schools are observed—*istiḥsān* or "equity", *istiṣlāḥ* or "general interest" and *istiṣ'ḥāb* or "sound precedent". Furthermore, in the classic view *ijtihād* tended to put itself out of business in proportion as it operated, on the view that law was not interminable and once the gaps left by the other sources had been filled, there remained no more place for *mujtahids*. This assumed a static society. But even yet amidst the proliferating changes of life the notion lingers in some quarters that the door of initiative, *bāb-al-ijtihād*, as the phrase has it, is really closed.

Finally, and most seriously, all the foregoing, in the strongly conservative view, must relate only to matters of law and practical guidance. The whole realm of dogma and Quranic, credal, theological Islam, is excluded from its range in an authoritative immutability, immune from enterprising or initiating thoughts and thinkers. Yet in this actual world there is nothing so deadly as having only a past—and nothing so futile.

These are the formidable issues in which we are immersed when the question is upon us about Muslims shaping Islam. These are the theories inherited from the past against which the claims and ventures of the Iqbals and *taqlīd*-breakers have been obliged to contend. One of their burdens has been that the Quranic ground of *ijmā'* is relatively scant. The chief textual foundation is Sura 4.115, in which failure to follow in "the path of the believers" is reproved, with the implication that such conduct means also opposition to the guidance of the Prophet.[14] Yet despite the paucity of sure proof-texts, there have been several other Islamic institutions, like the Caliphate, of undoubted actual authenticity, which lack specific Quranic ground. It is always valid for the upholders of *ijmā'* to claim that a *consensus fidelium* is a most appropriately Islamic thing. The community is in fact arbiter: *teneor* is *teneo* even in the most absolutist creeds. From its beginnings community and rightness have been coincident in Islam. The concepts of valid and invalid go with communal frontiers. *Dār al-Islām* and *Dār al-Ḥarb*, the households of faith and of unfaith, have been at the same time territorial and definitive. Even Tradition, it may be said, is a sort of communal mind in the form of a communal memory.

But if *consensus fidelium* has inescapable validity in real life, the question remains who are the *fideles* and how comes their consensus. The President of the *Jamā'at-al-'Ulamā'* of Pakistan, according to an answer quoted in the Munir Report, insisted that Muslim

> ". . . law is complete and merely requires interpretation by those who are experts in it. According to my belief no question can arise, the law relating to which cannot be discovered from the Qur'ān and *ḥadīth*."[15]

This rigidity ties *ijmā'* strictly to exegetical matters and makes its "discovery" wholly the business of mullahs. And it is plainly barring and shuttering, in unwarrantable fashion—indeed with incredible naïveté—that "door" of *ijtihād*. Time itself has made such timid obscurantism ludicrous. While such opinions huddle round the doorways for a private and vested security, the walls themselves are broken through by a besieging world. "It must be admitted", writes Muhammad Rasjidi (Rashīdī), that

> "the problems of the world today are very different from those of the time of Muḥammad, and their [i.e. such an] attitude would make Islam a dead religion. Actually, Islam is a dynamic religion, based on the Qur'ān, the Sunnah and reasoning."[16]

But how is the easy assumption of dynamism and rationality to be worked out? What is the conjunction of reasoning "and" the Qur'ān? Is it an addendum, or an association or a qualification? More precisely, is the age-long distinction between practical directives (*fiqh*) or jurisprudence, and theology or dogma, really any longer viable? Do not necessary questions of daily existence bear squarely on ultimate issues of theology? Can there be any dynamic direction and at the same time any final doctrinal immunities? Do not all serious questions of *fiqh*, as the modern world sets them for persons and communities, reach into sanctions and authorities of doctrine? Take, for example, the prohibition of *taṣwīr*, or visual representation of living form, as treated in the official periodical, *Majallat al-Az'har*.[17] The writer there insists that this veto can now properly be lifted. To believe that Muslims still need a radical prohibition of statuary, or a rigorous protection from photography, would imply a chronic idolatrous perversity of mind which, if it existed, would demonstrate that fourteen centuries of Islam had proved a total failure. One cannot, in other words, reach a particular legal verdict without, either way, impugning, or involving, the total nature of Islam, including the time relation of its revelatory source.

It is likewise with the now familiar reinterpretation of the proviso relating to plurality of marriage. The debate about "if ye think ye cannot do them justice" (Sura 4.3) is in one sense a purely textual matter for a strictly textual *ijtihād*. But the whole understanding of "justice" within the marriage relationship opens up a host of questions, sociological and "sacramental", for which there is no sufficient guidance in the phrase itself. The relation then between the letter of the text and the mind of the exegete is much more that of clay and potter, than of clock and mosque-timekeeper watching for the hours. In other words *ijmāʿ* truly functions as far as may be Quranically: but the writ of the Qur'ān runs by dint of *ijmāʿ*.

Scores of examples elsewhere might be cited to

confirm this fact of the living relation of thought to scripture and of opinion to authority, whereby it becomes impossible to draw any safe line behind which the Qur'ān, or Tradition, may somehow "speak its mind" to a wholly receptive, entirely unprepossessed community, exempted from sociological, spiritual, environmental queries of its own. This means that there is no ultimate immunity of Quranic sources from the factor of present community, either for *fiqh* or *sharī'a* or *īmān*. This is true whatever, precisely, may be made by individual exegetes of the distinction in Sura 3.7, between *muḥkamāt* and *mutashābihāt*. For in the last analysis even the categorical is in time and the metaphorical by nature turns upon the way it is taken. In either case the difference textually is more of degree than essence—a fact that is proved by the tendency either to allegorise the categorical, to consider it earlier misunderstood, or to "spiritualise" its absoluteness.

But if, as a perhaps unacknowledged consensus seems to indicate, dogma cannot be immunised from the consequences of admitted modifications of law, all the greater urgency attaches to the identifying of the *fideles in consensu*. Is *ijmā'* a technical, legal process for which the community relies on those competent and qualified? If so, what is the form of the competence, the measure of the qualities? Here the same factors, just noted, making for wider view of *ijmā'* make also for more open concepts of *ijtihād*. Indeed much of what underlies the whole theme of this book may be seen as something of a lay revolt within Islam against the special status of custodians of faith and law, and their long monopoly in the definition of Islam.[18] And, by the same token, it is impossible to resist the impression that much official resistance from mullahs and pundits to the broadening of *ijtihād* arises from a sense of threat either to prestige, or effective influence, or even economic status. There can be little doubt that the will to preserve the authority and position of shaykhs and mosque personnel lies behind the opposition, throughout the Pakistani constitutional debates, to the idea that legislation on the part of a Muslim house of deputies could possibly embody or represent communal opinion. The qualified ulema, said Mawlānā Abū-l-Ḥasanāt, earlier quoted, have their status by virtue of minute scholarship and expert training and are "in no way analogous or similar to the legislature in modern democracy".[19] Ihtishām al-Ḥaqq made the same point in respect of a government commission, of whom by this criteria he was the only valid member in an improper body (on which, however, he in fact sat), when the government commission studied family and marriage law in Pakistan.[20]

If this view is adopted it renders superfluous all the painful, yet appropriate, discussions in recent constitutional ventures in Islam about the place of the population, through electorates, by deputies, for legislatures, in the ordering of Islamic life. The attendant questions about minority voting rights, about devices to ensure non-repugnancy to the Qur'ān if assemblies of Muslims could not be relied upon to assure it, and about whether voting rights should be limited to good, observing Muslims, would all become superfluous if *ijmā'* and *ijtihād* are specialist preserves.

But life cannot have it this way. There are new states, established in the name of Muslim populations and in some sense associating Islam, territory, people and state, in one unity. This must necessarily find its organs and cannot be deprived by inward "ecclesiasticism" of the self-direction it has so hardly and so lately won from alien empire. In the practice of politics these abstractions of theorists about the workings of democracy may be inconsequential and doctrinaire. The frustrations of abstract "Islamicity" will be one of our discoveries in Chapter 7. None the less these ardent and enterprising discussions, having to do with the shape of the *shūrā bayna-hum* of our title verse, "the counsel among them which is their way", are symptomatic of a widening claim from a growing number in the articulation of Islam. The new nationalism has broken up the single *millet* that Qur'ān and Caliphate recognised. The old universalism is sundered. But what the recent fragmentation into nations destroys in the whole it revitalises in the parts. Statehood, as observed in Chapter 1, is a veritable forcing-house of popular *mujtahids*, aided and abetted, of course, by an insistent and ubiquitous modernity.

They have much force on their side. Why should the judgements about Islam be always and only given by those who know their "companion studies" in Tradition and the *nāsikh* and *mansūkh*, abrogating and abrogated, subtleties of the Qur'ān.[21] These obscurer arts, by their very remoteness, disqualify their practitioners from understanding contemporary physics or the intricacies of economic policy. If the centre of gravity, so to speak, of a community moves, as it undoubtedly has in recent Islam, from the theological experts to politicians or engineers, and if *ijmā'* is truly a community achievement, should not the changes reflect themselves in the criteria of "competence"? May not a worthy merchant, who, by long repute and steady discipline, practises Islamic ethics in the exacting spheres of business or administration, be thereby qualified to help direct its general counsels? Sura 4.58 observes: "Surely God commands you to make over trusts to those who are worthy of them". So we must beware of a monopolistic, "ecclesiastical" custody of Islam.

This plea is reinforced by the "equality" of Muslims before God. "In religious matters the humblest Muslim stands on a level with the caliph or his chief *qāḍī* and the ultimate control rests with the conscience of the people as a whole."[22] To make good this brave notion a critical egalitarianism must find voice and formulation. In doing so it has both theoretical and practical difficulties to surmount. Both are conspicuous in the substance of the chapters that follow. Both reach into sharp educational questions. For Muslim education tends to segregate two fields of discipline into two types. The mosque-school, Az'har or Deoband, style of training all too little serves the critical and knowledgeable fashion of mind, while the "secular" state-school, state-university stream of students are all too often intelligently ignorant about their precise doctrinal heritage. With them Islam tends to be an allegiance of will and assumption, rather than an alert conviction. Only slowly is the educational duality brought into one. Meanwhile theology, the mosque-sermon and the mullah-mind tend to be innocent of "informed worldliness"[23] and those who move freely in stock-banking, chemical research or oil engineering are unfamiliar with the world of *tawḥīd* and *i'jāz*. All such debate about who can, in status or skill, constitute a *mujtahid*, is simply part of the large issue as to what *ijtihād* has in fact to accomplish.

It is also important to keep in view in this setting the still heavy burden of illiteracy, which means that in many parts of *Dār al-Islām* the masses are necessarily unable for critical or deliberative opinions. They may, of course, be vital parties to fundamental acts of self-determination, as in the creation of Pakistan. But those choices arise from political action which needs to be urgent enough to reach its goals and so relies on slogans, emotions and open promises. "Governments", as

Albert Hourani has drily remarked, "do not exist in order to assent to true propositions."[24] This sober observation puts *ijmāʿ* and *ijtihād* into a sort of wry perspective. What Iqbal designates as "the principle of development in Islam"[25] must be understood like all other movement as a battle with inertia and a balance of forces.

They have, none the less, much solid achievement to their credit, some aspects of which await us in Chapter 6. The fast of Ramaḍān adapted, by President Habib Bourguiba, to the exigencies of a modern society, with factory shifts, wage structure and output patterns: *zakāt*, as a voluntary principle of alms-giving at least symbolically realised in fiscal methods aimed at social welfare and income redistribution: the position of women in life and society ameliorated by dint of joint exegetical and social reinterpretations—in these and other fields there is no doubt that a strong, practical consensus unto change is operating, even if, in shape and substance, it diverges far from what the schoolmen would recognise as either *ijmāʿ* or Islam.

Two reflections in conclusion may be appropriate. The one is the fascinating fluidity of the Islamic present. Remarkable revisions of Islamic order are happening on every hand. Community and consensus are, as Khālid Muḥammad Khālid has it in another context, "on the road together".[26] The institutions and attitudes of centuries are under active change, with scruples and theories in rearguard retreat. Yet, for all its exciting present postures, may not *ijmāʿ*—like its counterpart in every system and religion—conceal a hidden peril? Is not consensus in self-esteem, convergence of complacence, all too easy? Do not communities in fact all too readily agree on an error? Is the collective always the authentic? Are there not acts of *ijtihād* which no *ijmāʿ* rewards with approval, but which society nevertheless requires? It is all too possible for consensus to deny the creativity of the few or comfort the perversities of the many.[27]

Yet, either way, we come back to the importance of the Muslim in the personal. For good or ill, he is the raw material of the potential convergence of belief and practice. What Islam does is the cumulative decision of Muslims. Time is for ever holding its own census to decide its continuities. So we turn to a miscellany of mentors.

CHAPTER 6

# MEN AND MINDS

THE President of Egypt in his *Falsafat ath-Thawra*, or "The Philosophy of the Revolution", visualised with enthusiasm the use of the annual pilgrimage to Mecca as an occasion for ecumenical councils in Islam, where leaders in politics, literature, scholarship, science, commerce and youth, would confer together for the direction of Islamic destiny.[1] Whatever may be the merit, or the prospect, of this suggestion, Muslim history shows little liking for the conciliar pattern. Whether in the Ṣūfī fraternities which have often carried the main brunt of Islamic survival, or in the characteristic pattern of "cell" and "school" and *ijtihād*, Islam seems to have relied for its counsels on the local and intimately communal and on the group. At least there are in our time no universal consultations in which we can take unified cognisance of its common mind. Our task with "Men and Minds" involves the searching out of books and authors, trends and directions, the diffused *shūrā* of this or that initiative and the approvals which coalesce around it.

We must beware of over-estimating the intelligentsia. Yet it is with them that the issues which underlie the slogans of the streets or the stridencies of the radio find discursive and temperate form. Much in the living situation belongs with symbols and emotion, rather than ideas and reason. The former only become susceptible of scrutiny and debate when they are given rational expression. Our proceeding, therefore, is legitimate provided we are careful to restore the issues beyond such analysis to their full context of tension and hope. It seems appropriate to focus on Egypt—whose is the intellectual leadership of Arab Islam.

The foremost name in the Egyptian scene in the generation after 'Abduh's passing is that of Ṭāhā Ḥusayn (b. 1889), now the doyen of Arabic letters. His unique authority has been built up over the years by firm devotion to objective standards of scholarship and in numerous works of history and imagination. His name symbolises the steady pursuit of culture, a creative acceptance of Europe in art and scholarship, and a crusade for worthier educational standards. He is a lay scholar and, though graduated from Al-Az'har, has only indirect theological significance. In this very fact, however, he is symptomatic of the tentativeness with which the ultimate problems of the Muslim mind have in general been treated in this half-century. But he exemplifies in other realms the premises which need to be extended to the whole range of Muslim belief.

His artistic sensitivities were heightened by the tragedy of blindness which overtook him in his village home at Maghāgha, in Upper Egypt, when he was only two years old. His writing has that wistful tenacity which is born only of adversity. His childhood and youth are distilled into two volumes of autobiography, *Al-Ayyām*, which unfortunately break off at the point of his adult career.[2] The *taqlīd* which 'Abduh challenged can here be felt, in a mental régime at Al-Az'har which neither satisfied nor educated the mind. The foremost of his services to Islam is just the fervour of a repudiation of spiritual torpor and the skill to make it autobiographically. Here is a refreshing change of outlook from the slavish and stereotyped habits of mind to fresh springs of personal emotion and living experience. The reader knows himself to be close to the heart, in

*Al-Ayyām*, of the intellectual revolt provoked by conservative Islam. He reads it in the narrative of an alert student, from his first awed entry, in 1902, into the University, through growing bewilderment to passionate disillusionment. Lonely and nervous, the writer describes with vivid touches the manners and habits of shaykhs and students and other denizens of the Az'har quarter, the vehement and often sterile debates, the mingled lethargy and bigotry that characterised the whole system. His loss of faith in Al-Az'har was continuous: grudges, defamation, incompetence reigned. "Students, young and old, never stopped jeering at the stupidity of their teachers and their proneness to ridiculous mistakes."[3] These experiences aroused his interest in the lay intelligentsia outside Al-Az'har. Through the office of the newspaper *Al-Jarīda* he discovered the world of the tarboush beyond the world of the turban. In this field of literature and letters he was to find his *métier*.

His rebellion was, however, a wistful repudiation, as of one who had been cheated of his hopes but remained without venom. His sifting of Al-Az'har in the crucible of his own experience and his honest record of personal disillusionment are a most important example of critical counsel in Islam. They are also representative in another way. For Ṭāhā Ḥusayn has, with one or two exceptions, tended to let theology lie while exercising his scholarship in other fields, exemplifying there the sound intellectual integrity so urgent to faith yet not in fact directing it to issues of dogma. Thus, for all his virility of mind, he has contributed indirectly to that abeyance of theological criticism which is so marked a feature of current Arab Islam.

After a time in the new Egyptian University and studies in France, Ṭāhā Ḥusayn launched into the literary career that has sustained a spate of writings over three decades—stories, translation, articles and criticism. Three works are of particular relevance in this context. The first is a controversial discussion of pre-Islamic poetry, *Fī-sh-Shi'r al-Jāhilī*, withdrawn and reissued as *Fī-l-Adab al-Jāhilī* the following year.[4] Its significance lies in the furore which its modest contents aroused and in its illustration of the complexities of critical scholarship impinging on dogmatic preserves. The Az'har authorities demanded that he should be deprived of his post in the Egyptian University (since it was run on public funds) and in the end only the action of the Government in making the issue in the Egyptian Parliament a matter of confidence saved him.

His actual thesis was neither new nor very revolutionary. It concerned the date and character of Arabic poetry, traditionally taken to be pre-Islamic, with which Quranic eloquence (*i'jāz*) was contrasted to demonstrate the revelatory status of the latter as the surpassing text of an illiterate reciter. Ṭāhā Ḥusayn held on critical grounds that the poetry was in fact post-Quranic and this deprived the traditionalists of one line of support. His main argument was that the poetry in question showed a uniformity of dialect only feasible after the Qur'ān's wide influence had become operative. The point is said to be reinforced by a study of pre-Quranic inscriptions. It also fitted closely several Quranic considerations, notably the belief that it was Muḥammad who taught the Arabs monotheism, whereas this "pre-Islamic" poetry is almost entirely monotheistic. Allusions to Noah, the future life, and other features, seem to support the view that the poets in question must have been post-Quranic—not to mention the Qur'ān's picture of the earlier jinn poets. Nevertheless, the transference from pre- to post-Islamic date meant the loss of the traditional argument for Quranic eloquence, and this, notwithstanding the other "assets" Quranically, was damnable heresy to the conservative mind. The latter seemed to prefer losing Muḥammad's originality than their own mental securities.

Ṭāhā Ḥusayn also disputed certain traditional points relating to Abraham and his connection with the Ka'ba at Mecca, and the historicity, in Arabia, of a "religion of Abraham" of which Islam was said to be the final, perfect form. He claimed, in this and other issues, to pursue the proper liberties of scholarship without the trammels of dogmatic prepossession.

> "Literature was studied by the older authorities because it was a means to understanding the Qur'ān and religion . . . because it was sacred it could not be subjected to proper scientific discussion. . . . I wish to study the history of literature in freedom and self-respect, as the naturalist studies botany and geology, not fearing any authority in such study."[5]

He insisted that such independence of sacrosanct attitudes and a refusal to admit dogmatic immunities were essential to contemporary integrity of faith. The Arabic language itself had to be delivered from religious sanctity, and historical studies set free for doubt, analysis and independent judgement.

In another place, Ṭāhā Ḥusayn claimed that this work on pre-Islamic poetry, together with 'Alī 'Abd-ar-Rāziq's study on the Caliphate, had decisively established the principle of intellectual liberty in Egyptian Islam.[6] The verdict is over-optimistic. For there were serious corollaries of his attitude which needed urgently to be worked out in fields where he did not venture. But as a man of letters, if not as an exegete, he continued to appropriate the essential freedom which he took to be the birthright of the Muslim. The second major work in which he developed his crusade was *Mustaqbal ath-Thaqāfa fī Miṣr*,[7] a vigorous and courageous discussion of Egyptian educational needs and policy. Insisting that Egypt and Europe have a single intellectual heritage, he pleads for comparable patterns of teaching and approach. The state is seen as the sole responsible source of education. Al-Az'har must come into line with modern ideas, reform its concepts and methods and accept the leadership of the state as the condition of a vital Islam and a strong nation. The most interesting feature of his emphasis is the confidence in an Egyptian cultural self-expression as the key to any feasible modernisation of Islam. His own editorial activities and his subsequent roles as Director of General Culture (1940) in the Ministry of Education, and Minister of Education (1950), as well as a prolific output of articles and studies, have served well the cause of which through four decades he has been the symbol and the voice.

In *'Alā Hāmish as-Sīra*[8] he takes for his field the "margins of traditional prophetic biography". He disclaims any strictly historical scholarship, though his aim is to renew the ancient "hagiography" of Islam for the contemporary reader by retelling it in a fresh idiom and freeing it from archaic or forbidding guise. He is, of course, free himself, in this enterprise, of Quranic, and therefore dogmatic, necessities and it would seem in the light of his whole career that this choice is deliberate. He is anxious to recover for today's youth the moral lessons of heroic Islam without incurring the strictly academic or doctrinal issues. The vocabulary and tedious *asānīd*, or chains of attestation, encumber the old histories and deter the Muslim of today. Imagination and feeling must re-create the force and recover the vitality of the past of the Prophet and his Companions.

Ṭāhā Ḥusayn's achievement in this realm, though

deeply religious, is not in the strict sense apologetic, since by choice and temper he concentrates on the didactic to the exclusion of the critical. There is point in his plea that religion is much more than logic, and faith than historical scrutiny. Yet this stance, maintained through all his later works, means by the same token an abeyance of theological duty. His whole work and influence confirm the conclusion that Ṭāhā Ḥusayn's chosen role has been that of the scholar-layman for whom religion is essentially "feeling". His instincts, both of prudence and fulfilment, lie outside the orbit of the shaykhs, whose educational dominance he has done so much to qualify and amend but whose professional obligations he has left squarely in their camp.

If his career in the province of culture is here rightly assessed, he becomes an outstanding example, perhaps the first in Egypt, of a typically Western reaction to religion, the attitude which takes refuge in a scholarly detachment and leaves religious problems to those who care to burn their fingers or agonise their souls. There are suggestions throughout his writing that religion is for the sentient, not the critical, side of the duality said to characterise all human personality.[9]

Yet, if the "mental fight" for theology within religion is not to be sought or found in him, the climate which produces the reaction he represents with such distinction is already generating the temper of a valid apology. For such a pattern of reaction to dogma is at least sympathetic to the tasks of a more ultimate radicalism even though it refuses to broach them. Meanwhile the temperamental and practical faults of religious conservatism are being chastened and pruned. That Ṭāhā Ḥusayn has served and inspired a literary renaissance in the Egypt of his lifetime is indisputable. Its evidences are everywhere.[10] But careful concentration of that liberalism in the fields of literature and education leaves theology still unfulfilled.

A much readier instinct for the central citadels of belief was found in another writer of comparably liberal sympathies, Muḥammad Ḥusayn Haykal (1888–1956). His major works handle with great thoroughness the two exacting themes of the Prophet and the Pilgrimage. Haykal's *Ḥayāt Muḥammad*, or "Life of Muḥammad", first published in 1935, is the most ambitious and significant of twentieth-century Islamic biographies in Arabic, while *Fī Manzil al-Waḥy*, "In the Home of Revelation", presents a fascinating religious study in the experience of sophisticated pilgrimage.[11] Both works need to be set in the context of the author's literary development.

Haykal drew his main inspiration from Qāsim Amīn, the energetic champion of women's rights in Islam,[12] and from studies in France. He established himself as a lawyer and man of letters and in 1924 published the first Arabic novel on Western lines, *Zaynab*. His newspaper, *As-Siyāsa*, often crossed swords with *Al-Manār* in a crusade against *taqlīd* and for spiritual and intellectual renewal as Haykal conceived it. It was, however, his *Life of Muḥammad* which constituted his largest achievement in the new direction of Muslim thinking. Since its topic is the most sensitive realm of Islamic life, it deserves a careful assessment.

He set out to present the Prophet in the clear light of rational evaluation based on the principle that the Qur'ān, freed from the embellishments of the *Sīra*, was the sufficient source for the historian. The traditional accretions had de-Islamised the picture, while Western orientalism had tended to inhibit the loyal Muslim with the impression that scholarship was inimical to piety. Haykal aimed to combine a soberly critical scholarship with an intelligent devotion. It was not, of course, difficult to shed the traditional and the apocryphal, whether in the prophetic biography prior to the call to prophecy or in such subsequent events as the Night Journey. But it must be doubted whether the will to reason and fact did justice to the essential religious dimension of Muḥammad or to the implications of the metaphysical status Haykal affirmed of him. The discussion of the Mount Ḥirā' experience is disappointingly slight.[13] Muḥammad the shepherd comes upon his vision after years of meditation on the corruption of idolatry, the misery of disunity and the vanity of strife. He saw that neither Jews nor Christians could deliver his people. When he began his mission he proceeded in the way of modern knowledge, calling on his first hearers to clear their minds of prejudice and to test the credentials of his word. Responsively the early Muslims opted for this *islām* of reason. Let there be unity of worship, not idolatry. For unity binds man to man, tribe to tribe, planet to planet, in an appropriate order. Superstitious worship is vanity because it has mistaken the universe and God. What respect for human intelligence could be higher than this? Islam made a clean sweep of all factors in the relations of God and man save good works and piety. Each owes his brother what he owes himself: no idol, no priest, no mediator, remain.[14]

So to the obdurate irrationality of the Meccans and the Hijra to Medina and its sequel. Jealousy, pride of place, rivalry—these were for the moment too strong and stubborn. So the political development of Islam was indispensable to its spiritual triumph. Meccan recalcitrance necessitated a struggle to the death. Meanwhile, the Medinan achievement set a supreme example of ordered freedom, civil, religious and constitutional, built on the foundation stone of human brotherhood. The battles were ultimately defensive, in that they secured the victory of the just and the rational. It was only obduracy that required them. Islam is not pacifist, nor "personal". As a faith for life in all its parts it must attain the sceptre.

The reader is left with the uneasy feeling that there is a whole dimension of the "religious"—perhaps crudely yet validly sought for in the old "mystique"—which eludes this modern biographer. The impression is only deepened by those passages, notably the pages on the Night Journey,[15] which venture some "metaphysical" thoughts about Muḥammad. The Prophet stood, it is said, face to face with reality, beyond the veil of time and place. All human judgements are relative but the recipient of the Qur'ān sees the whole universe gathered to his spirit and knows it "from eternity to eternity".[16] Yet, allegedly, it is all congruent with modern science, for that too is forcing the secrets of the universe into the open. No attempt is made to reconcile the insistent humanity of Muḥammad with the claims that link him with cosmic universality.

Nor, strangely in a *Life* which sets itself squarely within the Quranic alone, is there any effort to assess the underlying question as to how revelations so sharply occasioned and particular in time and place are the locale of the eternal and the Divine. It is admirable to use the Qur'ān historically, but therefore all the more imperative to relate its history to its eternity. The reader is hardly reassured by the concluding plea for a committee of scholars to propagate Islam wisely and progressively in this modern age.[17] For has this academic venture, right as it is in its own province, sufficiently wrestled either with the mystery of its heritage or the dimensions of its contemporary business? Judged in the light of its own modest plea to have made only a beginning, *Ḥayāt Muḥammad*, with its fervour and candour, is a notable waymark.

Muḥammad Ḥusayn Haykal's other book, *Fī Manzil al-Waḥy*, aims to do for the Pilgrimage what the biography attempted for the Prophet, namely, to bring a "scientific" and rational judgement to its interpretation. It was inspired by a desire to reform some of the cruder circumstances of pilgrim travel and ritual, as well as to take stock of Saʿūdī Arabian Wahhābism and drink from the sacramental source of Islamic solidarity. The book breathes a deep religious feeling. Muslims must renew themselves only from their own past and not be deceived by the material seductions of the West. Overcoming a certain reluctance of sophistication, the author set out for Mecca.[18] His experience reinforced his vocation. For it gave him at once an object lesson in Muslim backwardness and obduracy as evident in the Meccan ulema and an overwhelming assurance of Islamic vitality as mediated in the ancient shrines. Mecca, he hoped would become the Geneva of the Islamic world, but it had still many obstacles to surmount to reach that goal. First hygienic and technical improvements, then a university: meanwhile the nurture of the vision which his own book would serve. Rekindling his spirit at the foothills of Ḥirā' and on the field of Badr, Haykal senses the aridity of much mosque preaching, deplores the atrophy of *ijtihād*, and castigates the formalism and neglect of self-sacrifice among his fellows.

But he still holds off from the deepest issues of theology. The faith, he insists, must offer rational arguments and confront the dangers implicit in the scientific climate with the loss of theological "immediacy", in the popular mind. Yet he still keeps dogma and science effectively apart.

> "It is our duty to take our stand on everything that science attains and surround ourselves with knowledge . . . but we must also tell people that God has

commanded them to believe in Him and it is not for them to question or oppose."[19]

There is more than has been here attempted in the assumption that science and dogma can make so easy a peace, with the one gently tolerating the assertion of the other. To state the partiality of science and for the rest proclaim that in the Prophet's life, its lessons and doctrines, lie the surest means to the universal spread of truth, beauty and goodness, is too large a generalisation to pass for theological apology in a bewildered age. Haykal's two long major works—some twelve hundred pages between them—are a generous measure alike of the scope and incompleteness of his purpose.

Another mentor of Arab Islam and a prolific popular writer is 'Abbās Maḥmūd al-'Aqqād (b. 1889). Born of a Kurdish mother, he is not directly a product of Al-Az'har, or indeed of any school beyond the primary education he received at Aswan. His own avid reading and literary aptitudes have made him an influential author in Syria and Iraq as well as Egypt. His initial concern, with Aḥmad Amīn and Ṭāhā Ḥusayn, was to raise the level and sharpen the effectiveness of Arabic writing. For this he argued in *Muṭāla'āt fī-l-Kutub*[20] where he deplored the stilted form and self-conscious cult of eloquence in Arabic style. Literature could only reflect the serious ends of man when it broke free from convention and imitation.

These strictures were well taken and find echo widely in the minds under review in this Chapter. On the more exacting ground of constructive Islamics, 'Abbās al-'Aqqād proves less adequate. His major work for present purposes is *'Abqariyyat Muḥammad*, "The Genius of Muḥammad", first published in 1942. Here the Prophet is taken as the epitome of the virtues after which all sincere men strive. The book may be rightly seen as a form of communal idealism in the shape of heroic eulogy. In Muḥammad Islam traces the equation between possessive memory and corporate ethics. So we do not look for critical history. Muḥammad is the paragon, as prophet, soldier, ruler, man, husband, father, preacher. Strenuous apology is undertaken at the points where sensitivity is most alert, namely, the defensive wars and the necessary marriages. What matters more than these details is the assurance that shaped the ancient Traditions. Here was the superb figure, whether as seer, thinker, orator or man of action, a man with whom there is no like among men and whose impact dominates all future centuries. No event that has happened since has been what it would have been had Muḥammad never appeared. Neither the discovery of America nor the French Revolution could have occurred without him.[21]

The book does not stay to deal with the metaphysical enigma involved in its own claims, assuming them historically verifiable. The author does not intend a critical apology. He is anxious to demonstrate that if Carlyle can do much Al-ʿAqqād can do more. There is no need here to reproach its intellectual silences. For it is important to appreciate that here in the ardent re-possession of the central figure we have the most zealous and crucial point of Islamic "counsel". ʿAbbās al-ʿAqqād is all the more forceful as its spokesman for his strong assurance. The significance of *ʿAbqariyyat Muḥammad* is in no way altered by the subsequent writings in the "genius" sequence on ʿUmar, Gandhi and Jesus.

An Egyptian "counsellor" of much riper scholarship was Aḥmad Amīn (1886–1954), essayist and historian, who, though not an original thinker, provides none the less a valuable index to Muslim mind through four decades. It may be useful to preface a review of his writing by some brief notice of an earlier essayist, Muṣṭafā Luṭfī al-Manfalūṭī (1876–1924)—not for any marked similarity of temper, but for the fact that each wrote out of a vigorous discontent with prevailing modes of life and relied on the essay form. They may be taken as reflecting the mood of Arab Islam in the period and the aftermath of the two great wars of this century.

Al-Manfalūṭī, who claimed descent from the Prophet himself and graduated from Al-Az'har, possessed a vivid imagination and a powerful prose style, in which he gave evocative shape to many of the ideas of Muḥammad 'Abduh, whom he greatly esteemed. His three volumes of *An-Naẓarāt*[22] became almost a *vade mecum* of their generation in Egypt. For they made articulate the latent issues of day-to-day Islam—the tensions with Western influence, the paradox of religious fervour and scepticism, the zeal and the timidity of reform. He attacked conservatism and superstitition, decried saint worship and gave sharp focus to social criticism.

> "I saw religion, that great spreading tree of peace under which is shelter from the blasts of life and its sighs, and it had changed its role in the hands of men into poisoned arrows with which every one tries to wound his brother . . ."[23]

Inertia and decadence and inward dishonesty impede and distort the true Islam, to which Egypt, and all Muslims, must seek, against the encroachments of Western malaise. There can be no salvation westwards. With Haykal, Al-Manfalūṭī is sure that European manners, luxuries and habits of mind, where Muslims lack discrimination, will only unhouse their souls and dig their graves. It is the Prophet, not Rousseau, Bacon or Newton, the Qur'ān not Herbert Spencer.

Yet the Muslim guardians of the unity of God have

themselves become idolaters. Organised religion is caught in its own pride. One wistful essay describes a journey to a perfect society, not westward like Bacon's New Atlantis, where all is harmony, discipline and peace, in a nation of simple monotheists among whom no prophet has gone and to whom no scripture has been sent. Their pure, natural, rational moralism shames the subtleties of the theologians, the niceties of lawyers and the pretensions of mystics.[24] Public opinion is sound and unselfish and prisons and police unknown. On other occasions Al-Manfalūṭī's writing breathes an almost Hardy-like defiance of a hard deity. His own tragedy of four lost sons lent a strangely moving pathos to his pen.

It is this same ardent questioning, combined with a like set of devotion, which characterises the much more erudite writing of Aḥmad Amīn. Formerly Professor of Arabic Literature and History at Cairo University and a mainspring of the Committee for Authorship, Amīn played a large role in the revival of Egyptian scholarship. His works on Islamic history do not directly concern theology or the Qur'ān but exemplify a new attitude to historical studies. His autobiography, *Ḥayātī*, and the several volumes of reflective essays, *Fayḍ al-Khāṭir*, or "The Welling Mind", with their wide range of topics, provide a notable access to intellectual Cairo in his day. Here the reader may feel the currents of Islam. The essay form, of course, absolves the writer from obligations he may not wish to assume and leaves him free to wander casually, or reflect diversely, to allude, to ventilate and to opine, at will. This perhaps is its merit and the choice of the form may itself be symptomatic. Where responsibilities sit thus lightly, the pen is alert and ambitious, the mind critical and venturesome. But there is no sustained reconstruction of Islamic thought, sociology or theology.

Aḥmad Amīn insists on the urgent need for religious conviction. The Muslim East must believe again, as it will if given leadership in belief. Mosque preaching must be vital, informed and positive. Secularity is rampant: there is worship of mere quantity: quality languishes. Arabic still lacks a valid literature for today. Preoccupation with the past jeopardises the future. Islam must renew in *ijtihād* its proper principle of movement, distinguishing between elemental obligations and their changing application. On science and faith, he contents himself in the main with the familiar division of provinces and the partiality of the merely rational. His mind is conservative, yet too lively to be obscurantist. He is acutely aware of the need to disseminate culture and to break down the aristocraticism both of Arabic writing and Islamic theology. In *Ḥayātī*, he analyses the contrast between the disciplined piety and erudition of his father and the temper of his own children. The same lesson underlies the narrative of his own emergence from the turbaned world of Al-Az'har into the new and strenuous climate of "liberal" studies. In this transition he expresses in autobiographical terms the major personal problem of Islamic letters in this century. Few held together as well as he the educational dichotomy which has so often and so long kept apart the classical lore of the shaykhs and the new learning of the sciences. In *Al-Ḥalqa al-Mafqūḍa*[25] he sought for a bridge of culture through a group of scholars who truly knew both worlds and could link Quranic memoriter with chemistry and Al-Ghazālī with Bergson and Shaw. Aḥmad Amīn exemplified his own plea in his careful fostering of Islamic research and his painstaking self-initiation into French and English. Both are described in *Ḥayātī*, with simple directness and candour.[26]

These considerations lead further into the definition

of the Muslim in himself. Given the tensions of circumstance and the dichotomy of loyalties, who and what is the authentic Muslim? *Ḥayātī*, it might be said, is a sort of reverie on this issue in memoir form. Take, for example, the urgent passage in which he ponders the secular "transformation" of one of his most pious friends,[27] a movement from the meticulous to the casual, from mosque to cinema, with its underlying question about feasible, not to say valid, continuity. Who is the twentieth-century Muslim and by what may he be known? How does he maintain what the past bequeathed and the present requires?

Amīn searches for the answer throughout his *Fayḍ al-Khāṭir*, in all the realms of his interest. But he rarely carries it into the central citadels of Quranic authority and the discussion of the Prophet. The great need is for religion made intelligent and intelligence made religious. As a "counsel" of contemporary Islam that motive is unexceptionable. The author of *Fayḍ al-Khāṭir* ardently and amply commended it. But should we seek his like elsewhere it would be in Erasmus and not Luther.

A more tempestuous counsellor in Egyptian Islam is KHĀLID MUḤAMMAD KHĀLID (b. 1920) whose *Min Hunā Nabda'*[28] aroused a vigorous controversy in the early nineteen-fifties in Cairo. In this author the reader soon learns to expect only an ejaculatory, crusading fervour, not a dispassionate analysis. His style is much given to the use of the exclamation mark. His terse and emphatic manner, however, serves a lively mind. He wants to galvanise his brethren into a repudiation of the dead weight of officialdom and traditionalism, and a recovery of what is for him their true, rational, spiritual identity. The undoing of Muslims, he argues, lies not primarily in the political or external factors where apologists so love to set it. It springs rather from inward atrophy of true leadership. This is evident in social evils, in poverty and injustice. Official faith is often in a conspiracy with wealth against justice and mercy. Unlike many writers, he begins not with an ideal 'Umar age and delinquent comparisons, but with present miseries and culpable disloyalty. He wants to purge Islam of what he provokingly calls "priestcraft". He brushes aside the hypocrisy of the "if only" pleas of idealists who take comfort in institutions which are a dead letter, in *Zakāt* which is neither paid nor payable, in exhortation which is a soporific or a sham. Alms may proclaim, but they must not impede, socialism.

The ulema, therefore, must be renewed in genuine honesty of social thinking and must emerge from the shelter of their vested dogmatic interests. Islam must become altruistic, democratic, rational. Sermons must be entrusted only to enlightened preachers, and a few well-chosen mosques. External national ventures must not be allowed to divert attention from clamant interior ills. Nationalisation of production is thoroughly Islamic. The spate of births must be limited and women emancipated. Marriage may be the "proper" thing for a Muslim, but it need not be taken for a hatchery. Did not the Prophet say that the worst of calamities was to have a big family on scant means? Quality must win out over mere quantity.

Religion should not be in meticulous charge of the proper affairs of the law and the state: its purpose should be to guide the wills of men in a due social liberty of self-direction. The true goodness cannot be legislated, nor can virtue be equated with mere law-abiding, nor evil with indictable offences. Woman is safe and secure, not in a dungeon of purdah but in moral self-respect among both men and women which true responsibility generates. "Traditions are but the social appearance of the nation: they constitute no eternal, immutable and absolute principles to be unquestionably observed by all generations to the end of time . . ."[29] Islam can and must "inform" the state and society only in the right "religious" form of personal character and rational belief. Other sanctions such as Islam has so long invoked and erected are barren, futile and mischievous.

This spirited manifesto raised a considerable controversy. Sayyid Quṭb's earlier *Al-ʿAdāla al-Ijtimāʿiyya fī-l-Islām* had given full exposition to the traditional claims which Khālid rejected. MUḤAMMAD AL-GHAZĀLĪ entered the fray with his *Min Hunā Naʿlam* in which he reverted to assertive "if-only" idealism and vindicated anew the old patterns of mind.[30] Khālid had been too round with evils which did not truly exist and the solutions he sought were basically un-Islamic. Statehood and Islam were insolubly joined. True religion must have sure power. Islam cannot and will not be a "defenceless" faith. As one trained in Al-Az'har, Khālid showed a renegade cast of thought.

> "Khālid's contention—that religion consists merely of road signs intended to orient life's travellers and, as such, has nothing to do with the state—is pure fiction. The truth is that the road is full of gangsters. Unless religion moves along it as a strong, well-defended caravan it will surely meet its end."[31]

For the rest, Al-Ghazālī fortifies himself with Western examples of the evils vested in the systems Khālid would emulate. Let Islam only be true to itself and the evils he deplores will find their sufficient answer. And meanwhile woman's fertility remains her most important function and asset.

Khālid Muḥammad Khālid has continued with a flow of publications, all in the same ejaculatory vein. Space is lacking to pursue the debate further, in that phase of counsel. A far more sophisticated analysis of Islamic self-definition is found in ʿAbdallāh ʿAlī al-Quṣaymī (b. 1910, c.) whose *Hādhihi Hiya al-Aghlāl*[32] begins with a condemnation of *al-jahl al-iʿtiqādī*, or "credal" ignorance. Islam must throw off the stagnation that arises from equating Divine exaltation with human depreciation. Man must reject a piety which obscures or impedes his true genius for dominion. There are echoes of Iqbal in the plea that a true humanism, or *insāniyya*, alone befits man's place in the universe and in revelation. Dogma and eschatology have been falsely allowed to frustrate the real human destiny. Shaykhly Islam sees perfection in the retrospect and decay in the prospect. This in fact is a denial, a *kufr*, of the Divine will within which man must be seen as the bearer of an evolutionary glory. The one Islamic predicate is development but too many Muslim religionaries are its impediment.

So there must be a change of heart. A new Islamic will to power must be organised and energised, for which purpose Western activism must be imitated, not, however, as in Ṭaha Ḥusayn, because the West is seen as intellectually within an Islamic view where Europe and Egypt have one Mediterranean matrix, but because only so can Islam's entirely self-sustained history be now restored. Al-Quṣaymī aspires to renew an optimism within Islam and to refute the ancient, inhibiting tradition by which "never will there be a time but that a worse will follow it".

The frustrating influence of falsely held religious dogma is also the theme of ʿAlī al-Wardī of Baghdad. In *Wuʿʿāẓ as-Salāṭīn*[33] he castigates mosque preaching as notoriously subservient to state and property interests and so open to the charge of hypocrisy, a theme pondered too in Yūsuf aṣ-Ṣibāʿī's *Arḍ an-Nifāq*.[34] The preacher is the mouthpiece of a godliness which fails men. Indeed, for ʿAlī al-Wardī, it does not begin to understand them. Human nature is properly a field for psychological treatment not hortatory eloquence. The new logic brings a new realism, not to say honesty, into our affairs and for Al-Wardī only a religionless sort of Islam will survive.

A necessity of selection which can hardly avoid being arbitrary imposes itself on all the foregoing. But the fundamental search after self-awareness and the struggle to state it with authority are surely clear. There is almost no space to illustrate from imaginative literature. Since choice must be drastic, let it turn to North Africa. Morocco and Algeria in the last two decades have produced a lively crop of novelists whose evocation of the contemporary Muslim soul is as telling as anything to emerge from Egypt or Asia. KATIB YACINE (b. 1929), of Constantine, writes, in French, in a sort of Kafka-esque style. His *Nedjmeh* anticipates Algerian liberation but returns back to Carthaginian things and scouts a merely Muslim "nationalism" which would hand the country to the ulema and perpetuate superstition and the *marabouts*. DRISS CHRAIBI (b. 1926), a Moroccan, has set down in *Le Passé simple* an even more powerful anti-clericalism, with equal wistfulness for "belonging" and "acceptance", such as MUḤAMMAD DĪB (b. 1920) demands in *La Grande Maison* in a vivid portrayal of agrarian poverty and the "hunger for brotherly love". Chraibi's story is largely autobiographical. His hero's despair is his own.

> ". . . despair of a faith. This Islam in which he believes, which speaks of the equality God ordains unto tolerance, freedom and love, for every individual in creation—this Islam, he saw it now, as a young man full of zeal shaped in French schools, reduced to Pharisaism, a mere social system and a

means of propaganda. And so he set out for France. He needed to believe in somebody or something—to believe, love and respect."[35]

The novel describes the tension of the generations, the revolt of the son against the tyranny of the father. The one satirises formal religious practices and brands pious subservience to injustice with the passion of a James Baldwin:[36] the other symbolises legalistic rectitude and commercial opportunism. Thus the underlying issues are expressed in passionate overtones. *Le Passé simple* is a study in polarity, between the *ḥajj* and the *lycée*, between the rigid and the restless.

Another North African writer, whose major novel is a story of spiritual conversion through the *ḥajj* (*Lebbeik: pélerinage des pauvres*), has taken up Chraibi's problems in analytic discussion in *Vocation de l'Islam*. MALEK BENNABI (b. 1905) refuses to despair of Islamic adequacy to the twentieth century. Indeed he turns the tables, insisting that the supposed scientific "gift" of technology by the West to the Muslim world is in fact the fruit in part of Islamic rationalism. He believes that the long Western submission of Muslims under colonialism lies only in the fact that they were in temperament and by dogma "colonisable".[37] Mere political rejection of this role is useless unless it be accompanied by religious renewal, critical, alert and progressive, which alone will end the proneness to be imperialised. To find this Muslims must seek the future, as Al-Quṣaymī demands, not revere the past. Surprisingly, Bennabi is ready to anticipate this happening more vitally in Asian Islam, in Pakistan and beyond, rather than in the dogma-prone, self-admiring, Arab segment of the Muslim household. For him the *shūrā* of promise lies in breaking out of the contradiction whereby the West is at once maligned and imitated, into a new maturity in which it can be both recruited and judged, within the meaning of Islam.[38]

Miscellany of mentors was the modest phrase used to describe this chapter at the conclusion of the last. There is one further representative to add, whose notice may be prefaced by two observations arising from these pages. The first is that their incompleteness may be to some extent atoned for, vast as it is, by the effort of a later chapter to assess the present status of recurrent themes. For there are many minds, particularly of the conservative temper, whose significance may be more satisfactorily "taken" there than here—in so far as they are not reflected in Chapter 7. The second is to note the degree to which the "minds" reviewed are "lay". This had been anticipated in the discussion of the widening claims to *ijtihād*. What goes with it is the relative immunity of the central areas of Islamic theology and dogma from critical penetration. The impulses to thought, authentic and urgent as they are, seem to derive mostly from social conscience, political fervour, cultural confrontation or artistic awareness. All these are validly "religious" in their intensity and integrity. It would be a damnable view of the "religious" that sought to isolate it from motives that belong with being human. Yet it remains true that all too little Islamic *shūrā* proceeds from a religious primacy of purpose. So much apology is "Islam and . . ." With many writers it is defence, or utility, or "value" that are in mind, rather than the *islām* of Islam, the irreducible and inalienable quality of faith and, shall we say, "seriousness" which constitute the Muslim as God's.

Some, as in the Christian parallel here, would say that there is, in fact, nothing but the "Islam and . . ." stance, or, going further, that life and society, nation and person, would be safer and sounder in a kind of religionless dissolution of this ultimate "Islam" *per se*.

But, refusing without here refuting both these positions, what of this "religious" Islam in self-scrutiny? It seems right to include at least one voice that speaks a "mind" on this.

Muḥammad Kāmil Ḥusayn (M. Kamel Hussein) (b. 1901) is a "lay" writer, a surgeon of distinction, an educationalist with active interests in literature, archaeology, psychology and ethics. His two volumes of miscellany, *Mutanawwiʿāt*, cover many themes,[39] with perception and enthusiasm. In our context, his most striking characteristic is a will to bring the definitive concepts of religious Islam into living relation to contemporary existence. *Shirk*, *ẓulm*, *fitna*, *islām* itself—all are terms which it is easy to leave in their historic and even "fossilised" connotations, and so rewarding to explore and apply in their whole implicit reach and range, as critics and correctors of empirical Islam itself. Here is a voice, not of course wholly unique, but refreshingly original, insisting that there is an Islam that disqualifies Islam, not merely in that it is obscurantist, or illiberal, or socially effete, or archaic, or retrospective, or unproductive, or whatever else may be laid against its effects, but because it is a religious way of escaping from religion, a form of worship which eludes encounter with God, a sin that is in the very sanctity. Here is the deepest form of self-awareness—when the religious man knows that his very sanctuary may be a hiding-place from his Lord. Should it not be the first concern of Islam that God be most great even over Islam?

The intriguing fact is that Kāmil Ḥusayn has thought in these terms in conjunction with his deep interest in the phenomena of the religions in general. Though there is no space to explore it in these chapters, a large element in the duties of all the religions to themselves is their duty towards each other. Their dialogue or mission is their own souls' integrity. It is in this sense that Kāmil Ḥusayn's *Qarya Ẓālima*, "City of Wrong",[40] is, with his kindred writings, so rich and rare a document of Islam. It sets out to ruminate on the collective sin of Jesus' rejection on Good Friday, which it takes as an epitome of "the sin of the world", a sin conceived in communal pride and perpetrated in the name of religious security and Divine loyalty, and reinforced by quotation from infallible scripture and by the philosophy that at any cost in evil the triumph of the good must be ensured. All these can be seen as oblique criticisms of the stance of historic Islam itself, even to the point of actually echoing Quranic phrases, yet in a clearly culpable intent. The issues of Islam are thus vicariously examined within a wholly different context, that of the Jews, the Romans and the disciples in Holy Week, and still consistently within the Quranic view of that rejection as being foreclosed by Divine intervention.

The device of critical examination of one ethos under the guise of the history of another is no new thing. It was practised prudently by several medieval thinkers. But from *Qarya Ẓālima* and its author's other writings emerges a quite articulate concern for *islām*, within, beyond and even against Islam, for God's sovereignty through and yet against Muḥammad's people. The potential of this kind of writing is immense, its promise exhilarating.

Take the definition of *shirk*, the cardinal sin of "associating" anything with God. How fixed, and barren, and merely controversial, this concept has been since first it splendidly dislodged the literal, pagan idols of Mecca and the Arabs. How exciting the realisation that all false absolutes are *shirk*, whether in the market-place, the palace or the laboratory. Even the mosque itself may commit it whenever its pride or its claims, or simply its continuity, usurp what gives it being, namely, the will and authority of God. Iqbal said something like this in his own allusive way. Kāmil Ḥusayn gathers it into a searching and dispassionate critique.

Or turn to the Quranic notion of *ẓulm*, and *ẓulm an-nafs*, which

> "... does not make the acceptance of right guidance turn upon probable reward, nor the avoidance of evil or some feared retribution. It does not forbid the forbidden merely on the ground that it harms the social order ... it summons men to right conduct on the ground that the evil-doer wrongs himself ..."[41]

By this movement from what I do to what I am as the gist of sin, the way is ready for an ethical understanding of *islām* which, while fulfilling "law", is yet beyond legalism, and has an inward ally taking God's part against us in the very way that we are for Him. The door is thus opened to a quite new kind of *ijtihād* by which the Islamic intention that God should be all in all may be sifted, energised and fulfilled.

It may be risky to borrow that term. But it is the more revolutionary in that Islam has been for so long inured, by the Quranic concept of *fitna*, to take hostility to itself as hostility to God, to see in the established order or doctrine the shape of the Divine "interest", to depend upon an identity between its ideal self and the realisation of God's will. This had made it the more difficult to confront its real self with adequately radical criteria. It is to these, beyond external influence, circumstantial necessity, or even doctrinal defence, that Kāmil Ḥusayn is pointing the way. It is thus, surely —though returning as we must to the crowds, the tumult, the wistfulness and the flux—that the mind of a faith is to be read and esteemed.

CHAPTER 7

# THE MUSLIM BROTHERHOOD AND JAMĀ'AT-I-ISLĀMI

"THE spirit soars to the lofty heights of 'Umar's time but eyes are fastened on the spires of Westminster." Lyrical language, without a doubt, but given its sentimentality a fair expression of the two levels on which Islam has to be estimated today.[1] There are the basic ideals of the pristine period when under the second great Caliph Islam enjoyed its golden age of moral and political fulfilment: and there is the fact that, for the most part, existing régimes in Islamic states find practical models in Western-style government. Military rule, it is true, has in several countries superseded party politics. But whether or not this has happened, the actualities of authority are almost everywhere pragmatic, opportunist more than dogmatic, and generally "Western" in their assumption that government is a business for realists. It is the deeply religious ideologies, the movements most akin to the spirit of 'Umar, which have been denied the sinews of power.

Existing régimes must certainly be seen as "Muslim" and for the most part would not want to be thought otherwise. Heads of State go on the pilgrimage and there is a clear intention after religious relation. But the inner temper seems often akin to that suggested of the first Prime Minister of Pakistan, Liaquat Ali Khan, namely, that if "the body of the constitution was mounted on the chassis of Islam, the vehicle would still go in the direction he chose". "State", where constitutions are still pending or mending, would stand equally well in the sentence.[2]

Our study in this chapter has to do with those bodies of opinion which would "go in the direction Islam would choose", men and groups with clear, sustained, inflexible ideals as to the nature of Islamicity and a firm determination to apply them steadfastly to the entire order of Islam in state and society. The *Ikhwān al-Muslimūn* or Muslim Brotherhood of Egypt and the *Jamā'at-i-Islāmī* of Pakistan are akin in this quality and can stand for other smaller bodies of similar character and intent. Despite well-disciplined efforts to operate politically they have both quite failed in this realm. The *Ikhwān* are proscribed in Egypt and the *Jamā'at* through stormy vicissitudes has been quite thwarted of its ends in Pakistan. Both have had to submit to the frustration of seeing other régimes actually in the saddle who do not share their ideological convictions and by their sights fall lamentably short of the "lofty heights of 'Umar". Yet these groups, in their zealot reaction to modern pressures, know their Islam and represent its inner temper with an intensity which, at worst, we cannot afford to ignore and, at best, presents an image of Islam that commands respect and even admiration.

There is an element of paradox in their involvement in politics as parties. Though there was, of course, no other feasible way to be involved, party politics may be seen as directly contradictory of the truth that in Islam the body of believers is the only "party". Precisely because of their puritan and conservative stance, the *Ikhwān* and the *Jamā'at* felt this dilemma keenly. Unable, like the Wahhābīs and Sanūsīs in other circumstances, to identify government with themselves in unity, they had to debate and campaign, within a partisan situation and a Muslim population, for their own views as one angle among others from which questions of the day and society could be broached. Yet it was part of their philosophy that "each and every adult Muslim belongs as a matter of right" to the one party—Islam, "whose ideology is the Divine law of nature".[3] We have met elsewhere the disparity in the terms "Muslim" and "Islam". For the *Ikhwān* and the *Jamāʿat*, the ambiguity had to be *de facto* conceded, by taking "party-part" in politics, while it was *de jure* denied by their view of the true Islam of which they were the custodians. This is simply their form of the dilemma attaching to all authoritarian philosophies entering a practical competition which must necessarily imply, and proceed by, relativity. There is, in other words, a debate about what is not properly debatable: a partisanship about what is not partial. It was as if orthodoxy had to consent to become a sect, or fundamentalism share a status with conflicting opinions.

This inner theme has a further irony when in fact the political action meets defeat. When in January 1954 the new régime in Egypt (then headed by Muhammad Neguib) dissolved the Muslim Brotherhood, after a sequence of events, it was the final knell. Several months earlier the *Ikhwān* had been exempted from a general ban on all parties, on the ground that they had "religious" purposes (of Y.M.C.A. style, i.e. Y.M.M.A.) which deserved to be permitted as non-political. But the Brethren found it impossible to refrain sufficiently from politics to satisfy the régime and the ban was extended to them. That interlude, brief as it was, at least points up the idea of being required to operate "just as a religion" and how odd that demand is for anything Islamic. But so it was, and failing to be only religious marked, in the circumstances, the public end of the organisation. Ought building mosques and educating the young in Islam in fact to have sufficed them? Yet how could it, as long as they compared their reading of the state with the ideal of ʿUmar?

A similar theme, in differing circumstances, runs through the *Jamāʿat*. Like many conservative elements, it had been suspicious of "Pakistan" as a notion. But when statehood was achieved it could not forbear to buy up political opportunity or abstain from the chorus of its definition. But here also, the imprisonment for a time of its leader and the non-success of its partisan efforts have thrown it back on the sole strategy of communal disciplines, devotion and education. If it was ever a paradox that Muslim peoples should have been ruled by non-Muslim aliens, is it not something of a like paradox that true Muslims should be thwarted by indifferent or worldly ones in the seats of power? The detail of these two bodies and the thinking of their leadership must be briefly reviewed.

Ḥasan al-Bannā' (1906–49), founder and first Supreme Guide of the Muslim Brotherhood, was twenty-two years of age when he launched the movement at Ismailia, a town on the Suez Canal, where he took appointment as a school teacher. Throughout his youth he had been strongly devoted to an active practice of Islam and had ardently campaigned for reform of moral laxity and the inculcation of Islamic ideals. He belonged during his studies at *Dār al-ʿUlūm* in Cairo to the circle that gathered around Rashīd Riḍā, whose journal *Al-Manār* he tried for a time to carry on after his death. But from an early date he sensed that the real task of revitalising Muslim society would demand a vigorous crusade among the masses, rather than student and literary ventures. To this he found his talents and the growing magnetism of his personality aptly suited. With a few original colleagues he held bi-weekly sessions in three capacious coffee houses in the town, where he carried on preaching and teaching Quranic interpretation and training in religious disciplines. The "spirit of militancy", as he described it, gathered momentum. Other branches were founded in near-by villages, including a plan for Muslim Sisters. The house in Ismailia became the headquarters of a growing fraternity and the symbol of a new quality of religious fervour and dedication. The Muslim Brotherhood in these pre-political years represents one of the finest modern examples of deep Muslim piety, finely aggressive against formalism and complacence and earnestly set for religious renewal. The mosque, as Ḥasan al-Bannā' used it, became a vital centre of social conscience and moral antiseptic.

In 1933 he was transferred to Cairo by the Ministry of Education. Some fifty centres were the fruit of five years' effort. With the move to the capital, the reach of the *Ikhwān* was enlarged and its energies in organising schools, beneficent clubs and instruction classes redoubled. A journal was launched and general congresses convened to concert the work of branches, which enjoyed considerable local autonomy. The movement reached out into other parts of the Arab world, especially Syria, Palestine and the Sudan. The secret of its success lay in the force and dedication of its ideals and in the extraordinary energy, almost charismatic in its quality, of Al-Bannā' himself. He combined the meticulousness of a watchmaker (his father's profession) with the drive of a prophet. He was aided perhaps by the fact that he had never been part of the scholastic tradition of Al-Az'har, with its immersion in schools and texts and controversies. It was the Islam of the *dhikr*, or *ṣūfī* emotion, which drew him. But he was an assiduous reader, gifted with a retentive memory and a robust practical sense of simple religion and its effective propagation. His powers of oratory were remarkable and he knew how to develop the maximum fervour in his audiences, avoiding the idly controversial, releasing the inner yearnings and translating them into discipleship. All these endowments were energised by a tireless industry and an incredible capacity for action. His speeches were said to have numbered over thirty thousand in the seventeen years between 1928 and 1945, and he was an indefatigable visitor through the whole Egyptian dispersion of the *Ikhwān*, from Alexandria to Aswan.

It was after the move to Cairo that Ḥasan al-Bannā' developed his movement into a political instrument. But he aimed to reach political goals by his own characteristic means. A political party in the usual sense it would have been quite unthinkable for the *Ikhwān* to become. Al-Bannā' regarded the machinations and coalitions of political parties as both despicable and futile. The Constitution of 1922 in any event was Western and un-Islamic. Political parties should be abolished and the whole structure of the *sharīʿa* and the state brought into conformity with a true Islam, its education mosque-centred and its social order fashioned to rigorous purity. Moreover, Muslims must reach out beyond "nationalism" into a unified expression of their ideology, culminating in a renewal of the Caliphate. The mission of Islam demanded the end of the "partiality" both of the party politician and of the domestic nationalist.

There are those who believe that "their object was to generate popular energy in order to seize power rather than to restore the rule of Islamic virtue".[4] But this could be a hasty judgement, since the two ends were no alternatives. "Power" for the most part, as the *Ikhwān* conceived it, meant a nation in self-direction according to their principles,[5] a kind of "totalitarian" acceptance by a suffrage of will, a popular consensus, for which the Brotherhood must work by cells of action, by "fabian" propaganda, by calls to kings and ministers, by vigorous journalism, and, under pressures of frustration, perhaps by subterfuge. There were moments of flirtation between the "parties" and the Brethren. For the one found the other's organising strength a fascinating potential ally, while for Al-Bannā' there remained the problem of the elusiveness of power on his own ideological conditions. When eventually in 1952 a régime arrived claiming popular will beyond the parties, it had military form, and after an uneasy interlude, the *Ikhwān*, led after Al-Bannā''s death by Ḥasan al-Huḍaybī, found themselves proscribed.

There is no space to trace the vicissitudes of their external history through the thirties, the period of the War, the Palestine campaign, the Wafd ascendancy and the Revolution, or to assess the truth of its alleged "terrorism" before and after the assassination of Al-Bannā' himself. The logic of the whole lay in the fact, already noted, of their failure to attain power by their chosen concept of a popular take-over of their ideology by the nation which would be synonymous with a take-over of the government by their hands. And until this failure was decisively confirmed by the advent of military rule, their powerful religious, economic and social crusade, with its strike action, its cells, its journals and its vows of group loyalty, inevitably drew out the intriguing suspicions of the politicians.

In the immediate aftermath of the Revolution in Egypt in July 1952 it might have seemed, superficially, that opportunity had dawned for the *Ikhwān*. The general amnesty freed their prisoners, the army officers were known to share some of their social and economic ideas, and the old order had been liquidated. But tensions rapidly developed. The new régime was not ready for the kind of ideological measures the

Brethren required, nor did the latter relish negotiations with the British. The new rule seemed to them only another version of compromise over Islam. The gulf widened and, after a brief reprieve, the *Ikhwān* found themselves deprived of all those assets on which they had most relied—corporate order, recruitment, active instruction and social clubs. Their trump-card of the futility of party strife has been itself trumped by the Revolution, while their anti-imperial, anti-foreign *animus* has found fuller vent from the same source. Their claims for *sharīʿa* supremacy became less viable and less intelligent than in the forties with the abolition of the *sharīʿa* courts themselves.[6] For the rest, where their ideology has attained its ends, it has been by other hands and means, and where it has not, its frustration seems complete.

Nevertheless, in the teachings of the *Ikhwān* contemporary Islam has found counsels most congenial to its history and championed them with a thoroughness no "liberalism" can equal. They hinge, according to Al-Bannā', on three principles: there is, and must be, a single Islamic community, *Dār al-Islām*, to which nations are subordinate; Islam legislates in the *sharīʿa* for all human affairs; Islam is brotherhood among all nations and classes. There are some six propositions on which the policies of the *Ikhwān* rest. They claim to be scientific: the Qur'ān must be interpreted rationally, as ʿAbduh affirmed, and its contents are abreast of the spirit of every age. Anti-Westernism does not include technology, which is proper and necessary to Islam. Secondly, unity is paramount between Muslim groups and can be had if all will submit to the Qur'ān and the *Sunna*; factiousness must be relinquished. Thirdly, there must be economic equality of resources and opportunity, standards of living must be raised, exploitation, foreign or local, eliminated and a true

*Falāḥ*, or Islamic order of prosperity, actualised. Fourthly, society must be made self-responsible, through compassion and a struggle against disease, poverty, illiteracy and crime. The two final propositions have to do with disciplined national pride in the service of universal peace, as a fulfilment of world Islam. Through all these, the Qur'ān is seen as itself an effective constitution.

These counsels may be found not only in the numerous speeches and pamphlets of Al-Bannā' but also in Sayyid Quṭb's *Al-ʿAdāla al-Ijtimāʿiyya fī-'l-Islām*,[7] "Social Justice in Islam", and the response of Muḥammad al-Ghazālī in *Min Hunā Naʿlam*, "Our Beginning in Knowledge", to the work of Khālid Muḥammad Khālid, noted in Chapter 6. Al-Ghazālī rebuts the argument that religion must be separated from politics. On the contrary: power is indispensable. When Muḥammad became head of a state it was not a temporary expedient but the essence of Islam. The notion that Islam can be merely religious is a ruse from Europe to undermine the faith, and nationalism is a perversion from the same source. Sayyid Quṭb, for his part, defines social justice as the proper Islamic harmony between all departments of life. The Islamic state is *sui generis*, and bears no comparison with other political systems.

> "Islam proposes independent solutions to human problems. . . . Islam is a comprehensive philosophy and a homogeneous unity and to introduce into it any foreign element would mean its ruin."[8]

Here, as elsewhere in the thought of the *Ikhwān*, is the voice of the "immuniser"—the mood which demands the total distinctiveness of Islam so as to isolate it from all other human experience. Greece, Rome, old Egypt, Confucius, Plato, Zoroaster, alike, all can be neglected. To find other realms or sources relevant is apparently taken for inferiority. Self-sufficiency must always prevail.

*Islamic Law: its Scope and Equity*, by Sa'īd Ramaḍān,[9] is an interesting venture, from within these same traditions, to explain and justify for a non-Muslim the principles of Islamic law. He makes a bold attempt to hold fast the sole authority of Qur'ān and *Sunna* and also "fully to subscribe" to Iqbal's view that legislative assemblies are "the only possible form that *ijmā'* can take in modern times" and that *ijtihād* may be transferred to them from the individual *mujtahids* of the schools.[10] Much, for him, seems to turn on the point that

> ". . . it is an accepted principle in Islamic law that everything is allowed unless explicitly prohibited and not the other way round."[11]

This may readily provide a means to development, if positive sanction does not need to be found. But the operative issue Dr. Ramaḍān states as follows:

> "Legal speculation for an ever changing world has been left undetermined except for the authority of the *sharī'a*. Whether this legal speculation can be accepted as 'Islamic' or not is always dependent on how convincing to Muslims the particular attitude of mind is, both in its compliance with the basic texts and in its comprehension of the relevant issues."[12]

The provisos here are broad enough to reserve whatever the reader would wish to reserve, while leaving room for a progressive attitude, which the writer proceeds to elaborate with special reference to Islamic law and minorities. It is perhaps fair to see in Sa'īd

Ramaḍān some indication of how thinking elsewhere in the *Ikhwān* tradition has been moving since the suppression in Egypt in 1954.

Mawdudi, more fully Mawlānā Abū-'l-A'lā al-Mawdūdī (b. 1904), leader of the *Jamā'at-i-Islāmī*, resembles Ḥasan al-Bannā' in a number of ways. He is not strictly one of the ulema, having started his career as a journalist. The *Jamā'at*, founded in 1941, like the *Ikhwān*, intends vigorous service to the community in education, social action, the earnest propagation of Muslim doctrine and practice, all with efficient organisation and publications. The leader commands something of a comparable personal ascendancy and has, through imprisonment and misrepresentation, held on to a courageous course. Like the Muslim Brethren, his followers insist that Islam must come to terms with modern life but must do so by a renewal of sound faith and pure discipline.

Mawdudi's *Tarjumān al-Qur'ān*, an Urdu monthly begun in 1932, is a magazine of wide repute. His position has been set out in numerous pamphlets and books and also in the statements made before the Court of Inquiry into the Punjab Disturbances of 1953 in which the *Jamā'at* figured prominently. Broadly his political action reveals the same basic disavowal of partisan politics, his yearning and strategy concentrated alike on ideological success. *Towards Understanding Islam*[13] is an early but useful *confessio fidei*. He begins with a reflection on the *islām* of the universe and the whole animal world—a favourite theme with many writers.[14] Blood circulation, the stars in their orbits, and other "motions", are instances of a natural *islām*, or subordination to law. Even the unbeliever, bodily considered, may be said to be *muslim*, for his organs are under law. Full, volitional, free *islām*, however, is the moral obedience of the rational will. Then the voluntary as well as the involuntary is conforming, and man as such is God's vicegerent on earth.

This *islām*, however, characterising all men of conformity to Divine will, is finalised and given its definitive constitution in human history in historical Islam (i.e. "Muhammadanism"). God has set forth the final Prophet and commanded that he be believed. Such belief is at once enjoined and rational. To reject "Muhammadan" Islam is to go against natural law. Arabic was the best language for revelation. Muḥammad's authenticity is self-evident, his achievement incontrovertible. Thus, Mawdudi concludes, Muslim adherence is both natural and rational. But it must also be entire and fundamentalist. This quality of utter faith makes for dignity in man, courage, humility, patience, self-reliance and breadth of mind. The five articles of Muslim faith and the five pillars of religion are wholly binding: objection to them on any ground is an offence both against nature and against God. The *sharīʿa* remains inviolable: it is applicable for all time.

Mawdudi does not face man's defiance or probe the significance of a world in which the option of idolatry is open to men. He shares the traditional Islamic neglect of "the mystery of evil", and claims the approval of reason while excluding the possibility of non-persuaded-ness when it is exercised. In other works and in his Quranic commentary, he holds that the whole order of life and society has been revealed in the Qur'ān and the *sunna*—a principle derived from the *shahāda*, or confession, itself. "There is no god but God" means, among other things, that there is no other lawgiver for men. It follows from this that Islam, the universal law under God, must transcend nation. In *Nationalism and India* and *Muslims and the Present Political Struggle*, he argued strongly against both the Muslim League with its "Pakistan" policy and Muslims in the Congress.

He anticipated, with considerable ground, that "Pakistan" would not prove a true Islamic state as long as it merely replaced Empire, or the Hindus, by "Muslims". In this he was a better "disciple" of the universalism of Iqbal than many of those who freely invoked his name. Oddly enough it was Iqbal who, admiring Mawdudi's literary and debating skill, had brought him from Hyderabad, Deccan, to Pathan Kot in the Punjab, though he was scarcely settled there before Iqbal died. After the creation of the new state, the *Jamā'at* was inevitably involved in its shaping. It might deplore the concept: it could not ignore the fact. In the midst of much surrounding ambiguity and confusion, it began with a clear notion of what Pakistan should intend when it claimed to be an Islamic state. It meant a state under the whole *sharī'a*, interpreted by its proper trustees and making actual the full religious system of Islam. The Qur'ān and the *sunna* must control, in the contemporary *ijmā'* and *ijtihād* of the qualified. Unlike some of the ulema and their *Jamā'at*, Mawdudi argued that legislation in the normal sense was possible in an Islamic state, at least on matters not covered by the Qur'ān, the *sunna* and previous *ijmā'*. This counsel he sustained by appeal to the *shūrā* of Sura 42, which he took to be

> "... a body of persons whom the Holy Prophet, and after him the *khulafā'* [caliphs], consulted on all matters relating to affairs of state."[15]

This account is corroborated in the *Jamā'at-i-Islāmī*'s own critical publication on the Report of the Court of Inquiry into the Punjab Disturbances of 1953, which will be noted in a later chapter on the Aḥmadiyya, over whose "heresy" and agitation they arose. Mawdudi's view here is in line with that of Sa'īd Ramaḍān, noted above.[16] It is plainly a far more progressive view than the one which refuses to expect adequate Islamic conformity of thought from a legislative body of Muslims elected by the suffrages of Muslims.

But if allowing *ijmā'* in some form to popular assemblies, the *Jamā'at* has been under no illusions about the obstacles to its own orthodoxy in such allowance. It protests, for example, at the "intolerance of secularism", the pressures and vetoes, like those of Atatürk in Turkey,[17] which loyal religionaries have to suffer and resist. Such readiness for "hard-going" is one of the most attractive features of the *Jamā'at*'s history and of Mawdudi's own career. He has himself been under sentence of death. Nor has he attempted to purchase easy victories. He courted sharp unpopularity by declaring the Kashmir situation outside *jihād*, or holy war, and he disappointed progressives, with much less right, when he resisted state appropriation of land and socialist programmes of redistribution on the ground that private property was secured by the Qur'ān and the *sunna*, including that of the excessively rich. The *Jamā'at*'s social concern is, in this light, more philanthropic than radical.

In his *Process of the Islamic Revolution*, Mawdudi shows himself acutely aware of the massive obstacles confronting Islamic renewal. True revolution demands a great mental transformation and leaders who will refuse demagoguery. It hinges on piety and the sense of God, and the virtues of early Islam, newly exemplified in men and women. He found the clamant pleas for "Pakistan" wrongly identifying the ancient enemy and fighting for office, power and economic interest, and against Hindus, when a true Islam meant a struggle against the inward perversities by the weapons of ideology, preaching and steadfastness.

These virtues the society has aimed to foster.

Though it has never achieved the numbers and dispersion or thrust that took the *Ikhwān* into, by some estimates, between a half and one million members, the *Jamā'at* has stood with dignity for an Islamic integrity.[18] Its appeal has been mainly to those who, like the founder, had little or no acquaintance with Western languages and learning, but counted themselves intellectuals and men of prayer. Membership involves a probation and promises of religious and doctrinal loyalty.

The counsels of this chapter are not politically operative, except in so far as they activate social concern and conscience in the seats of power. Their own ventures are either clandestine, as in the case of the Brethren, or dogged, and hampered by ill-favour. It is all too easy, as the writers of the Munir Report in their less judicious moments show, to treat them with cynicism and contempt.[19] Yet there is a kind of integrity, despite serious compromises, which contrasts favourably with the opportunism of the secular Muslims and the airiness of the liberals. Given, of course, the fact that the *Jamā'at* has never carried the burden of responsibility and has only the opposition role of a critic, consistency, it could be argued, is easy enough, and very scholastic at that. None the less, if one is looking for a serious Islam, making a sustained effort after loyalty of worship and the sense of God, in the midst of bewilderment and shifting passions and much time-serving, one may find it in the discipleship of Al-Bannā' and Mawdudi. Ameer Ali's *The Spirit of Islam* has with good cause been castigated as failing, in its ethical poverty, to make active demands on the Muslim and to summon him to anything more than admiration.[20] Whatever their faults and failures, that is not a charge of which either the *Ikhwān* or the *Jamā'at* could be accused.

CHAPTER 8

# MAWLANA AZAD AND INDIAN ISLAM

"IF by chance old memories were revived for him, he would simply say with a sigh: 'Why expose the scar on one's own heart? No one is to blame. I alone am to blame. I was so incompetent that I could not succeed in keeping back the Muslims of India from committing deliberate suicide.'" So writes Syed Mahmud (Sayyid Maḥmūd), a Muslim Indian M.P., and a close lifelong friend of Mawlānā Abū-'l-Kalām Āzād, reflecting on his attitudes after the partition of India.[1] The acceptance of onus and reproach should be taken more as the proof of a generous sorrow than a historical verdict. But its intensity certainly measures the depth of post-partition feeling and judgements. Though in one sense the shaping of Pakistan ostensibly freed the two communities, thus two nations, to go their several ways, the "Pakistan" philosophy inevitably perpetuated a decision, made concrete in independent statehood, which *ipso facto* set a question-mark over the very survival of Indian Islam. If that statehood was truly indispensable then Islam in India could have no sure ultimate hope. One Pakistani leader conjectured a century, perhaps less, before Muslim people there[2] might cease to be. By its very existence in the terms of the antecedent justification of its partisans, Pakistan called into question the whole future of those whom its frontier lines unavoidably excluded from its Islam-validating auspices. The unavoidability could not alter the implications externally as long as they were authoritative internally. And outside Pakistan were some forty million disciples of Islam.

They, for their part and through their leadership, were, one might say, existentially required to go on devalidating the Pakistani account of Islamic security and expression. For only so could they prepare themselves to survive effectively, if not creatively, in a situation of permanent and irreversible minority status. This was the paradox. Partition, necessarily, was non-recurring. The "Pakistan" way of salvation was eliminated as an option or policy for those outside its actual incidence at the determined frontiers. There could conceivably be no further territorial statehoods to save Muslims, either in prospect or in event. Ironically, then, the genesis of Pakistan obliged Muslims outside it to persist only in terms of its refutation.

Thus far negatively. But the Muslims of India had equally to sustain their *raison d'être* by positive co-operation and living co-existence under the new conditions with their Hindu fellow-citizens. This vocation was both arduous and unprecedented: arduous because both states were engaged in a desperate battle for sheer survival and by the circumstances of their origin were saddled with innumerable potential issues of friction, suspicion and ill-will;[3] unprecedented in that no other Islamic minority had ever in history faced quite the same quality of destiny. When earlier, by those aberrations of Islamic order noted in Chapter 1, Muslims had been called to live without their own statehood, the circumstances, imperial or otherwise, had never been those of multi-religious unity under secular statehood, as a continuous minority, set, either for doom or glory, in a historic decision to which they had been a party. It is important to see this uniqueness of the situation in which Indian Islam is found. Accepted as a new form of Islamic fact, it may yet be productive of surprising, even disconcerting, developments, in an Islamic response to the necessity to be itself *just as a religion*—a vocation it has never hitherto either faced, or, by its own consent, embarked upon.

The chief mentor of that embarkation, the outstanding pilot, or Columbus, of this enterprise was Mawlana Azad, whose career and authority span the fateful partition by many years. In the magnanimity of grief, he may have accused his own incompetence. But the open mind of history will find little to reproach in the temper and effort of his mind, and can exonerate him from the blame he was ready to assume. Azad's counsel on contemporary Islam presents the surest foil to the case for Pakistan and represents with more authority than any other the significance of Muslim India in the years since 1947. An account of him may well be prefaced by some discussion of Muḥammad 'Alī, brother of Shawkat 'Alī and exponent of an Islam approving the Hindu-Muslim unity that Azad's leadership embodies.

Muḥammad 'Alī (1878–1931) during internment in 1923 projected a four-volumed work which was to have the title: *Islam, Kingdom of God*. Because of intense political preoccupations in the cause of Khilafatism and Hindu-Muslim unity, it was never fulfilled. Only a prelude of autobiography was in fact published, with the title: *My Life, A Fragment*.[4] It is a document of deep religious feeling, a *confessio fidei* set down during imprisonment and serving to illuminate the inner self-awareness of Islam in the heyday of its determination for common action with Hindus against the British Raj. "Pakistan" was still a distant unknown, and the separatism which gave it birth firmly disallowed as inimical to its true genius. Islam, Muhammad Ali believed, had never as a spiritual force been dependent on temporal power.

He is all the more impressive as a witness, for the crisis-quality of his prison awakening to the Qur'ān. Aligarh, followed by Oxford—an education in the tradition of Ahmad Khan—had somehow left him ignorant of his real heritage in Prophet and Scripture. A journalistic and political career caused him to fall foul of the government and in confinement his Islam kindled into warmth and fervour. He became, as he put it, intoxicated with the force and grandeur of the Qur'ān which he read in Naẓīr Aḥmad's Urdu translation.[5] *Tawḥīd* grew upon him as a personal reality, man in the dignity of his "service" as vicegerent of God, and himself as part of this great strength. "This was my unique discovery in that small volume revealed some thirteen centuries ago to an Arab of the desert whose name I bore."[6] The devotional ardour of his writing has a grateful quality. All too little of the counsels of Islam are autobiographical, whatever significance ought to be attached to the fact.

The familiar notes, of course, are here. *Taqlīd* is the obvious villain. "Formal renunciation of a mildewed scholasticism" will set Islam "right with the progressive world of science" and "right with itself".[7]

> "Metaphysics and anthropomorphism are alike foreign to the whole spirit of the Qur'ān and if we just let it soak into our consciousness as . . . into the consciousness of the Arabs (then) we shall get all the philosophy we need."[8]

H. G. Wells, whom he also read in prison, and met in London, has the right activism. Orthodoxy, in Islamic terminology, means just this vigorous freedom from credal impositions and subtle speculations. Muslims must beware of double standards as between sophistication and simplicity. Muḥammad's career supplies as much theology as is needed to be a true Muslim and is the best commentary on the Qur'ān. This, it must be conceded, might lead to confusion, the more so as Muhammad Ali claims: "I have as much right to interpret God's message as any other man, except the infallible messenger who brought it."[9] But for all its incompleteness, *My Life, A Fragment*, assertive and activist as it is, was a forthright manifesto, a personal credo from gaol.

Some of the external factors recur in Mawlana Azad—prison, the Qur'ān, communal fervour with unitary policy—but the mind and the pen are incomparably more adequate. Abū-'l-Kalām Āzād (1888–1958) had a distinguished ancestry and was born in Mecca, where his father, Muḥammad Khayr-ad-Din, had emigrated after the Mutiny, marrying a daughter of the Arab shaykh Muḥammad Ẓāhir Wītrī. He returned when his son was a boy of ten and settled in Calcutta. Early evidence of talent ripened into prodigious learning. He studied briefly at Al-Az'har in Cairo, though he did not graduate there. He did not take up English until he was in his twenties, but he had early seen the wisdom of Ahmad Khan's insistence that Muslims should get abreast of Western thought and technology. He radically rejected, however, the Ahmad Khan, Aligarh, tradition of anglophile co-operation with the British. Only, it seemed to him, by ardent unity of political action with Hindus could the future be assured. He, therefore, founded in 1912 a journal *Al-Hilāl* to propagate these views, with such effect and force of satire, wit and rhetoric, as to create a new chapter in the history of Urdu letters and to incur the anger of the British authorities. The weekly reached a circulation of 25,000, and when its permit was withdrawn he substituted another, *Al-Balāgh*. He was expelled from Bengal in 1916 and interned at Ranchi where he began his famous *Tarjumān al-Qur'ān*, manuscripts of which were successively lost, or impounded, during intermittent imprisonments, so that its completion was delayed until 1930. Detention also saw the production of his *Tadhkira*, a biography of unusual shape, elicited in parts by an importunate publisher, from whose unwelcome attentions the author protected himself by literary and poetic devices.

The result is a document of self-revelation and reflection, written with great command of language and metaphor, and a rich sense of family history. With precedents from the days of Akbar and Shāh Wālī-Ullāh, he upheld the freedom of men of grace and the spirit against the strictures of time-serving, legalistic ulema. Spiritual authenticity must not be decried or denied by institutional rigidity. He ruminated on the three stages of experience—desire, love and truth. Beyond the year and five months of "profane love" in his twenty-first year, he passed, he says, from a half-way house into the discovery of liberty and truth.

> "The world in whose tavern of oblivion had been poured into me the wine of heedlessness, whose visions tempted my eyes, whose melodies charmed my ears, that same world so transformed itself now that every little piece of it was a picture of sobriety and wisdom, a lesson for the seeing eye and the knowing mind, every particle was eager for converse, every leaf was a document . . . the heavens descended to answer questions . . ."

So Love

> ". . . opened the door of learning, it taught me the truth of action, it had the books of Divine wisdom on its tongue, the treasures of true knowledge were in its generous hands. It taught me the profundities of the *sharīʿa*, it guided me across the hills and

valleys of the *ṭarīqa*, it revealed the secrets of the Qur'ān and initiated me into the mysteries of the *sunna*, it gave me wisdom, it bestowed on me a sensitive heart . . ."[10]

From such sensitivity of religious experience Mawlana Azad's leadership derived. It was in this temper that, as long as the Caliphate policy was feasible to Indian Muslims, he held to it, and when Arab nationalism and Turkish developments terminated its hopes, preserved intact the Hindu-Muslim joint action it had favoured, on the ground that while religion was God's a homeland was for all. Doomed as it was to ultimate defeat as a policy for Islam in undivided India, his reading of Islamic loyalty was based on the deepest integrity, of a far more articulate and lively kind than the slogan-ridden mentality by which the masses were otherwise persuaded. It could be that in this imperfect world its very quality was its undoing.

This very distinction between a religion and its followers was an important point of departure in his commentary. In *Al-Hilāl* he wrote:

> "We cannot take a single step towards the truth by starting from those ideas and beliefs which are actually found in the minds of the followers of any inculcated religion."[11]

These, he insisted, were distorted by vested interest or sheer continuity of the sacrosanct. So it is that followers always deviate from their prophets and teachers. When we come to the unadulterated teachings of the latter, purged of "popular" accretions, we discover the inner unity of all faiths. Diversity, in other words, arises from institutionalising. Spiritual essentials are unitary. Part of this institutional "shape" in Islam was the unfortunate involvement of the Qur'ān in Greek, non-Arabic, categories in the early centuries of

Islamic theology.[12] So gradually its natural and direct simplicities were lost in a warren of exegetical canons and categories which absorbed all attention but had no relation to the essence. Religion also took to itself sanctions of geography, or affiliation (as in a census), or custom, or heredity. All these must be discarded if true religion, and true Islam, are to be rightly identified and rightly held.

Therefore, in his commentary, Azad set out to recover the *fiṭra*, or true religion, of the first generation Muslims, the Qur'ān's original recipients, and to see with their natural unsophistication. His desire to set the Qur'ān squarely in the ethos of its time is in sharp contrast with Iqbal's inventiveness in finding in its vocabulary what no reader or hearer of Muḥammad's day could have conceived. The ulema who he claimed had well resisted political pressures, had sadly capitulated to philosophic ones throughout the Middle Ages. The resultant loss could only be restored by letting the Qur'ān interpret itself (cf. Sura 50.45) congruently with the fact that it was sent down part by part because it had to incorporate itself into a living, real environment of audition and apprehension. This truth of it needed to be the ruling principle of the present reader. It did not, of course, mean any exclusion on his part from his mind of the actualities of his own world, including science and culture, an attempt, so to speak, to primitivise himself. On the contrary: he must bring his own existence-context, but let the Qur'ān address him there out of its own. In these terms, as Azad claimed, he had himself given "prolonged thought to every chapter, every verse, every pause and every word". He added:

> "There is no conviction in my heart which the thorns of doubt have failed to pierce: there is no faith in my

> soul which has not been subjected to all the conspiracies of disbelief."[13]

This was a large claim, and some, perusing his free appeals to teleology in creation, or Divine action in history, might question whether he was not in fact impervious to certain perplexities of his time. There is a note of assured confidence about his lengthy discussion in the commentary on the Opening Sura, *Al-Fātiḥa*, of its great themes, Divine providence, benevolence, justice, unity and guidance, *rubūbiyya*, *raḥma*, *'adāla*, *tawḥīd* and *hidāya*. But no justice can be done here either to its flowing style or its broad sweep. Consider two passages:

> "And what is the objective of this order, this *rubūbiyya*? It is sustenance of life in the universe. But sustenance alone is not the whole objective. Something greater than this is in view. Sustenance is but a means to the development of beauty in everything. We notice that there is design in the life of the universe, and that there is beauty in this design. There is in its disposition the sense of balance. Its actions display specific attributes. In its visage there is beauty. In its voice there is music. In its smell there is perfume, and there is nothing about it which does not contribute to the upkeep of its edifice. This aspect of life is greater in its reaches than the orderliness (*rubūbiyya*) that dwells therein. And this reality the Qur'ān designates as *raḥma* . . .[14]

And this on the *Ṣirāṭ al-mustaqīm*, or Straight Path, of the *Fātiḥa*:

> "The fact is that no other term than the 'Straight Path' could have been chosen to signify the universal *Dīn* or the way of God that the Qur'ān speaks

of. You may chalk out any number of paths you like to reach a particular destination, but the Straight Path will be but one, and it is by following it alone that you can complete your journey with safety. It is only the straight path which is called the royal road. . . ." ". . . the character of the *Dīn* is so open, so easy, and so brief that the entire body of beliefs and practices is summed up in but two terms, viz. 'faith and righteous work'. Its beliefs do not baffle the mind: its practices do not tax the body. It is free from every form of meaningless subtlety. It is throughout a straight road. As the saying goes, its night is as bright as its day. Praise be to God who hath revealed the Scripture unto His servant and hath not placed therein any crookedness. (18: 1)."[15]

Do Azad's criteria of Quranic simplicity suffice him as an interpreter? Is he not to a degree involved in the consequences of *tafsīr bi-ra'y*, or exegesis by personal opinion, which in his analysis of exegetical dangers he had vowed to avoid? He is not guilty of the excesses of Iqbal in this respect. But is he not also less alert to the larger issues within his cosmological, anthropocentric theism? And if this be so, is he too assertive about his own right to "simplify" and "universalise" Islam? We find him claiming:

"I am under no obligation for guidance to any man's hand or tongue, nor to my family nor to any syllabus of education. All the guidance I have received has been from the Divine Throne."[16]

Can this pontifical detachment from community be surely Islamic? Were the scholastic disquisitions on the Qur'ān, for all their aridity and *taqlīd*, not in origin right in the instinct to find canons of definition and explanation. Azad's strategy is to leave it to the Qur'ān:

"The more I dashed my hands and feet against the
waves
The more woefully perplexed did I feel.
But when I ceased to struggle and lay motionless,
The waves of their own free will drifted me across
to the shore."[17]

But if others do likewise can we be sure of a corporate "drift"?

These questions lead on to a further and more serious issue. Have we here in Azad an Islam driven, by the demands of Hindu-Muslim co-operation, into an excessively accommodating interpretation of itself? For if so, this would only be another consequence of that "Pakistan" policy against the formulation, application and perpetuation of which the Azad school has been obliged to militate for its existence. Can Islam be appropriately equated with the common essence of all religions, merely by developing a distinction between what it is and what scholasticism or institutional self will have made of it? Azad seems willing to include under the Quranic theme of "To every people its prophet and teacher" the great figures of Hindu religion—a proceeding to which Indian Muslims were often tempted, but of which they were always wary prior to "Pakistan". Is Azad then, for all his attraction, at least a partial justification of the Pakistani suspicion that Indian Islam will at length be metamorphosed by Hinduism? Yet did not Iqbal write as if an inspired peace with polytheism was legitimately a policy for a vitalised Islam? It is a fascinating conundrum. Yet either way, there is "a shrinkage of the substance of Islam".[18]

Mawlana Azad, for all that, remains an intriguing and dominant figure of world Islam. He more than any other thinker has faced religious duty to religious otherness. Since being among the religions at large is rapidly becoming the prime test of each of them, it may well be that Azad's instinct will prove truer than Jinnah's. Meanwhile, there is no mistaking the theme of their disparity.

For these same reasons, however, Azad should not remain here as the sole representative of post-partition Indian Islam. His attitudes to Hinduism go further than others. ASAF A. A. FYZEE (b. 1899) provides a useful example of Muslim opinion, reacting to the necessities of co-existence with Indian religion and of acceptance of the secular state. In *A Modern Approach to Islam*[19] he identifies himself readily with the latter, insisting that religion and law are essentially different and that there can, rightly, be no state enforcement of religious conviction or behaviour. He is ready, too, to allow monotheism to Hinduism, "not a thousand deities, but one Supreme Being, the Absolute, the Creator, Rām or Raḥīm, by whatever name you call him, which was the *one* object of worship".[20] Situated as he is, he went on,

> ". . . the Indian Muslim has to test and compare his faith and actions with those of his other compatriots each day of his life. . . . An Indian interpretation of Islam . . . enjoys the advantage of a common religious life and a shared mystical experience which militates against bigotry and fanaticism and makes for eclecticism and catholicity."[21]

This "Interpretation" holds that law must be firmly separated from religion and if this involves upheaval and bewilderment for Muslims it will, none the less, be salutary and by it a truer larger loyalty will be expressed. Civil law or *qānūn* is inevitably intruding more and more into the *sharīʿa* anyway. Insurance laws, the law of the air and the road, public finance, international law, and much more, are making it less and less possible for life to be strictly controlled by the *sharī'a*. Fyzee, whose career to date has been spent in the study and profession of Islamic law, believes that this must be admitted and that it makes nonsense of the traditional *Dār al-Islām* distinction, by which the true Muslim could be identified. There are clearly wide disparities and diversities of attachment to Islam, in fact and spirit. The old criteria must go. Men who cannot perpetuate the old canons claim none the less that their repudiation is for, and in, a true Islam. *Takfīr*, or the practice of incriminating the unbeliever, is an anachronism.

> "It must be asserted firmly, no matter what the '*ulamā*' say, that he who sincerely affirms that he is a Muslim is a Muslim: no one has the right to question his beliefs . . ."[22]

For his part, Fyzee's Islam requires a careful distinction between the privacies, in conscience and personal allegiance, of religious doctrine and the obligations of public law and authority. Only when this is made can we have a right state of either doctrine or law. In arguing this separation, he is somewhat too ready to over-simplify the issue and to exclude the state too roundly from the moral and spiritual. Ethical norms he takes as subjective, legal rules as objective. Whereas law must be mutable, religion is unchanging in its inner kernel. So what is needed is a frank "secularisation" of law (including even a revision of the thesis that all land belongs to God: let sovereignty for purposes of law belong to the people)[23]—leaving religion in spiritual uncompulsiveness to direct and inform the minds and hearts of persons as such.

His view of the role of Islam in this may be gauged from his comments on Muḥammad and the Qur'ān:

> ". . . one among the elect was the Prophet Muḥammad. The history of his quest, his mental agony and final illumination is to be found in the Koran, and the Book is full of that inward perception of truth which shows the history of man's gradual cognition of God. . . . To me it is clear that we cannot go 'back' to the Koran, we must go 'forward' with it. I wish to *understand* the Koran as it was understood by the Arabs of the time of the Prophet only to reinterpret it and apply it to my conditions of life and to believe in it, so far as it appeals to me as a 20th century man. . . . We cannot make the Koran a book 'which imprisons the living word of God in a book and makes tradition an infallible source'."[24]

In short, he wants Islamic jurisprudence to be itself and faith to "keep to its last" which is the impregnation of the community with the right ideals and the dimension of consciously acknowledged mystery. Then both society and creed will be liberal, authentic and progressive.

These two notable figures in Indian Islam since partition, the one Minister of Education and twice President of the Congress, the other Indian Ambassador in Cairo and Vice-Chancellor of the University of Jammu and Kashmir, must suffice here. Less well known is MUḤAMMAD AJMAL KHĀN (b. 1897), whose Urdu works on the Qur'ān and Muḥammad are a powerful corroboration in exegetical scholarship of the views of Azad, to whom for many years he was private secretary. In particular he calls for careful, chronological study of the Qur'ān's contents and for an openness to scientific criteria of judgement.

The foregoing should not be taken to imply that

conservative voices are silent or absent in the new India. The Ḥanafite "Al-Az'har of India" at Deoband still maintains its repute and there are orthodox Sunnite or Shī'ite academies at Lucknow, Calcutta, Jaunpur, Vellore and numerous other centres. But it would be fair to say that they are dogged more than virile. The new day has brought many problems, material and psychological: minority status makes for serious loss of prestige and sometimes of revenues: there have been grievances, real or sensed, resulting inevitably from the legacies of partition and the tensions of a great new exposure to change. The Hindu secularity in politics is itself in battle with its own extremists and while its determination to fulfil its vision has for the most part held them at bay, the "risk" element is a latent emotion in Muslim psychology likely, according to its incidence, to develop either sullen tenacity of dogma, or excessive "hybridization of religious ideals".[25] And the end is not yet. Complications are legion, from language problems, from Kashmir, from physical dismemberment of the body of Islam in the sub-continent, from personal and provincial ambiguities and rivalries. Yet there is a real sense in which Indian Islam is confronting the demands of a destiny in modernity which in measure Pakistan was founded, if unconsciously, to avoid and evade. By the same token its task is sterner. It may be that minority status can do for Islam what even statehood would preclude. At all events, as Wilfred Smith has observed, "their faith—Islam—is the one thing . . . left to them".

CHAPTER 9

# THE SIGNIFICANCE OF TURKEY

"YOU have to think twice every time you think
In case what you think's a bit on the dubious
side."[1]

"A Sleep of Prisoners" or a muse of observers—the remark suits either equally, and a mosque as the place of it as well as a church, not least if it is in Ankara. For Turkey provides the most intriguing room for a variety of verdicts, which is one good reason for its place in our discussion. The Turks have been castigated as the most outright traitors to Islam in the twentieth century with their liquidation of the Caliphate and their secular society. In the same context and for the identical measures they have been hailed as the most realistic and creative of Muslims.[2] What is seen from one angle as the great repudiation is assessed from another as the bold reformation. As if this controversy about the deeds of Atatürk and the thought of Gök-Alp were not enough, the reversal of their main principle since 1950 yields its own further quality of paradox. For some critics it seems like religion vindicating its centrality to life by the acknowledged bankruptcy of the secular: for others it suggests the social bankruptcy of religion unable effectively to master the vagaries of men or to assimilate their modern situations. If we are honest, there's a dubious side to most of the solutions or opinions that are too neatly offered about the mutual relations of Turkey and Islam since the rise of Atatürk.

To explore them in summary fashion leaves little

space for second thoughts. First the bare historical narrative. It may begin with the Young Turks and their revolution of 1908, which terminated the long and bitter chapter of Ottoman history written by the régime of Sulṭān ʿAbdul-Ḥamīd II. Many areas of the empire in the Balkans had broken free of his tyranny. But Egypt apart, the Arab core remained in wretched subjugation to its inefficiency and cruelty, made all the sharper for the stirrings of Arab intellectual, political and literary aspirations during the same period. The Young Turks sought to vindicate the Ottoman idea by military action to stem further secessions and by liberal offers to the provinces in return for an imperial loyalty. They reckoned without the principle of nationality and failed to measure a situation that called for much more than a pan-Islamic constitutionalism. When, in 1915, with a flourish of *jihād* claims, they entered the First World War against Russia, the Arab Revolt replied, with its stake for an independent nationhood. It thus contributed to the complete prostration of Turkey. The end of the war found the hearth of Ottomanism at the mercy of the Allies at Versailles and, apparently, of the Greeks at Smyrna.

Out of this debacle, it was rescued from dismemberment by the genius of Muṣṭafā Kemāl Atatürk, but only by his decisive rejection of the Ottomanism of the Young Turks, which may be seen in turn as his shrewd understanding of the implications of the Arab Revolt. He at least saw the irrevocability of the Ottoman demise, though its shape had still not become plain to the Khilafatists of India, who continued for some years to plead and scheme for the renewal of an imperial, caliphal expression of Islam. His whole effort, military and political, was concentrated on a domestic salvation, in first freeing the soil of Turkey proper from invaders, exchanging or evicting the racial minorities, and gladly embracing the dissolution of an imperial estate. It was an ideological as well as a practical concentration. Its principle was Turkism, the divine right of the *umma*, or nation. Its chief philosopher was Ziya Gök-Alp. The discovery of the self-sufficiency of Turkishness and the unregretful relinquishment of empire were dual aspects of one salvation. In a real sense, the clue had been provided by the Arab Revolt itself in its preference for inter-Islamic conflict and action against the Ottomans, rather than the imperial *status quo*, however liberalised. The war, then, as seen in retrospect, was for both Arab and Turk, the one in "national" rebellion, the other for "national" recovery, a crucial repudiation of the Caliph's empire, and a decisive verdict on thirteen centuries of Islamic history.[3]

Mandated régimes, it is true, took the place of Ottoman sovereignty in the Arab areas, frustrating Arab aspirations and fulfilling the misgiving about ambiguous Anglo-French intentions. That sequel belongs to Arab history. But mandated or Arab, the Ottoman provinces were gone. Istanbul yielded to Ankara—the old order symbolically displaced by a new capital which had no Sublime Porte and stood squarely, and anciently, in the heart of Turkish Asia with broad hills around its citadel to house the new instruments of ministerial authority, away from the crippling and outmoded precedents. Turkey became a laic, secular state and society. The offices of Imamate and Sultanate were first separated (November 1922) on the ground that they could not properly be combined, and the Sultanate was vested in the National Assembly. After a brief interlude, the entire caliphal structure was terminated (1924). The *sharīʿa* was abolished and new civil and criminal codes substituted, based on European, mainly Swiss, models.

Nor should it be assumed, whatever subsequent

interpretations may be proposed in retrospect, that these measures were purely pragmatic and "political". They represented a deliberate and resolute attempt to reconstruct the whole fabric of national ideology. The Ministry of Justice promulgated the legal revolution with explicit repudiation of the principle, taken to be emphatically Islamic, of the religious derivation of law. Laws based on religion, it insisted, belonged to primitive societies. The first essential of progress was to emancipate law from religion, and hold the latter strictly to the province of conscience. Even there it was assumed that its writ was running out, a process which state action seemed designed to expedite.

Turkish education became by decree wholly secular. There thus exists in Turkey today a phenomenon surely unique in the history of Islam—an entire generation reared in an abeyance of official religious teaching, a period of two decades in which Muslims have been deprived by their "Muslim" state of the means to learn their faith and practice. It is true that in the rural areas, and in clandestine fashion, mosque-schools contrived to outdo the ban. Nor is it, admittedly, possible to arrest simply by state decree the whole continuity of Islamic devotion and to make a cleavage in the sequence of generations. Yet the intention and the policy were there, and that, not as a temporary hiatus to take better stock, but as a purposeful moratorium on all Islamic self-inculcation. It may indeed be right to see this in longer perspective as Islamic reform. But by centuries of Muslim criteria it was treachery. Laicisation and secularity became complete in 1928 when all religious terminology was eliminated from the Constitution. The very verse (Sura 42.38) which supplies a title-theme in these pages was removed from its place of honour in the great National Assembly and was replaced by a tablet, in Turkish, which carried the inscription: "The power of the State proceeds from the people".

The script changes of the late nineteen-twenties—a lively example of Atatürk's dynamism—marked a great psychological revolution, bringing the claims of Turkish solidarity into the minutiae of everyday life and decisively affecting the sanctities of traditional religion, with the sacrosanct Quranic text and the associations of Arabic calligraphy and vocabulary. Similarly drastic in its effects was the suppression of the dervish orders though they were so deep a part of the Turkic culture the ideology proclaimed. Yet there is no doubt that for secularity they were a most powerfully inimical force with their hold on the religious imagination and their tightly knit fraternities of emotion and economy. A régime prepared to count them among its first enemies had gone a long way from venerable criteria of Islam.

The debate deepens when we take the measure of the philosophy justifying the revolution. If it is accepted, for present purposes, that ZIYA GÖK-ALP (1875–1924) is its main exponent, his ideas must be briefly reviewed. Born in Diyarbekir in south-east Anatolia, he developed a critical scepticism from which neither traditional orthodoxy nor Ṣūfism could retrieve him, and in which he turned to Western ideas, not least in the sociology of Durkheim[4] and the notion of national culture. Under the Young Turks he became a considerable intellectual force and a vigorous publicist. Among his many poems one, *Turan* (1911), enshrined the core of his ideas, developed also in a series of articles in 1918 on "Turkification, Islamisation and Modernisation". He was for a time an exile in Malta in the interval between the Allied Occupation of Istanbul and the successful campaign of Mustafa Kemal. He sat for his native town in the new Parliament of

1923 but survived only one further year. His relations with Atatürk were never very close, partly because of his academic reticence and partly for his long association with the Union and Progress group in the war years. But in fact the recovery of Turkey as a territory shorn of empire provided exactly the opportunity for which his ideas and concepts were meant. It is fair to say that he had in part been forced to them, as a scholar might in reflection, as Atatürk had been forced to them by the dire necessities of practical and military leadership. Many of the items of the latter's active revolution in the twenties—language reform, abolition of *waqf* or religious endowments, homogeneity of population by minority elimination, even the abolition of the Caliphate—had all found vent in the former's poems or journalistic blue-prints. He had in theory "Westernised" the Turkish people well before Atatürk's physical redemption of the nation opened the way for it in fact. Of first relevance here is the part his ideas of Islam played in the whole.

"Islamisation", in his famous triad, meant a return to what he believed to be the intellectual freedom of the first days. Islamic institutionalising must be undone. Even the commands of the Prophet himself should be jettisoned if, and where, they had become outmoded. This was a far more ruthless suppression of *taqlīd* than anything advocated in Arab circles, and was sustained by a national assertiveness which no Arab could muster, in view of his unique cultural ties with the very being of Islam. In measure Gök-Alp's notions meant a conscious de-Arabising of Islam. In this context must be set his intriguing, if dubious, understanding of the role of *'urf*, or customary law, in Islam. The classical legists recognise "local custom" as a valid source of law within Quranic paramountcy. Such customary law is in fact very extensive throughout Islam. But Gök-Alp took it to mean the value-judgement of a cultural entity, a sort of sociologist's *ijmāʿ*. He goes further and claims that indeed a great deal of the sacred *sharīʿa* is in fact of such customary origin in essence. Save for matters of conscience between man and God all "religious" obligations really derive from *ʿurf*. Social consciousness gives them sanction and can change them. They can still be regarded, if we are so minded, as divine, but only by a bold form of the *vox populi, vox Dei* equation. *Uṣūl al-fiqh*, or sources of jurisprudence, in fact become the social sciences rather than revelation.

From this follows the separation of religion and the state. For the nation is the source of all law. The way will then be open for a wholesale and unimpeded absorption into Turkishness of Western science, technology and secular temper. With this he calls for a rigorous demarcation of spheres. The ulema, who, from early, though not original, times in Islam, had become influential in state affairs, must be firmly excluded from the political realm. There must be no curb on the democratic sovereignty of the people or the rule of the state from religious factors, whether doctrinal or "ecclesiastical". This is almost a reversal of the "repugnancy" idea we have met hitherto. What is "repugnant" to the national will is excluded. It is as if the door of *ijtihād* is turned around, not to admit the conformable, but to scrutinise the dogmatic, and all is done within the sociological notion of Turan, or Turkic, being. This, of course, is the context for the abolition of the Caliphate, the end of *waqf*, as an *imperium in imperio*, and the revision of family and marriage law. It is also the inspiration of the denial, in his developed thinking, of pan-Islamic culture.[5]

It leads to the deepest point of disparity between Atatürk's achievement and Gök-Alp's beliefs. The great Ghāzī, the dictator-hero, opted for complete secularity. For all practical purposes he carried his Turkism into irreligion. The poet analyst, had he survived, might have become the subtlest critic of this handiwork. For, within his sociological principles, he had a considerable pragmatic and relative appreciation of Islam once "Turkified". It may be that we should see in subsequent developments beyond Atatürk a sequel partly after Gök-Alp's heart, though denied his mental direction. In his youth he had known deep religious experience, and warmed to Al-Ghazālī's autobiography in search of faith, and he acknowledged the "values" of *zakāt* and of prayer. He would have approved that definition of deity which sees it as a symbol of our need to have our highest values beyond the reach of harm. This for him would have been the inner sense of the most characteristic of Muslim attitudes, *tawakkul*, or reliance upon God. Doubtless the warmth of these attitudes was for him depreciated by the temptations of Comte's theory of the "theological" as something to be outgrown by man and having only a phased validity. But his poems have enough of the wistful and the perceptive to sustain the suggestion that the "phase" after all might be of right perpetual.

Doubtless there were strong pragmatic considerations in his justification of Islam as a national religion. But it was a two-edged argument. Patriotic criteria made Islam Turkish over against seceding Christians in the Balkan wars or the Armenians and Greeks in the aftermath of defeat. But Islam itself came from alien, non-Turanian origins and had subdued Turkish culture at a late point in its career. Patriots like Madame Halide Edib could easily conclude that Islam and Turks had never truly been compatible, and this view could all the more readily be held[6] once the Ottoman sequence had been written off as Turkey's calamity. Nevertheless, Gök-Alp was for the most part ready to concede the necessity of religion and, for religion in the Turkish context, the irreplaceability of Islam. The conviction was reinforced by certain palliatives on which he taught Turkish feeling to insist, such as the *adhān* (call to prayer), the mosque sermon, the feast greetings, the prayers and ritual, the chants and recitals, to be in Turkish, and the text of the sacred volume to forgo its hallowed Arabicity for the language of the Turks.

The thought of Ziya Gök-Alp sufficiently epitomises the issues here to dominate the exposition. With

> ". . . the vision and role of a Biblical prophet in the Young Turk revolution . . . to him more than to any other one man belongs the credit of producing both historical facts and the inspiration to revive the native pride . . . which Atatürk later employed so successfully . . ."[7]

And in him are concentrated as well as anywhere the questions that have accompanied the religious vicissitudes of Turkey since Atatürk.

Before he died in 1938, the leader effectuated a secular state and society far more radically than the legacy of Gök-Alp indicated. The proposals of a committee formed in part of Gök-Alp's disciples in 1928 were summarily rejected.[8] Policy became anti-Islamic and Turkish Islam went into educational, practical, ritual, and in part emotional, abeyance. We should be very far "on the dubious side" to claim Atatürk and the Kemalist régime as in any way an essay in Islam, even by the wildest paradox about "the wounds of a friend". What he did achieve, religiously, was to create a situation for Islam quite as unprecedented, though in very different terms, as that set for Indian Islam by partition and the prospect of permanent minority status. He left Turkey the testing legacy of a quarter of a century's interlude[9] of Islamic existence and the burden of emergence from a kind of catacomb of repudiation by state, by education, by policy and symbolic, even mystical, autocracy.

It is always difficult for dictatorship to go into reverse. This is not the place to relate or assess the political story of the sequel to Atatürk, the gradual restoration of party politics, the renewal of electoral contest and the emergence to power of the Democratic Party in 1950, unseating the heirs of Atatürk, the Republicans. Nor is there place to trace the later evolution of Democratic Party dominance and its supersession in personal tragedies by military authority. We need in any event a longer perspective in which to set these developments. But within them, interacting and eddying in the current, are Islamic themes and forces of great interest and some complexity. They have to do, essentially, with the form of the equation between Islam and Turkey, in the post-Atatürk scene.

Though Gök-Alp, as we have seen, insisted on the separation of state and religion and on the subordination of Islam, as religion, to the nation, he nevertheless defined the Turkish nation as made up of Turkish-speaking *Muslims*. He did not regard other religionaries, though they spoke Turkish, as members of the *umma* but only as citizens. So "the ultimate identification of Muslim and Turk remained".[10] Whereas Atatürk left it severely dormant, his successors began to re-activate it. There is no doubt that the Democratic Party's strength in the rural areas at least turned on their growing willingness to give the rein to renascent Muslim feeling. The initial overtures were tentative and guarded and the sanctity of the Atatürk legend persisted unimpaired. But latent forces of conservative religious sentiment proved something like an electoral gift from the gods, which politicians in either camp learned to take seriously. In a cumulative process, religious expression and religious activity began to take open form. Whereas in the University of Istanbul the 287 students in theology in 1926 had been reduced to 10 in 1932 when the Department was abolished, 80 students had enrolled in 1948 when theology was again introduced. A law of July 1947 allowed schools to offer elective courses in Islam if they first received approval of the teacher selected. Since 1949 the Ministry of Education has introduced Islamic teaching, under its own syllabus and direction, at primary, secondary, teacher-training and university levels. In village mosque-schools, where teaching had been illegally maintained, it is again open and popular.

There are numerous other signs of the renewal of Islam in Turkey: a great spate of mosque building and repair, the vigour of religious journals, a widespread open return to the popular festivals of the Muslim calendar and saints, the recovery of Ramaḍān, and very considerable numbers of Turkish pilgrims to Mecca. The de-Arabising of Islam ceased to be pressed. Nineteen-fifty saw the return of the Arabic call to prayer which had been prohibited from 1933, and Arabic Qur'ān recitals were permitted over the government radio. Restraints have been lifted in practice from the dervish orders and the religious capital of Ṣūfism at Konya has experienced a remarkable revival. Yet all these measures, open or tacit, have eventuated without any explicit modification of the secular principle written into the Constitution, and, ill-defined as it is, that secularism remains ostensibly as a pillar of the Turkish state. The sense in many quarters among thinking Muslims that the religious issue could all too readily become a means to political exploitation and so to hypocrisy, has helped to keep the secular ideal strong, if only as an insurance against obscurantist theology. The ambivalence here is perhaps best illustrated in the career of Adnan Menderes, Democratic Prime Minister in the fifties, who frequently warned against politicians capitalising on religious feeling, yet himself yielded in opportune circumstances to that very temptation.

The renewal of Islamic vigour in Turkey has forced into prominence the whole issue of the temper and presuppositions of dogma. Drawing back from the radical solutions of Atatürk and setting state and Islam in some mutual relation, the Turkish mind has been busy with the "image" of Islam. Wanting Islam, for this variety—even confusion—of motive, what Islam does it want? If religion is again to "season all sorts of men" what shall be its savour? The old issue of Islam *versus* secularity has been metamorphosed into secularity *cum* Islam. But what in practice does the mutuality mean and what should it do for each? Secularity, at least unofficially and tortuously, confesses that it needs more than itself. How is the more, which for Turkey must be a Muslim "more", conceived and attained? Islam, for its part, tacitly accepting this *modus vivendi*, has to work out its mission in a relenting secularity.

It may be fair to look for the microcosm of this theme in the new (since 1949) Theological Faculty in Ankara, the launching of which was something of a deliberate symbol of the new day. If obscurantist moods and perils are to be excluded it will be by attention to *quis custodiet ipsos custodes?* The primary business will be with the teachers of the teachers. Education must be shaped at its source. Hence the careful effort in the Divinity Faculty at Ankara, with its impressive budget and considerable body of professors, to generate a progressive, scholarly, alert quality of Islamic religious custodians. One significant circumstance impeding its purpose derives from the situation it is commissioned to redeem, namely, religious ignorance. There has been great difficulty in recruiting a student body of the calibre to sustain the venture, and for lack of whom the mission itself has suffered some eclipse. The educational dichotomy noted elsewhere has its peculiar Turkish form and it is proving immensely difficult to rehabilitate theological disciplines in the manner required with the human material available.[11] In the end it may be that the strength of Islam, and of its current response to its Turkish destiny, will lie, not with intellectual and academic finesse or competence—though these it cannot ignore—but in the deeper levels of mystical and practical piety which have always been the strength of Ottoman Islam, and whose indestructibility is one of the lessons of recent history. We must test the promise of current Turkish Islam not merely by the journal of the *Ilāhiyat Fakültesi* at Ankara but by such a *cri de cœur* as Mahmut Makal's rugged picture of the Turkish village.[12] The writer is an outstanding product of the Village Institute system begun in 1940 to help eradicate illiteracy and inculcate the ideals of the Republic.

To set the materials of this chapter in the broad perspective of Muslim history and assess its meaning is a hard business. Islam can be seen as at once the victim and the beneficiary of a revolution which exceeded in radical thoroughness its own philosophic antecedents. By many essential Islamic criteria it was a devastating conspiracy against the Qur'ān, the *sharīʿa* and the agelong instincts of Muslim dogma. It substituted the state for the Prophet as the seat of authority and rejected the traditional view of the former as instrumentally under and within the Divine order. It asserted nationality over against the universal and linked religious practice at best with social utility, at worst with primitive and outmoded attitudes.

Yet for all its dislocation and forthright rebellion, it may reasonably be seen as an episode in the unbroken theme of Islam. It can certainly be claimed that the

Caliphate was a dubious symbol, if only for its cynical exploitation by ʿAbdul-Ḥamīd whose tenancy wrought it no honour. Its demise could be greeted with consternation, but hardly with inconsolable dismay. "The disappearance of this wraith from the Middle Ages"[13] —if one is content with H. A. R. Gibb's phrase—could even be taken as opportune. It is entirely possible to describe Islamic culture in Turkey in our time as if no upheaval had occurred. Ḥasan Baṣrī Çantay blandly does so in the symposium, *Islam the Straight Path*, citing the very verse which had been removed from the National Assembly's walls, because it had a religious qualification for the takers of counsel (Sura 42.38), as being the plain charter of the secular state. Such double interpretation of Quranic meanings is by no means rare, though it is odd the writer did not recollect the ceremony of removal undergone by the passage he takes for justification. For him the fact that ninety-nine per cent of the Assembly are "Muslims" suffices and since there are no clergy in Islam everyone "with religious authority can speak about the Faith". He does not stay to give any precision to "Muslim", "religious" and "secular" in his narrative. But he is clearly intending to acknowledge the current Turkish situation as "Islamic".[14]

But aside from the ambiguities latent in these contrasted ways of reading the same events, there are two other factors, in conclusion, which leave the counsels of Turkish Islam, or rather their reviewer, in dubiety. These are the degree of government control and the religious dangers that make it a practical necessity. In the period from the entrenchment in power, in 1954, of the Democratic Party, until its tragic discrediting in 1960, there were many ugly elements in the political exploitation of religious conservatism. It would seem that Turkish Islam in general could not secure itself from the reactionaries within it and that the Menderes régime could not forbear the political gains that accrued, because of this fact, to the party prepared to induce them through the sinister use of the wide government powers over religion and education it enjoyed—powers originally designed to ensure that only progressive Islam would reoccupy the places made for it by the steady modifications of secularity in the years before. As it eventuated, partly no doubt through the rural factors and peasant conservatisms, governmental Islam (if the phrase is allowable) succumbed to the inherent compromises of political exploiters and religious reactionaries. Since the military régime of 1960, demands have been renewed for a check on traditional Islamic expression (Arabic in mosques and the like), and for a new campaign to wean the villager from his static mentality. Such ends, of course, presuppose a maintenance of governmental direction over religion, and thus, in turn, religion must remain a central political theme. A pessimist might be forgiven for concluding that the issue is really back where it was in 1950, only with the added embitterment of the inevitable quarrel about the "image" of Menderes, its vindication or vilification, as the case may be.[15] It is ironical, and yet perhaps also inevitable, that a régime setting out in the twenties to relegate religion to the realm of mere private conscience and exclude it from the state's majesty, should in its sequel have engendered a history in which faith and government should have been so much entangled. One thing is clear, namely, that Islam in Turkey is far too virile for secularism to ignore and too unpredictable to hold free rein. The fact of its survival is undoubted, the temper still in doubt. It has outlived Atatürk but is yet in the toils of his legacy.

## CHAPTER 10

# AḤMADIYYA

NOT seldom in the history of religions a divergent community serves to precipitate issues of an importance out of all proportion to its own numbers or the quality of its inner achievement. Its presence proves a catalyst whereby implicit questions take explicit shape and become themes of public controversy with a sharpness and provocation they might otherwise lack. Sectarianism is often a significant clue to stresses within the psychology and institutional forms of a religion. It poses, in excessive or assertive ways, the inherent dilemmas of mind that belong with more responsible or respectable orthodoxy. Such a role in the life of contemporary Islam has been filled by the Aḥmadiyya movement which derived from Mīrzā Ghulām Aḥmad in the last quarter of the nineteenth century or, more precisely, in the closing years of the thirteenth century of the Islamic calendar (1300 A.H.—1882/3).

The alternative dating is noteworthy. For Muslim tradition has anticipated that each turn of a century would be marked by a *mujaddid*, or renewer of religion, by whose initiative and *charisma* new vitality would be released into the legacies of the orthodox years. Mirza Ghulam Ahmad believed himself to be such a revitaliser as the nineties of the thirteenth century A.H. moved towards the grateful time. The consequences of his claim are such that the sequel, both doctrinal, emotional and communal, deserves inclusion here, though otherwise the numerous sectarian diversions and excesses within

Islam find no treatment within the limits of this survey.

Aḥmadiyya is exceptional on several counts—the vigour of its propagation, its reliance on heretical or at least dubious theology to break the authority of the mullah conservatism, its will to carry the warfare into the enemies' camp, and the strange pretensions and career of its founder. Here is a campaign against *taqlīd* and obscurantism of a very different temper from the co-operative Westernism of Ahmad Khan or the staunch orthodoxy of Mawdudi. It is as if, unconsciously perhaps, Mirza Ghulam Ahmad held the conviction that a real Islamic breakthrough worthy of the new century, and adequate to unseat the ancient authorities of schools and shaykhs and to turn the tables on the West, would have to be equipped with something more than reason and a conventional proceeding. At all events it was just the elements of shock, of mystery and of provocation that he was well constituted, by context and by temper, to provide.

Mīrzā Ghulām Aḥmad (1839–1908), born and bred at Qadian in the Punjab, believed himself to be in receipt of special revelations from God as he neared the age of forty—always for Muslims a crucial time of life, since it was at that point the Prophet himself had begun to receive the Qur'ān. Ahmad's claims were linked with thought of the *mujaddid* and also later with the Islamic notion of the *mahdī* or guide. Later still, he associated his vocation with the ideas of messiahship and with the name of Krishna. This eclecticism may have been an inverted form of concern about the multiplicity of religions (cf. the title of his journal *The Review of Religions*, founded in 1892) and a pattern of response to the Indian context. His later theories about Jesus may have been part of a desire to "Asianise" the Saviour of the Gospels. But from the outset his most serious potential heresy was the precise import of his claims to

Islamic revelation. For the finality of Muḥammad as the seal of the prophets is a cardinal, and most sensitive, point of Muslim belief. The word *nabī*, or prophet, was certainly used frequently of him and by him. By a vigilant orthodoxy he was taken to have undoubtedly impugned the sacred dogma of *Khatm an-Nubuwwa*.

The precise truth here is a matter of some perplexity, because of the subsequent controversy with which it was surrounded both inside and outside Aḥmadiyya itself, and for the inner obscurity of the usage. In so far as prophethood presupposes a caliphate in succession to it, Aḥmad founded one and it still survives, though part of his following divided on this issue at the death, in 1915, of the first Caliph, Ḥakīm Nūr-ad-Dīn. Prophecy, in any event, hinges, in turn, on the nature of the continuity of revelation. It involves the issues which have been reviewed in Chapter 5. There can be little doubt that Mirza Ghulam Ahmad did intend to supersede that communal form of "Islamicity" there examined as being the gist of Sunnite belief about ongoing truth. He also makes sharp contrast with the Shīʿite reliance on the hidden Imām, for which he substituted his own *charisma*. God, he avowed, had in some sense linked him with prophetic mediation of truth, and this, it was argued,[1] was because God still called and sent spokesmen of His unceasing word. How the unceasing word was related to the once-for-all Quranic is a subtle point. The ambiguity may be assessed from the following:

> "A *mujaddid* is in one sense a prophet, though he still does not possess perfect prophethood: but still he is partially a prophet, for he is endowed with the gift of being spoken to by God, matters relating to the unseen are revealed to him and like the revelation of prophets and apostles his revelation is kept

free from the interference of the devil . . . and he is commissioned just like the prophets . . . and it is incumbent on him that he should announce his claim at the top of his voice."[2]

This, whatever its reservations, was enough for apprehensive conservatives. That immunity from the devil seemed suspiciously like full prophetic status. But opposition, strident and strong, seemed only to get Mirza Ghulam Ahmad the more readily to "the top of his voice". He certainly aroused vitriolic foes, while asserting a magnetic fascination for his disciples. The result was a bitter controversy which often deepened into a sinister conflict of wills as well as words. There are several stories of his uncanny power to "will" evil on his detractors by imprecation and deliberate "curses". Antagonism only sharpened when they came true. These occult successes of vituperation enhanced his repute with some contemporaries and sadly disfigure his biography for the historian. It is only fair to add that with the passing of time many of his followers have outlived and outgrown these compromises of their genesis.

Accessions to his ranks, and growth in his pretensions, proceeded together. In 1889, he proclaimed a divine revelation empowering him to accept *bayʿa* or caliphal allegiance and in 1891 came the claims to be *mahdī* and messiah. But the *nabī* issue continued to be the sorest. As the Report of the Judicial Inquiry concluded, in 1954, it could be held that Muḥammad's finality was not impugned, but only if it is also agreed that a provocative ambiguity was present in the history and terms of the claim.[3] It may be conjectured that this extreme, even bizarre, pattern of renewal has its character, not only for the obvious reason that it derives from Ahmad's personality, but that only by such temper is a static condition broken through. Excess is then in its way the measure of the fixity it challenges.

So it is that the whole career of Aḥmadiyya has been intermittently stormy. At his death in 1908, Mirza Ghulam Ahmad is estimated to have had over fifty thousand followers, though his own assessment was ten times that number. His birthplace at Qadian had become the centre of a disciplined community. Seven years later schism resulted over the question of a successor to the first Caliph. The founder's eldest son by a second marriage, Bashīr-ad-Dīn Maḥmūd Aḥmad, of long reign, assumed the caliphal title against the opposition of a powerful segment who broke away and became the Lahore Aḥmadiyya. Having abandoned the caliphate, they have steadily approximated to a sophisticated orthodox Islam, save in the one point of the "death" of Jesus. They had differed with the Qadianis, as the "loyal" group came to be known, over the question of participation in the Muslim League which Mirza Ghulam Ahmad had forbidden. They ceased to regard non-Aḥmadī Muslims as *kāfirs* or unbelievers and drew steadily closer to the mass of Muslims, on whose behalf they have harnessed the vitality of the Aḥmadī impetus in mission and propagation. They have by now long disembarrassed themselves of the dubious features of their origin without forfeiting its *élan* and energy.

Both groups have pioneered the translation of the Qur'ān in the languages of the West and have established mosques in many European, American and African centres. Qadianis, in particular, seem to be distinctly unwelcome in Arab states and the heart lands of Islam. But the ventures of both movements are far flung in the periphery of Islam, not least in West and East Africa and in South-East Asia. For many in these places and in the West, they represent the only form of Islam to which there is access. In this sense they have inaugurated a new tradition in Islam, that of specific, organised mission sustained by offerings of the community and carefully directed and planned with personnel, literature, schools and sometimes clinics, etc. Aḥmadiyya initiative in this way has been in part a factor in arousing similar projects of dissemination on the part of venerable bodies like Al-Az'har, either in emulation or correction of its zeal.

The chief propagandists of the Lahore section have been Khwaja Kamāl-ad-Dīn and Muḥammad ʿAlī. Its journals *Light* (at Lahore) and *The Islamic Review* (at Woking) have sustained an alert presentation of their cause. *Review of Religions* has greater asperity and sectarian temper. The two Aḥmadiyya renderings of the Qur'ān[4] are, of course, involved in the Christological deviation from orthodox Islam which characterises them both, and this vitiates their otherwise painstaking and ambitious attempt to mediate the Qur'ān to the outside world.

Some estimate must therefore be made of the whole posture of Aḥmadiyya in respect of Christian faith. Inevitably Christian relations have been involved from the beginning in the temper and pre-occupations of the period here studied. It could not be otherwise, given the ancient antipathies between mosque and church, the traditions of controversy, and the religious overtones of the struggle with the West and its imperialism. Muḥammad ʿAbduh, like his predecessor, Jamāl-ad-Dīn al-Afghānī, addressed himself to Christian comparisons and the concern has been perpetuated throughout the apologetic history of modern Islam. It is as if Islamic repossession could not proceed without conscious and often sharply assertive reactions *vis-à-vis* Christianity, or perhaps more correctly, Christendom. The fact of

Christian missions, in the sometimes ambiguous context of political dominance, has, of course, intensified the inter-religious situation.[5] There is neither place nor occasion to explore the resultant issues here.[6] But at this one point of the Aḥmadiyya literature they confront us where they are most clearly focussed within the interior counsels of Islam, with which alone we are concerned. For with the Aḥmadiyya, specific and bold innovation in respect of Christian relations is manifestly central to the self-direction of Islam, as the Aḥmadīs believe it should be.

In brief, following their founder, their thesis is to make Islamic eschatology self-sufficient by eliminating from it the "Christian" dimensions implanted in it by orthodox Muslim tradition. By the latter, Jesus (in Islam ʿĪsā) was raptured to heaven by Divine intervention at the Cross without having suffered crucifixion at all. From thence He will return for a millennial role. This role admittedly is traditional and not Quranic: but its denial is certainly heresy. The nub of the matter is the interpretation of the crucial passage in Sura 4.158, about the apparentness of the crucifixion.[7] According to the Aḥmadī view, Jesus was actually crucified but did not succumb, was buried, without having died, and by dint of healing ointment revived and emerged from the tomb. He survived to a ripe old age as a preacher and prophet in India and his tomb has been identified near Srinagar in Kashmir. This forecloses all apocalyptic significance for Jesus and bypasses the whole Christian meaning of a redeeming Cross and the Resurrection. This, in Muhammad Ali's words, means "the crumbling of the whole (Christian edifice) like a pack of cards . . . to undo the influence of Christianity and to open the way for the conquest of Islam in the world".[8]

There is no doubt that they have chosen the vital

issue. The only point here, however, is to recognise a major doctrinal deviation and heresy in contemporary Muslim counsels and to note its context and purpose. Muslim progressiveness in sectarian form has undertaken a bold and deliberate revision of its own Muslim Christology. By eliminating the eschatological it streamlines the Islamic version of Jesus, but in so doing violates his Muslim, as well as his Christian, status. It weighs what it sees as a present handicap against a traditional continuity of belief and elects to relieve itself of the one by jettisoning the other. A tomb for Jesus in Asia is better for Aḥmadiyya ends than a throne in Christendom or heaven. Islam shall be revitalised, not by a new sympathy for the dimensions of the Cross but by a more purposeful antipathy. The Aḥmadi decision here is at least a forthright deviation.

The same militancy of mind characterises another aspect of Aḥmadī counsels, when we turn from debate about tradition and Jesus, to controversy within statehood and Islam. It was the Qadianis who directly or indirectly precipitated into sharp quarrel the unresolved ambiguities of Islamic statehood in the new Pakistan. Theories turned into contentions and contentions into riots. The substance in the passion was distilled, in turn, into judicial proceedings and report. What occurred in the Punjab in the spring of 1953 was a violent eruption of the inner ambiguity of the new state. Since it gave rise to one of the most interesting documents of Islamic analysis in our time, we must take brief stock of its implications.

Once Pakistan had been established as an Islamic state, sectarian movements which earlier had little or no political significance became bones of contention of the first order. If heretical, their being tolerated within citizenship, which an alien empire may have assumed, emerged as a salient issue for every purist. Qadianis held that theirs was the true Islam[9] and formally avoided all other Muslims. Conservative Islam reciprocated with demands, not for the liquidation of the Aḥmadiyya, but for their being denominated a non-Muslim sect outside the Islamic citizenship. Liberals and secular Muslims saw in this demand a direct claim on the part of conservatism to adjudicate on the Islamicity of every Muslim, which, if conceded, would hand over to the die-hards the effective determination of Muslim description, and so, destiny. This would have become of course an intolerable situation. Liberals were therefore compelled, not for any particular affection for them, but for the sake of the very possibility of freedom and progress, to resist the formal de-Muslimisation of Aḥmadis.

The essentials of this situation were embroiled and complicated by endless factors, local, personal, partisan and political, into which there is no need to enter. The Punjab Riots of March and April 1953 brought down the provincial government. After a period of martial law, order was restored. The subsequent inquiry probed not only the role played by the complex of groups and passions, but the fundamental question of the definition of a Muslim. It decided that there was in fact a chaos of authority. The judges may have been indulging in some shaykh-baiting, an all too easy practice,[10] when they concluded:

> "Keeping in view the several definitions given by the 'ulema,' need we make any comment except that no two learned divines are agreed on this fundamental? If we attempt our own definition as each learned divine has done and that differs from that given by all others, we unanimously go out of the fold of Islam. And if we adopt the definition given by any one of the ulema, we remain Muslims

according to the view of that *'ālim* but *kāfirs* according to the definition of every one else."[11]

Though the position is not quite so hapless, the statement captures its bewildering quality. The Report, commonly known as the "Munir Report", explores other areas of Islamic belief and practice, such as *jihād*, prophetic finality, apostasy and *dhimmīs*, or subject minorities. It is both intriguing and suggestive to find these topics figuring in a judicial inquiry into public disorders. Yet in fact the latter were simply the violent potential of Islamic issues in the chosen form of "Pakistan" and the latent forces of fanaticism with which all politics has to reckon just below the surface of events.

The Report laid the major blame on the *Aḥrār* and other conservative elements, but held that the Qadianis had not avoided to be provocative. Perhaps even more reprehensible than either was the evasiveness shown by governments, both provincial and central, in relation to the extremist demands.

"... in view of the emphasis that had come to be laid on anything that could even be remotely related to Islam or Islamic State, nobody dared oppose them, not even the Central Government which, for the several months during which the agitation had, with all its implications, been manifesting itself, did not make even a single public pronouncement on the subject."[12]

The Qadianis had certainly not of themselves made the fact within this illuminating comment: but they had contrived to make it evident.

Aḥmadi communities, both Qadiani and Lahori, resemble conservative groups like those studied in Chapter 7, in the firmness of their corporate and personal discipline. They share the ideals of strict practice and "puritan" pieties that belong with the traditions most hostile to them. A most notable symbol of this capacity for industry, and spartan loyalty, is to be seen in the re-establishment of the Qadianis at Rabwa after partition had left Qadian on the Indian side of the frontier. The second caliph, in response to a directive dream, led the movement to new headquarters, deliberately located in a barren tract of country, which careful toil and rugged will have made habitable by a community of several thousands, and in turn the focal point in the allegiance of a following estimated by the caliph in 1953 at a quarter of a million. The *chanda* system operates by which adherents pay one-sixteenth of their income to the communal purse. The caliph expects and evokes a total loyalty and the whole appeal of the movement inwardly is to sturdy communal identification in which the individual has both the strength and the weakness of all such corporate unities of dogma and attachment.

Aḥmadiyya counsels, then, in sum, compel the attention of the analyst, as a vociferous, intense, ambitious, yet strangely contradictory, expression of contemporary Islam. Its origins and, with the Qadianis, its continuing ethos, turn upon esoteric, mystical ideas of a seer-leader, yet its propaganda claims to be rational and scholarly. It is by character highly provocative and yet purports to be the vanguard of the religion of peace. It makes bold with an exhaustive erudition and yet perpetrates deep and serious lapses from objectivity in scholarship.[13] It has the hope of increasingly widespread dispersion in the world and yet seems oddly unconcerned about the cultural heritage of other peoples. Its attitudes to evolution would appear progressive and liberal, but it fails to take the full measure of the scientific revolutions of the time.

But perhaps in the last analysis the Aḥmadiyya goes

further than its specific apology or policy know. Behind its controversial form is the final question of the nature of Muḥammad's finality. What is the relation of the sealed Scripture to the open future? How do we relate the admittedly urgent dimension of religious certitude, which is the core of Muḥammad's Quranic status, with the perspectives of time's incertitudes? Can the last prophet rightly be a long time ago, and the nature of revelation "some everlasting echo"? Can a retrospective assurance serve a prospective mystery? Was it with these unspoken perplexities that Mirza Ghulam Ahmad's shaping of Islam into his own version of renewal unwittingly belongs? Or was his reaction to Muslim lethargy and the modern scene no more than a personal pretension that gathered momentum among the currents of Islam? In either case, it is at once an enigma and a clue.

CHAPTER 11

# THE STATUS OF RECURRENT THEMES

ABLUTIONS before prayer, it is said, must be done briskly. But the turban takes a long time to wind. Here is the paradox with which we are confronted—the necessity for activism and vigour in the face of the modern human condition and in the name of the dynamic "worship", yet the instinctive reservations and traditionalisms of a long enduring, deeply sacred, system. From counsel to counsel the mood shifts, the safeguards vary, the initiatives are offered, the themes persist.

As part of what is no more than a cursory survey, the previous chapters have attempted only to take stock of a crowded panorama at a few vantage points, where events, or books, illuminate its course and content. The paragraphs that follow venture another tack, namely, a review of how the Muslim "possesses his possessions" gathered, as they may well be for this purpose, into the custody of the holy Qur'ān. How do the recurring themes stand, within the equation of change and continuity thus far studied, as may be measured by Islamic thoughts with, of and through, the sacred Scripture? This gives the opportunity not only to notice certain other names and journals, but to assess their counsels at the inclusive and central point of Muslim existence. For in the Qur'ān meet the primary questions of Muḥammad's prophethood, the sources of the *sharī'a*, the vocabulary of worship, the authority of doctrine and the criteria of Muslim society. *Fidei coticula Coranus* as the Latins might have said.

The problems are formidable. There is no doubt that the classical view of the Muslim Scripture, assumed and aggravated by orthodox exegesis, is of a supernaturally revealed corpus of words, vouchsafed to an illiterate Prophet, constituting a final, and single, miracle of eloquence and guidance, inalienably Arabic in form, untranslatable in its real Quranicity and the unquestionable source of all authority in all the matters, doctrinal, social, legal, biographical, with which it deals. Here, in a deep sense, is a fundamentalism *par excellence*.[1]

The situation, however, is far more flexible than this proper statement might seem to admit. As will appear below, the Qur'ān itself may be taken as the surest emancipator of its contents from their own incubus of dogma and discipleship, tentative as much of this liberation at present seems. Meanwhile, the first great hurdle has been that of translation itself. Despite the long and wide dispersion of Islam for fourteen centuries, and more lately the various Western renderings (which orthodoxy regarded as mischievous and tendentious), the traditional mind has only in this twentieth century relented on this issue. Its dilemmas are understandable. For on the purely literary basis, translation is a sort of destruction. Even if the meaning is successfully conveyed the inimitable form is likely sacrificed.[2] But to this must be added the dogma of the Qur'ān's Arabicity and the related belief in the heavenly tablet, *Umm al-Kitāb*, not to speak of the danger that all translation is of necessity interpretation.[3] Marmaduke Pickthall, an English Muslim, received specific approval from Al-Az'har in 1930 for his intention of publishing an English version, provided he gave it the safeguarding title "The Meaning of the Glorious Qur'ān". He commented: "The position that all translation of the Qur'ān is sinful has been quite abandoned. This is a great step forward."[4] Muṣṭafā al-Marāghī about the same time denied that translation corrupted the "miracle" of the Qur'ān.[5] The "regrettable necessity" atmosphere about these concessions can, of course, be overcome if one bears in mind that on the Qur'ān's own showing its Arabicity is with a view to intelligibility, and that therefore where Arabness is not present but other races and languages are, translation becomes mandatory. So it is that the very passages so long thought to render the Arabic sacrosanct, in fact require its supersession.[6] But this is only one, if the most obvious, of the ways in which the Qur'ān and its custodians are involved inextricably in the equation of time and place, and the eternal both there and then and here and now.

The real brunt of this problem is, of course, evaded by the familiar practice of some liberals to turn Quranic content to their own will and to their heart's content. We have noted earlier the acute question raised by the assumptions of Iqbal that philosophic meanings can be read in the Qur'ān's vocabulary in neglect, or even defiance, of its original import. The potential range of such inventiveness is great. Ghulām Aḥmad Parwez (b. 1903), for example, takes the theme word of Sura 74: *Al-Muddaththir*, which relates to Muḥammad's practice of withdrawal and contemplation "wrapped in a cloak", and giving it an ingenious turn makes it denote "a world re-orderer", subsequently taking the imperative that follows, *Qum* ("rise", that is, to preach and warn), as a directive to global revolution.[7]

Cruder forms of this habit of mind are sometimes founded on a concept of Quranic prescience—a theme which often figures in journals like *Majallat al-Aẓ'har* and *Liwā' al-Islām*. What sciences have established and applied, even material ones like hygiene and metallurgy, may be read into the words of the Qur'ān. Such thinkers are only antagonised by the suggestion that since the purpose of the Scripture is moral and religious it cannot be expected to adumbrate modern discoveries and must thereby be absolved of scientific bearings. On the contrary: what is inerrant must be uniformly abreast of all knowledge, however much this claim may lead into the circularity that argues inerrancy from Divine guarantee and proves Divine guarantee by inerrancy.[8] Much is made in this connection of the very general call of the Qur'ān to attention and responsive awareness. But it is not always remembered that this very real Quranic "naturalism" in the right acknowledgement of the "signs" of God in phenomena is primarily a religious "controversy" of God with His people, and not an injunction to empirical science, except by very strained "extension" which has honestly to take account of so much else in the stance of orthodoxy before it can say with integrity: "The Qur'ān enjoins the scientific mentality which only believes what it has made subject to experiment".[9]

There are thinkers, of course, who invoke the specifically religious intention of the Qur'ān and depend on the reasonable separation of provinces.[10] But there is all too little Islamic scholarship dedicated to the same sort of critical textual study familiar for more than two centuries to Christian Biblical reception. The major work on the foreign vocabulary of the Qur'ān comes from outside Islam, in part perhaps because theoretically there is nothing but Arabic in the Qur'ān.[11] A far greater effort is needed to delve into the immediate context of Muḥammad's experience of *tanzīl*, to ascertain the connotations among the Qur'ān's first reciters of the terms it employs and to search in the hinterland of speech, usage and poetry, for the likely and primary significances within its rich and recondite terminology. But such linguistic and "archæological" studies of the Quranic environment have been deterred by assumptions of dogmatic "slumber", and the long ascendancy of the commentaries.

They are also complicated by the mystery of its incidence in the Prophet's mind, and by the interests of *iʿjāz*, the Arabic miracle of the illiterate instrument, and the Muslim instinct to assume that things are the more Divine the less they are human. Muslim veneration has long taken Muḥammad to be in some deep sense a cosmic reader of the universal Mind and several Muslim philosophers have understood prophecy as the supreme form of rationality. Yet there is everywhere a disinclination to take up with studied care and patient scrutiny the psychic, cultural and mental circumstances within which the Qur'ān came and within which the Prophet had his being.

Writers like Ameer Ali, though "heretically", have seen the Qur'ān as Muḥammad's achievement and its rules as his "prescriptions". But such writing fails to face the issue to which it leads, namely, whether the circumstantial context so vital to these proper historical studies yields a more disconcerting implication when taken account of in exegesis. The question, simply phrased, has to do with *that* time and *this* time. If we need the former to pursue contextual research what changes must exegesis wrestle with when facing modern situations? It is, of course, on this account that the conservative mentality prefers the immutable word, binding on all generations and only arbitrarily, not inherently, sited in its first generation. In this mood it is that some have even welcomed the non-chronological (and from the scholarly point of view highly vexing) arrangement of the Qur'ān. For this serves to detach its contents from any precise immediacies of place or time, and it is thus, allegedly, the more ready for timeless reassertion.[12]

Yet to plead this way is not only craven and wooden in itself: it is contrary to the Qur'ān. Non-chronology, as far as it goes, may symbolise that points of time are not the *only* setting of Quranic relevance. But it is any way far from entire. Indeed, it could be said to be no more than accidental. Sūras, perversely, may be composite and succeed each other in diminishing length in tedious neglect of when they came. But there is the watershed of the Hijra, the Meccan and the Medinan divide. There are inerasable events, like Badr, Uḥud and the *Barā'a*. There are the *asbāb an-nūzūl*, or occasions of the Qur'ān's descent. History cannot be escaped. A great turn in Islamic Quranic scholarship may be on the way when it is appreciated that by its own criteria it is a book immersed in events and that its meanings cannot be isolated from them, or carried beyond them, negligently of what they are and what they heard. This "historicity" of the Qur'ān is rooted in its own "piecemeal" character, as a book which had to be allowed to accumulate.[13] Here in this basic fact of the Qur'ān's genesis and structure, its incorporation of time's texture into its text, resides the still latent clue to its perceptive custodianship, by which sooner or later the Qur'ān will free itself and exegesis breathe anew.

Meanwhile the contextual principle in another sense makes headway—the interior comparison of terms and the idea of letting the Qur'ān test the Qur'ān.[14] So much of its content is controversial: the deliverances of Muḥammad are called out in encounter with his detractors, in the formula: "They say! Say thou!" What then can be learned from the Qur'ān's interior tensions and conflicts, even aside from the events *per se* within them? The same criterion may largely be applied to the burden and point of patriarchal and prophetic precedents which figure so frequently in the middle period. It can be extended also to the legal sections, for these also, often explicitly and always necessarily, *belong* with and to an empirical shape of affairs. Thus, for example, the famous directive of Sura 4 about appropriate plurality of wives within the limit of four belongs to a context about the care of orphans. The "translation" of the Qur'ān in the largest sense, for the direction and disciplining of life today, turns upon the full application of this responsible principle that honestly, bravely (if need be), and imaginatively, concedes and pursues a fully contextual interpretation.

Two early and immature efforts in this line may be cited. Ya'qūb Ḥasan, in 1927, in an Urdu commentary claimed that the Qur'ān should be interpreted by reference to itself and that this should be done for each succeeding generation anew. He therefore deplored an exegesis that relied wholly on the traditions of the Companions, which bound it to their own limitations. He tried a chronological arrangement and claimed to find harmonies in the text with modern science. Despite its tentativeness, this was a pioneer work in that it disputed the insistence that tradition was the only proper guide to *tafsīr*.[15]

A parallel venture was that of Muḥammad Abū-Zayd in 1930. In a brief commentary which caused a stormy controversy he called for the casting off of petrified forms and an exegesis of the Qur'ān by itself. He gathered cross-references and decried the old grammatical pre-occupations. He took the angelic worship of Adam to represent in myth the amenability of the order of things to man's dominion. Some of his explanations, such as Solomon's ants being his mobile cavalry or the Queen of Sheba's scouts, were less happy. He used his principle to try and eliminate the miraculous and quite failed to see that it would have been better applied by a search into the sources of Quranic stories in the apocryphal literature or Christian traditions. Abū-Zayd had a considerable following among younger shaykhs but an official committee of Al-Az'har condemned his "innovations".[16]

Initiative of another kind in taking the Qur'ān within itself is to be found in *Al-Fann al-Qaṣaṣī fī-l-Qur'ān al-Karīm*, a doctoral thesis in the Cairo University in 1947, by Muḥammad Khalafallāh. It addressed itself to the shape of the Quranic stories of the patriarchs and argued that their divergencies from the Biblical were not due, as Western scholarship often alleged, to the Prophet's misinformation, but to his deliberate decisions of authorship. He was in fact handling earlier material, for a didactic and artistic purpose, very much as, for example, Shakespeare handled the story of Hamlet or Macbeth. He was exercising a proper literary initiative and creativity. Khalafallāh's arguments, of course, proved highly offensive to the conservative mind, for which conscious authorship on Muḥammad's part was unthinkable. One could not speak of "sources" if one believed in *tanzīl*, or of literary creation if one accepted *waḥy*. How could the Qur'ān incorporate creative art and remain factual? Can there be even prophetic inventiveness in that which God sent and whose "original" is in the heavens?

The question whether, in fact, the Quranic stories have a livelier dramatic "shape" need not here be discussed. The issue in Khalafallāh's thesis, which became a test case of academic freedom, plainly focusses the central problem of the sacred Book as from God, unto men, *via* the Prophet and in time.[17] The copious output of Quranic commentary still revolves around the meaning and obedience of its revelatory status. 'Abbās al-'Aqqād's *Al-Falsafa al-Qur'āniyya* finds a kinship between the great themes of ancient philosophy and the spirit of the Qur'ān and claims its temper for the congenial tasks of science and sociology. Muḥammad Yūsuf Mūsā, likewise, in *Al-Qur'ān wa-l-Falsafa* cites the Qur'ān's call to "a people who cogitate" as proving its philosophic harmony. In *Naẓarāt fī-l-Qur'ān*, Muḥammad al-Ghazālī makes an extensive restatement of the conservative view of the Qur'ān's nature, authority and content, elaborating its doctrine of God, prophecy, man and society, and its threefold *i'jāz*—spiritual, intellectual and rhetorical, adding: "The Qur'ān is entirely in line with everything that science has unveiled and disclosed—a fact which is undoubtedly one of the proofs of its veracity and miracle".[18] Ḥāfiẓ Ghulām Sarwar, in *The Philosophy of the Holy Quran*, experiments with hidden implications of words, equating "Lord" throughout with "Vital principle". Sura 55.29's "Every moment He is engaged in some new affair" means the progressive evolution of Bergsonian philosophy. Man's making from wet clay is the origin of species related by the Qur'ān "long before Darwin ever noticed it".[19] *Lā ilāha illā 'llāh* is translated: "The Real is One". So though

> ". . . . the days of the prophet are over, Reason the ever-living prophet is still alive in the breasts of men. Reason is as wide awake as ever and the philosophy of the Qur'ān is everlasting".[20]

Malek Bennabi's *Le Phénomène Coranique* by contrast focusses on the prophetic and religious aspects of the Qur'ān and ventures some conjectures about the psychic bearings of vocation by reference to Jeremiah. There are echoes of Buber in his discussion of the "I" of Muḥammad's call in the confrontation with God which declares: "Recite . . . in the Name of thy Lord", and that to an "illiterate" who never conceives of himself as "reading". In the same sense he stresses the Prophet's solitariness and the characteristics of *waḥy*, its intermittent nature and the unity of its design. With this venture on Bennabi's part into the study of the psychological phenomenon of the Qur'ān goes an effort to examine the relation between the "I" within the consciousness of the Divine address and the personal "I" within the concrete incidents that sometimes incorporate the revelation (though it may be noted how many and heavy personal circumstances, e.g. the death of his sons, find no echo in the Qur'ān). This psychoanalytical study of Muḥammad and *waḥy*, is however, rare in Muslim writing.[21]

Another form of Quranic disquisition, of which Kāmil Ḥusayn in the opening essay of *Mutanawwiʿāt* is the best example, relies on the literary and emotional impact of the Scripture. This was perhaps its first effective quality. For it was by hearing that the Beduin tribes obeyed its call.

> "It is a most astonishing thing that these illiterate Arabs were entirely ready to sacrifice their lives and goods for nothing but their faith in the gracious Book."[22]

So we have a new criterion of the literary virtue of the Qur'ān and must be aware of its appositeness to its time vocabulary-wise and know that this underlines its essential religious intent which is to lead us to the praise of God. To subject the Qur'ān to the sort of logic appropriate to another context than its own would be like mistaking the caravan roads of Mecca for an autobahn.

Even where commentators have been ready to allow time and place to the Qur'ān in this liberating and constructive way, and to agree that historical accuracy is not everywhere indispensable to religious intent and validity, they have in general been reluctant to admit Western methods of comparison of texts and discussion of literary parallels or suchlike aspects of the historical setting. But there is little doubt that exegesis is on the move and that the Qur'ān is increasingly undergoing, if we should not also say inspiring, an exegetical emancipation, and the end is not yet.

That the story inspires reservation at some points may be indicated by reference to Ismā'īl al-Fārūqī. He writes in *'Urūbah and Religion* of an "axiological return to the Qur'ān", that is, a call to the values of Islam identifiable in what he calls "the Islamic, not the Arabic, meaning of the Qur'ān". It is "the basic and primordial source of everything evaluational".

> "There is no subject matter to which the Qur'ān is not relevant. Not that it instructs regarding every subject matter, but that by identifying the final values that ought to determine human purpose and destiny it conditions the valueness of every other value that any subject matter could have. Moreover, it provides the principle of ordering values into a hierarchy. . . . Besides this, a return to the Qur'ān has the advantage of over-arching an endless labyrinth of exegetical, theological and jurisprudential disagreements which have long troubled the mind of the ummah . . ."[23]

But perhaps here we are travelling down Kāmil Ḥusayn's autobahn, assured, however, that "when such axiological systematization of the Qur'ān is completed, the Holy Book of Islam may be looked upon in a new light".[24] The end, again, is not yet.

These brief excursions into Muslim reception of the Qur'ān in recent decades are intended as a feeling of the pulse of thought. Or to vary the metaphor we have taken ourselves into the counsel chamber for the most sensitive item of agenda. There remains time for only two other items of concern, Muḥammad and *Dār al-Islām*.

What is happening this half-century to the "image" of the Prophet? There have been more lives of him in that period than in any of the earlier Hijri centuries. The answer, in part, is latent in the foregoing discussion of things Quranic. For in the end the marvel of the Book cannot be isolated from the mystery of the man. Simple laudatory lives abound.[25] This is natural, for Muḥammad is inevitably the mirror in which the community sees and sets its own ideals. But for that very reason the emphasis is changing. What the earlier historians understood as the criteria of his uniqueness are largely metamorphosed in today's esteem. Directions have been noted earlier in the most thorough of the Egyptian biographies. The meticulousness of the tradition gives way to the large and broad evaluations, deriving from the Prophet's status and authority the elemental human rights and dignities. With the gradual recession of the insistent literalism of the understanding of *waḥy*, interest grows in the enigmas of his prophethood, the psychic reaches of his vocation and the massive achievements of his personality. In this field of the *sīra*, Western orientalism has for long inhibited the free pursuit of Islamic enterprise. For all too often, wittingly or otherwise, it has involved Muslims in vindicating controversy and aroused susceptibilities that impeded inward initiative while burdening the debate with peripheral, if explosive, topics. As the emotional overtones of this situation improve, with the new self-assurance of independence and the wiser patterns of religious relationship, Islamic biography will feel less compulsion to be assertive and raucous and find more occasion for historical penetration and spiritual mediation.

A variety of opinions exist on the finality of Muḥammad. The great-by-the-standards-of-the-time hypothesis is naturally unpopular, and deservedly. For it is a dubious, left-handed acknowledgement and misses the massive achievement that the time demanded and received. And though the argument claims notice where perfection and timeless ideality are in view, it otherwise must concede that extra-contemporary criteria can exercise no writ. In proportion as historical criteria of the Qur'ān grow and prevail they will take care of the issue of Muḥammad. For the rest there is the line of thought that starts from the principle, "After Muḥammad no prophet", but goes on to ask, with Ismā'īl al-Fārūqī:

> "But is prophecy the only way at God's disposal to communicate with man? Is direct, immediate verbatim revelation the only way a new value may be discovered and recognised . . .? Is God's omnipotence bounded by the limitation that 'there shall be no prophets after Muḥammad' puts upon the means at His disposal?"[26]

Simpler souls may well feel some disquiet in this sleight of mind, and it leaves many profound issues still outstanding. That God should communicate extra-prophetically and yet make it *kufr* to expect any more prophetic revelation may seem like begging questions by exchanging words.

But whatever the pundits do with finality, Muḥammad abides in the Arab vision of history and the Islamic awareness of God. With a less defensive mood and some relaxing of the present dominance of the political, we may anticipate new Islamic penetrations into the large territory of Muḥammad's personality in the action of the Quranic whole.

There remains the topic of *Dār al-Islām*—that

frontier of Muslim humanity over against the world still unsubdued without. An old tradition quietly identifies it with the turban sign, with which this chapter began. "The turban", said the Prophet, "is a frontier between the faith and unbelief."[27] How impossible to draw the line there now! Multitudes of Muslims do not wear it: it has become in truth a symbol of the ecclesiastic or the devotee, as remote from daily life as a tonsure in the West. How much like a Rubicon Aḥmad Amīn found it to lay it aside and take up the tarboush.[28] The puzzle of secularity has pushed far into the Muslim scene and soul. All through the previous chapters we have encountered it in one guise or another. There was once a recognisable boundary, even if only geographical, by which the Islamic could be known for certain and the hostile identified unerringly.

True, there arose very early a controversy about faith and works and whether conformity alone sufficed to designate the true Muslim and how that conformity could be indisputably known. It is also true that here and there the Qur'ān suggests a distinction between believing and belonging.[29] But, these apart, the Quranic instinct is to see the discrimination plain between the faithful and the faithless, the *mu'minūn* and the *kāfirūn*, the loyal and the hypocrites. It is just this quality of simplicity about the Qur'ān's knowledge of the good and of the evil, the sheep and the goats, which is so great an item in its assurance and its guidance.

Yet how is it ascertainable now? and how enforceable? Have we not here the deepest problem of the Islamic soul, in and beyond all the questions of *sharī'a* and *fiqh*, *dīn* and *īmān*, with which its modern analysts have to deal? Or who shall now say with the old clarity and ruthlessness where and when there is apostasy—that *irtidād* for which the faithless soul was cut off from the community? "'Tis all confusion, all coherence gone", one might almost say with Donne, echoing different bewilderments.

For Islam is nothing if not the place and pledge of the Divine kingdom, the collectivity in which an undivided worship is brought to the only Lord and sheltered by the single solidarity of a politico-religious unity, the people of the guidance; and, outside that proper orbit of the true conformity, the wayward world still waiting for the right mastery of doctrine and obedience, of Prophet and Caliph. Yet in our modern perplexities these simplicities, remaining as a spur and a summons, are yet perpetually fragmented and frustrated by the real world. The Islamic state, instrument though it be, must confess, "It is not in me". For just as crime and sin cannot rightly be identified, neither can the state and the good. Islamicity in statehood is still, moreover, in critical debate. Nor can society, or sects, or counsels, say assuredly, "It is in us". For their consensus persuades only some and antagonises many. We need to compare adjectives—Islamic, Islamist, Muslim—to cover the divergent things which their users want to qualify—all in the name of Islam. The Herodian and the Zealot persist and the pressures of the secular ethos multiply.

In measure, truly, the question is perpetual and, diversely, it besets all faiths and gives them, harshly perhaps, their most evident common factor in this day. But for each it is an inward crisis. What is the meaning of *Dār al-Islām* and what its means? How do we *intend* the *shahāda* that "God is, indeed, most great"? Perhaps amid the tumults and the tensions, the states and the rights, the pleas and the advocates, it would have to be confessed with old Lear, beyond all his passionate comings and goings,

"O! I have ta'en
Too little care of this!"

CHAPTER 12

# REFLECTIONS IN PROSPECT

"THE Herodian and the Zealot persist."[1] There was much to be said for the parallel when Arnold Toynbee drew it a quarter of a century ago, defining his Hellenist precedents in these terms:

> "Zealotism . . . a form of archaism evoked by foreign pressure: Herodianism a form of cosmopolitanism evoked by the same agency."[2]

And such a writer as Muḥammad al-Bahī, of the Az'har, still uses it, though he calls the two reactions "resistance" and "collaboration", seeing Ahmad Khan and perhaps more oddly the Aḥmadiyya as examples of the second and ʿAbduh of the first.[3]

Yet is there not coming to be an outmodedness about the analogy itself, the archaists, so to speak, becoming themselves archaic? For the comparison was developed in the time of what Toynbee calls "the inexorable 'western' question"—as it was for Arabs, Turks and Asians. It fitted the spectacle, familiar to a historian of the Peace Settlement of 1919, of an "Islam . . . facing the West with her back to the wall".[4] But Muslims in the nineteen-sixties are in a much stouter position than their fellows of the nineteen-twenties. There is about the panorama of lengthening independent Islamic statehoods something to make the Zealot a little late in his defiance. If Herodianism consists in being cosmopolitan, and absorbing the irresistible, then, to adapt a famous phrase, we are all Herodians now. The names, at their fullest, suggest a beleaguered minority-entity, precarious and dismayed—a picture which hardly fits Islam today with its wellnigh total political emancipation and its flowing tide of self-direction.

So there is much to be said for moving away from the suggestions of a state of siege, at least in a conclusion that intends to look ahead. In this generation, Islam is in charge of Islam, however circumscribed with queries the keeper and the kept may be. There are doubtless military disparities. But what nation does not know them? Even the vast continentalisms require their allies. Economic and social contrasts there certainly are between East and West. Glaring inequalities in living standards across the world persist and sharpen. Yet, despite or with all this, Islam, as the first chapter argued, is in command of itself. Muslims have long ceased to be merely Europe's "eastern question". Even the disenchantments and forebodings which still argue the Zealot's case, or breed his mood, can only rightly be understood as disappointments or frustrations within a self-ordering society. We have seen as much in Chapter 7. What a wholly defensive society might characterise as Herodian has in large measure become the habitual pattern, the natural assumption of men in so far as they live with the modern scene and with the alien factors which have everywhere induced it.

Alien *factors* we must say. For there is nothing inherently un-Islamic in the spirit or the mind of Western technology. And there is nothing non-Muslim about the aegis of authority or the shaping of destiny in contemporary *Dār al-Islām*. *Istiʿmār*, or imperialism, one of the busiest words in twentieth-century Arabic, has only an emotional lease of life. What Mr. Tom Mboya calls "colonialism's twilight" has set in almost everywhere in the Muslim world. When the psychological and spiritual gears have shifted from negative repulsion and reproach to positive construction and fulfilment—however strenuous the change may be—there is surely the hope for a flowering of culture and renewal, for philosophers, artists, poets, musicians, even theologians, to adorn and vindicate the independence. All the techniques and technicians are available—abiding from what is irreversible in the old imperialism. It is therefore urgent to have this great reversal in proper and constant perspective and to see world-Islam as master in its own house, unless we are to perpetuate criteria of judgement and expectation which history has left behind. This remark applies both within and outside that house. Its very survival means that the Zealot has to become Herodian and the Herodian a Zealot. It is just this which the conservative mind finds so hard and the secular so galling.

That Islam has the resources of doctrine and tradition to take its present destiny is certain. What is in doubt are the capacities of leadership and will. When Bernard Lewis remarks that it is "very rash to assert that the secularisation of Islamic sentiment has passed the point of no return",[5] the crucial matter lies in where, and how, the "point" is seen. Islam, it can be said, has two great assets for the surviving and absorbing of modern pressures. The first is its fundamental doctrine of man in dominion. Unlike the other faiths in Asia, Islam has no need to modify or revise its account of man to accommodate a scientifically ordered world. It is not world-renouncing. Activism, provided it is under God, requires no break with its dogmas, properly held. Technology can rightly be seen as the realisation of that "caliphate" given to man in the Quranic view of him.[6] The quarrels of modernity with Muslim ways may be said in large measure to concern the perversions of its full meaning which those ways entail. What Islam loses by science are the distortions, in fatalism and apathy, which its people tolerate. What abides is its assurance about the "empire" of man whom the Qur'ān says God has made the proper imperialist of nature.[7] There are, of course, reaches of sin and evil, thrown up by man's very works, into which characteristically Islamic theology never penetrates. One does not expect a Herbert Butterfield in Islamic musings on foreign policy, wars and power and all the other political mirrors of our human nature.[8] This "optimism" may be the Achilles' heel of Quranic man.

But the illusions of human omnicompetence, which are so sore a folly in our present scene, Islam is superbly qualified to explode. No sane Muslim could possibly consign God to ever-shrinking gaps in explicability which man is shortly due to close and eliminate for ever. The Qur'ān talks repeatedly of "the exclusion of God", but it is not this which it means.[9] It is rather its conviction that the end of adoration is the beginning of idolatry. Islam, as doctrinally furnished by the Qur'ān, ought to be more than adequate for the right welcome and the proper discipline of the scientific and the modern, without dividing nervously into Zealot stridency or Herodian expediency. The condition, however, is leadership.

On the same condition the other asset turns. It belongs with that dominant role of community, and perhaps one might add, of circumstance, that characterises the Islamic tradition of things. An often forgotten source of law in the early and medieval centuries lay simply in the customs that obtained. When the "proper" sources in Qur'ān, *ḥadīth* and *sunna* had spoken, there remained that vast corpus of accepted behaviour which Islam was ready, often very hospitably, to perpetuate, once its fairly limited but quite insistent demands were met. Non-repugnancy, though from some points of view, in constitutional debates, a menace to democratic will, is in other senses a criterion of indulgence. What does not contravene is permitted. Short of its arbitrary, religious and legal obligations, Islam admits what the generality do. The pattern of its progress in Africa gives modern form to this ready tolerance of all non-incompatibles and these are often less than radical and far removed from social revolution or cultural disturbance.

> "It may sound paradoxical, yet it is a fact that on the one hand Islam claims the entire allegiance of man and on the other it leaves a vast field of human activity free from all shackles. Where the mind would benefit from following its own inclinations and exploring new avenues, it has been left free."[10]

The second sentence of this judgement from the former Education Minister in Pakistan is clearly capable of endless application in the areas of modern technology and scientific mores, where "freedom from shackles" is just what scientists and exploiters want. "Following one's inclinations and exploring new avenues" is a fair working description of the modern mood. "The goal of the law", says Shaykh Khallāf, "is only the welfare of men and wheresoever lies the welfare of men there is the law of God."[11] This gives an obviously wide occasion to change and, incidentally, a broad justification for the choice of title in this present study. So conservative a thinker as Farīd Wajdī takes the *shūrā* to mean the universal "democracy" of Islam where the individual is responsible for his own salvation.[12] Given this broad and hospitable place for communal welfare, collective and private judgement, and ready "tolerance" of what is or what comes, conditional only on "repugnancy", and with "repugnancy" itself creatively or accommodatingly tested, the way is plainly open, not only for the widening of the Consensus, studied in Chapter 5, but therewith for a larger metamorphosis of Islam in the light of what Muslims say, or shape, it to be. To acknowledge that the freedoms are not total is to admit that they are real, and certainly, as even conservatives bear witness, they are operative. Bernard Lewis' "point of no return" may well be never reached, though there will be a constant and strenuous battle for the religious dimensions of the continuity.

And it will turn, no less crucially than the other asset, on leadership. Here then the rest of our reflections must concentrate. The first consideration is when may there come some easing of the persistent pre-occupations with political passions? These have for so long, and at such costs in mind and spirit, prejudiced the energies of Islam. Such political "priority", allowed if not justified, is at once the symptom and the consequence of the self-ordering within it which we have argued. Surely, however, the time has come for creative thinking and active consecration that transcend the political.

Conservative religion, as evident in Chapter 7, suffers many frustrations. Almost everywhere political opportunity is wanting. In this situation what some writers call the neo-Islamic, when they mostly mean the old Islamic, can easily lapse into quietism and aloofness and stagnate in neglect of its real tasks. Or it might conceivably erupt into violence—the sort of violence engendered in frustration which the present "secular" monopoly of power holds firmly in subjection. As long as it finds no emotional satisfaction it will be liable to negative passivity or wild explosiveness. In neither case will it get beyond the old Zealotism failing to understand what it still sees as the old Herodianism. Can it blossom into responsible leadership of mind unless it has the stimulus of actual opportunity to shape things and until the persistent dichotomy of educational background is more radically overcome? For these custodians of the old Islam are still largely naïve or irresponsible in their Islamic judgements, and, as James Baldwin has it in a very different connection: "It is the innocence which constitutes the crime",[13]—the "innocence" of an inadequate perception of issues. It is, however, in large measure more sinned against than sinning, in that it has been shaped by dogmatic slumbers and enfeebled by political impotence, save among Wahhābīs and Sanūsīs. This intellectual situation in conservative Islam is the major factor in the current crisis of leadership.

Something of the same frustration, for very different reasons, besets the "modern" intellectual in the Muslim world. The unresolved dualities in the thought, for example, of Iqbal, persist in the spiritual and mental disquiets of the student and professional classes. With authoritarian régimes installed in many countries and electoral processes either acquiescent or non-existent, the *shūrā* of contemporary Islam has little formal chance of democratic definition. The reasons, of course, are much more than intellectual and go back into stubborn facts of economic and political life. But the intellectual consequences are hardly short of disastrous. Much potential leadership atrophies. It either declines into dilettantism, quits in emigration or waits gallantly for a better day, knowing, however, that so many of the factors that day itself waits for are beyond its reach. Or it gives up an unequal struggle and opts for irreligious secularity or conservative nostalgia. In either case the loss to Islamic creativity is enormous. There is much point in Muḥibb-ad-Dīn al-Khaṭīb's remark that if ʿUmar were alive today he would devote himself to enlarging the middle classes.[14] For by this tactic, he might slowly make feasible an ordered, democratic, political framework in which consensus could genuinely operate and the intelligentsia find the opportunity to be hopeful and active mentors of society and for Islam. Nothing would the more likely equip them for such responsibility than the real chance of it.

The background of this situation has been incisively discussed by Hishām Sharābī in "The Young Arab Generation". His sentiments have been echoed by Christian Arab thinkers also. He questions whether Islam as a metaphysic any longer "exercises a genuine hold on the mind of youth" as distinct from supplying a point of national cohesion. After noting how the promise of Muḥammad ʿAbduh and of Ṭāhā Ḥusayn has been unfulfilled in its real measure, he deplores the unreality which attaches to Arab intellectual life by reason of the political absolutisms, and the consequent self-pity, or compensating pedantry, or mere propagandism, which muddy the waters and disserve the spirit. The only form in which intellectual service to the revolution is possible is to approve the silence it enforces. At the mid-century which "has brought to an end the humiliation . . . of foreign rule", he finds "the new hierarchy of wealth, rank and power, where conversation is dead and silence reigns, despite the clamour of voices".[15]

Whether or not the whole judgement of this eloquent evaluation is admitted, the urgency of virile, and viable, intellectual leadership, compassionate with the masses, honest with the issues, and operative in the states, is plain. Without it there are no "counsels" properly to be had or seriously to be followed. The present duties of such leadership would seem to be threefold.

The first is the adequate deployment of the doctrinal and spiritual resources of Islam, even if to some degree Islam itself is reshaped in the process. This has already widely happened in the realm of the *sharīʿa*, including its most central and stubborn areas, namely, those that have to do with personal status. These transformations, justified as they must be by the alleged "intention" of the old forms (for this is the only way to maintain the continuity), themselves imply and involve a like, if less complete, renewing of the specifically religious presuppositions belonging with the law. The old unity of dogma and law cannot be turned into a convenient divorce when the one is changed. If it is argued that a modern, western-born, rational code, replacing the law of revealed status, is a consistent perpetuation of its meaning, the concept of revelation in *all* its reaches is radically revised. Any other conclusion is inconsistent with the characteristic unity of the Islamic scheme.

But the doctrinal, Quranic, Prophetic, exegetical, philosophical corollaries still lag behind the lawyers and the reformers. Literary emancipations have been accomplished to give new flexibility to language. Potentially, in the doctrines of God and man in Islam, of Lordship and loyalty, of dominion and adoration, lie many of the resources its theologians need to recover a metaphysical authority for faith. But the frailty is in the will and the mind. It is not so much a crisis of Islam as of Muslims. The apologists, of course, have often said as much, but they have proceeded to exonerate themselves.

The second duty concerns the problem of power, the relation of the state to nation, and of nation to Islam. Power makes out of date those metaphors taken from provincial underlings of Roman empire. Islam is now again its own *imperium*, but fragmented into national states. What relation do these have to the community of Muslims? Both Muḥammad ʿAbduh and Muhammad Iqbal were wary of them.[16] Is there hope that the old *umma*, or people of the Quranic Book in solidarity, could again take shape? Or is power only feasible in territorial diversity? Which has precedence, the unity in race or the unity in Muḥammad? What bearing does the Arabness of the unifier have on the cohesion of the present whole? These are the general questions of power and its locus. They have important repercussions for the minorities within Islam. But it is their meaning for Islam itself which is of first significance.

Within these territorial themes of statehood, what of the exercise of power domestically, its forms of accessibility, its connection with the popular will, the nature and accountability of its mandate? Is there really to be a general *shūrā* other than the accidents of advantage or conspiracies of force? Within these again, what of the responsibility of power towards evil and injustice, the wretchedness of human multitudes and the factors that degrade and weary them? For power must needs be "gentle" if it is truly to be under God.

Beyond the circle of the Muslims' solidarity and their domestic world lies the wider *oikumene* of man, the diversity of creeds and culture. How is Islamic power to see itself in the present implications of its will to universalise? Will its human mission be ready to die to any of its treasured particulars for the service of its fuller values?

And what of Africa, the great opening occasion of Islamic decisions? Another volume in this series deals with this field. Nowhere in the world is the white man's recession of authority more exciting or more fraught with drama than in Africa, the continent that came so late to modern destiny and was more totally than any other the test and patient of colonialism, and so on many grounds the point of utmost reckoning. As Africans move into their tumultuous, continental surge of destiny and life according to Africa, and do so in the wake of a retreating white and Western dominance,

Islam, numerically, emotionally, culturally, is well poised for vital consequences in the shape of their wills and the temper of their future. Whether that role is constructive and compassionate, imaginative and disciplined, or the contrary, seems likely to be the largest theme of Islamic decision in the rest of this century. Everything about Africa is big, and for better or worse all that have to do with her are taken up into that bigness.

This, like all else, turns finally on compassion. To persons and their poverty, people and their hopes, the responsibility of power relates. The ultimate test of all dogma and religion lies in its writ of compassion running through the forms and patterns of the social order and the dispositions of political authority. Many of the writers cited earlier in this study have voiced the social conscience of their faith. Much of the force and sanction of ʿAbduh's leadership derived from the dignity of his outlook on his fellows and the humanity evident in his *fatwā* decisions. Successors like Al-Manfalūṭī were lively in their sympathy with the oppressed, for whom Ṭāhā Ḥusayn, to cite only one work of imaginative writing, pleaded in *Al-Muʿadhdhabūn fī-l-Arḍ*.[17] There is compassion, too, and realism, in Driss Chraibi, for the stresses not merely of the poor but of the disquieted and the dismayed. Tawfīq al-Ḥakīm's study of the bewilderments of the old minds amid the new ways is a fine example.[18] And there are many. The literature of social concern in contemporary Islam makes the more urgent the need for integrity of mind in the search for the answers within the economic and social institutions of Islam. Too much writing on *Zakāt* and the Qur'ān's veto on hoarding eludes the hard realities of the money world and the complexities of life. Its comfortable panaceas amount too often to an evasion of thought or action. Too much "Islamic socialism" is not yet living in the twentieth century, and accepts a static even complacent account of economic wrongs.

But the ultimate in these realms takes us to the stuff of sacrifice and the real measure of human burden-bearing, in a word, to the shape of the cross. It is here that Islam's resources both of life and doctrine face their largest question. If its central doctrine stands in the compassionateness of God, as the *Bismillāh* affirms, then it cannot fail to be caught up into the nature of a compassion that is worthily Divine. If we are concerned with the sovereignty of the good, we cannot finally miss the fact that it is constantly being confronted with decisions like the cross as the condition of its self-consistency.

The final crisis of the counsels by which Islam is defined and discharged in this time has then to do with the capacity to judge itself, radically, by its own criteria. For these are God and judgement, the twin themes of the living Muḥammad. And when he preached them it was the illusions which departed. The first "counsel" to the idolaters was to let God be God: it remains the perpetual test and crux of all His worshippers' debate.

# NOTES

## CHAPTER I

## CHARTING THE DEBATE

1. *Letters from a Traveller*, London, 1962, p. 124.
2. *Ibid.* p. 66.
3. See M. M. Thomas, in *Christianity and Crisis*, New York, Vol. 22, No. 22, December 24, 1962, p. 236.
4. Literally "the house of Islam", signifying territory ruled in accordance with Islamic principles (and usually under a Muslim ruler). The opposite is *Dār al-Ḥarb* (p. 17), "the house of war", where Islam is not yet supreme.
5. The passage occurs in Shakespeare's *King John*, Act 2, Sc. 1, lines 562-88. Readers may also recollect Ezra Pound's *Usura* in the same sense.
6. The question is part of John Steinbeck's portrayal of the wistful misery of uprooted people deciding which of the family and household things to jettison in their trek to the west from their confiscated homesteads in *The Grapes of Wrath*. His picture of the Middle West evokes many parallels for the contemporary Middle East, not least the profanations of earth by the new ruthlessness of science and mechanisation, and with the profanations of earth, the hardening of men. "All of them were caught in something larger than themselves. Some of them hated the mathematics that drove them, and some were afraid and some worshipped the mathematics because it provided a refuge from thought and from feeling." How close all these themes are to the inner meaning of Islamic *Shirk*, or life that has lost the fundamental venerations.
7. Ismā'īl Rāgī al-Fārūqī, *On Arabism, 'Urubah and Religion*, A Study of the Fundamental Ideas of Arabism and of Islam

at its Highest Moment of Consciousness, Amsterdam, 1962, p. 172.

8. *Ibid.* p. 204.
9. *Ibid.* p. 125.
10. There has been a long running battle in Pakistan between strong and vocal, legal and social, conservatism and the social reforms of successive governments. The Report, in 1956, of a Government Commission on Marriage and Family Laws, was bitterly opposed by Ihtishām al-Ḥaqq, a member of the Commission. He and others resisted its proposals for a minimum age for marriage and compulsory marriage registration, on the ground that they constituted an unwarranted extension of proper "initiative" or *ijtihād* (see Chapter 5, below). More recently, there has been a move from the same quarters to repeal the Family Laws Ordinance, the promulgation of which arose out of the Report and has been one of the most cherished achievements of the Ayyūb Khān régime. The ordinance, which dates from 1961, makes it difficult for a Pakistani to take more than one wife, makes sixteen the minimum marriage age for girls and liberalises divorce procedures. It is odd to realise that this measure could only elude antagonism under cover of the martial law. Since the end of martial law a standing committee of the Assembly has been involved in discussion for and against repeal.

    This issue, the reactionary attitudes for the sake of which it is joined, and the animus with which it is pursued, will be some indication of the diversities of temper and outlook which this survey has to comprehend.
11. This distinction with its intriguing parallels, was developed by Arnold Toynbee in *Civilization on Trial*, Oxford, 1948, chap. 10, "Islam, the West and the Future", pp. 185-212.

## CHAPTER 2

## COUNSEL FOR PAKISTAN

1. Percival Spear, *India, Pakistan and the West*, Oxford, 1952, 2nd edit., p. 91.

2. Syed Ahmad Khan, *Essays on the Life of Mohammed*, Vol. 1, London, 1870, p. xi.
3. Syed Ahmed (Ahmed Khan), *The Mohamedan Commentary on the Holy Bible*, Ghazipur, 1862, p. 66. *Nechari* is an adjective from the English word "nature".
4. See ch. 1, note 4.
5. B. R. Ambedkar, *Pakistan, or the Partition of India*, 3rd edit., Bombay, 1946 (originally published in 1940 as *Thoughts on Pakistan*), pp. 308-9.
6. Muḥammad ʿAlī, *Select Letters and Speeches*, ed. Afzal Iqbal, Lahore, 1944, p. 462.
7. *Ibid.* p. 57. He appealed to Hālī, the great Muslim poet, for corroboration.
8. Muhammad Iqbal, *The Tulip and the Rose*, trans. by A. J. Arberry, London, 1947, Stanza 118.
9. Muhammad Iqbal, *Javid Namah*, Lahore, 1932, p. 40.
10. Quoted in Khān A. Aḥmad, *The Founder of Pakistan*, London, 1942, p. 16.
11. Mahatma Gandhi, *To the Protagonists of Pakistan*, Karachi, 1947, p. 21. In a speech at Aligarh, Jinnah himself observed: "Pakistan was not the product of the conduct or misconduct of Hindus. It had always been there: only they (the Muslims) were not conscious of it. . . . Pakistan started the moment the first non-Muslim was converted to Islam in India, long before the Muslims established their rule." M. A. Jinnah, *Recent Speeches and Writings*, Lahore, 1947, edited by Jamāl ad-Dīn Aḥmad, Vol. 2, pp. 62-3.
12. Phillips Talbot in *The Middle East Journal*, Washington, Vol. 2, No. 4, October 1948, p. 397.
13. In a statement issued from Delhi, March 23, 1943.
14. F. K. Khān Durrānī, *The Meaning of Pakistan*, Lahore, 1944, p. viii.
15. *Ibid.* pp. 116-18.
16. Ziauddin Suleri, *Whither Pakistan?* London, 1949, p. 71.
17. Jinnah claimed in December 1943 in a speech to the All-India Muslim League at Karachi: "The Muslim League and Muslim India have now become shock-proof, slogan-proof, stunt-proof. In fact it is proof against every machination." And every reservation, being also thought-proof? See

*Recent Speeches and Writings*, *op. cit.* Vol. 2, p. 25.

18. Keith Callard, *Pakistan, a Political Study*, London, 1957, p. 200.

## CHAPTER 3

## MUḤAMMAD ʿABDUH AND TWO SUCCESSORS

1. *The Autobiography of Kwame Nkrumah*, Edinburgh, 1957, p. 164. He first made it in a speech at Lincoln University, U.S.A., on receiving an honorary degree. He adds: "This met with enthusiastic cheering from the audience".
2. "Peculiar" here in the sense that the "solution" of partition in Palestine had to do with the special issues created for the Arab world by Zionism. In another sense, it is in no way peculiar, inasmuch as the Zionists' demand for statehood is the same, in their view, as the Pakistani in its context. It is the common assurance of salvation by statehood, of security territorially achieved by a religion.
3. See *Al-Manār*, Cairo, Vol. 8, p. 893, for a clear statement of this fundamental choice.
4. The story is well told in George Antonius, *The Arab Awakening*, London, 1938.
5. *Ar-Radd ʿalā'd-Dahriyyīn*, Cairo, 1925, trans. from the Persian by Muḥammad ʿAbduh, p. 70.
6. C. C. Adams, *Islam and Modernism in Egypt*, Oxford, 1933, p. 16. Jamāl-ad-Dīn appears not to have been disturbed by the fact that his words were a quotation from Guizot's *Civilization in Europe*, the entity he had earlier identified with irreligion. *Taqlīd* is more precisely the obligation to follow earlier authorities.
7. Translated into French, with introduction, by B. Michel and M. ʿAbd-ar-Rāziq, Paris, 1925. First Arabic edition, Cairo, 1897, 5th edit., 1926–7, 18th edit., 1961.
8. Two vols., Cairo, 1929. Eng. trs., *An Egyptian Childhood* (1932); Ṭāhā Ḥusayn (see below) went to Al-Az'har three years after ʿAbduh's resignation and never met him.
9. *Al-Islām wa-n-Naṣrāniyya, maʿ al-ʿIlm wa-l-Madaniyya*,

being articles in *Al-Manār*, 1901, published separately, Cairo, 1902. 3rd edit., 1923, p. 132.

10. *Risālat*, p. 55.
11. *Ibid.* p. 10.
12. Margoliouth in his review of C. C. Adams' *Islam and Modernism* in the *International Review of Missions*, Vol. 22, No. 3, July 1933, pp. 421-2. Cromer in *Modern Egypt*, Vol. 2, 1908, p. 180.
13. H. A. R. Gibb in the *Bulletin of the School of Oriental Studies*, Vol. 11, p. 758.
14. *Majallat al-Az'har*, Cairo, 1935, Vol. 6, No. 7, p. 510. This was the second issue after the change of name from *Nūr al-Islām*. In a previous number under that title, Vol. 3, No. 5, in 1932 it had castigated him, pp. 330-40, as a potential atheist, a dabbler in Darwin, and, satirically, "a new *mujtahid*". This may be a measure either of the journal's mutability, or of Riḍā's growing conservatism.
15. Henri Laoust, *Le Califat dans la Doctrine de Rashīd Riḍā*, Beirut, 1938, p. 208.
16. Adams, *op. cit.* pp. 185-6.
17. Wahhābism derives from Muḥammad ibn-ʿAbd-al-Wahhāb, who, in the middle eighteenth century in the Ḥijāz, founded a rigorous "puritan" revival movement. Its influence, as noted in Chapter 2, was considerable in India, as well as in the Arab world. Had our dimensions here been wider it would have called for analysis. It was based on Ibn-Ḥanbal and the theologian, Ibn-Taymiyya, imposing a strong asceticism and militating fiercely against all Ṣūfī pietistic accretions. *Jihād* was understood in literal terms and in pursuit of it the Wahhābīs conquered Mecca with such other success as to provoke the Ottoman Empire into action. Muḥammad ʿAlī defeated their forces and by 1820 their political ascendancy ended, until revived by Ibn-Saʿūd in this century. Its principles, in his powerful hands, provided a vital element in the Saʿūdī state. It has remained a significant factor in shaping Muslim reactions in the direction of "Zealotism". Some aspects of action and reaction over Wahhābī attitudes will concern the later discussion, e.g. in the thought of Muḥammad Ḥusayn Haykal.

18. Cairo, 1933, 5th edit., 1948.
19. *Ibid.* pp. 32 and 39.
20. *Ibid.* p. 40. Albert Hourani in *Arabic Thought in the Liberal Age*, Oxford, 1962, p. 142, notes a similar evasion in ʿAbduh, who quietly dropped from later editions of *Risālat at-Tawḥīd* his statement in the first edition upholding createdness of the Qur'ān.
21. *Ibid.* p. 308.
22. *Ibid.* p. 40.
23. See note 7.
24. *Tamhīd*, p. 121.

## CHAPTER 4

## MUḤAMMAD IQBĀL AND HIS PRECURSORS

1. *Payām-i-Mashriq*, Stanzas 53 and 22. See bibliography for details of Iqbāl's works, their translators and interpreters.
2. Quoted by Jawaharlal Nehru, *An Autobiography*, London, 1936, p. 461.
3. K. M. Panikkar, *Survey of Indian History*, London, 1947, p. 283. Among Aligarh's famous graduates may be listed the poet Altaf Ḥusain Hālī (1837–1914), the novelist and teacher Naẓīr Aḥmad (1836–1912) and the historian Muḥammad Shiblī Nuʿmānī (1857–1914). See ʿAbdul Qādir, *Famous Urdu Poets and Writers*, Lahore, 1949.
4. He excluded himself from the committee dealing with religious instruction and even banned his own theological works from the curriculum lest they should alienate the orthodox. Like many textbooks since, the manuals of Islamic study were occupied with ritual directives on, e.g., cleanliness, and with exhortation.
5. Muḥammad ʿAlī, *My Life, a Fragment*, edited by Afzal Iqbal, Lahore, 1942, p. 30.
6. See Wilfred Cantwell Smith, *Modern Islam in India*, Lahore, 1943. London edit., 1946, pp. 152-3.
7. First published in 1890 as *The Life and Teachings of Muhammad*, based on a still earlier work *A Critical Examination of*

*the Life and Teachings of Muhammad*, 1872. One problem with the republication, through over fifty years, of this work is that time and issues have overtaken it. It antedates both in facts and temper so many developments since the turn of the century. Even in its final 1922 form it precedes the end of the Caliphate.

8. *Op. cit.* 1922 edit., pp. 183-6.
9. *Ibid.* p. 165.
10. *Ibid.* p. 34.
11. *Ibid.* p. 167.
12. *Ibid.* p. 171.
13. *Ibid.* p. 172.
14. *Ibid.* pp. 200-1.
15. *Ibid.* pp. 112-13.
16. *Ibid.* p. 122.
17. From "A Muslim View of Christendom", in *The Outline of Christianity*, edited by A. S. Peake and R. G. Parsons, London, 1925–6, Vol. 5, p. 254.
18. See his *Essays, Indian and Islamic*, London, 1912, pp. 24 and 13.
19. *Ibid.* p. 284. See also *Outline*, p. 253.
20. See his *Studies, Indian and Islamic*, London, 1927, p. 57.
21. See his review of Lothrop Stoddard's *New World of Islam*, New York, 1921, in *Studies*, p. 32, and compare pp. 270-1.
22. In two volumes, Lahore, 1937.
23. *Ibid.* p. xii.
24. *Ibid.* Vol. 1, p. 123.
25. See, for example, *Islamic Culture*, Hyderabad, Vol. 9, No. 3, July 1935, pp. 519 f.
26. *Fundamentals of Islam*, Geneva, 1929, p. 9. In this booklet Islam is expounded without a single reference to Muḥammad.
27. *Lectures*, Lahore edit., 1944, p. 167.
28. *Bal-i-Jabrīl*, p. 81, quoted in Saiyidain, p. 161.
29. *Asrār-i-Khūdī*, lines 86-90.
30. *Lectures*, p. 72.
31. *Ibid.* p. 91.
32. *Ibid.* pp. 162-3, also pp. 155 and 164, where he writes of "the inner catholicity of Islam" of practically boundless breadth. It is hard to dispute Mr. Nehru's opinion: "His [Iqbal's]

whole outlook on life does not fit in with the subsequent developments of the idea of Pakistan". *Discovery of India*, London, 1946, p. 298.

33. As, for example, Annemarie Schimmel has done in *Gabriel's Wing*, Leiden, 1963.
34. *Lectures*, p. 51. For other examples see pp. 131-5.
35. *Ibid.* p. 111.

## CHAPTER 5

# CONSENSUS AND COMMUNITY

1. *Modern Egypt*, New York, 1908, Vol. 2, p. 229. It was in line with his other remark in the same context about Muḥammad ʿAbduh, whom, he alleged, "was in reality an agnostic", *op. cit.* p. 180. The remark was, of course, grossly untrue and unjust. But that Cromer could have thought so indicates a fixed notion of what he supposed Islam had to be.
2. Cf. Ameer Ali, *op. cit.* p. 122, and also Muhammad Ali, who wrote in *Select Letters and Speeches*, edited Afzal Iqbāl, Lahore, 1944: "It is one of the fundamental doctrines of Islam, absolutely unalterable, that there should always be a Khalifa", p. 189. He was speaking in London, on April 22, 1920. Cf. also *My Life*, pp. 183 and 194.
3. The Turks had already declared for a spiritual Imamate, but had not yet abolished the entire structure.
4. See Henri Laoust, *Le Califat dans la Doctrine de Rashīd Riḍā*, Beirut, 1938, pp. 111-15, 116-22, 132, 220. Riḍā's work had the title, *Al-Khilāfa wa-l-Imāma al-ʿUẓmā*, Cairo, 1923.
5. Attempts to re-establish the Caliphate were discussed in conferences in Cairo and Mecca in 1926. See A. Sekaly in *Revue du Monde Musulman*, Vol. 74, pp. 1-213. Further conferences were held in Jerusalem in 1931 and Geneva in 1935. All four affirmed the necessity of the Caliph to Islam but found no way of action.
6. *Uṣūl*, Cairo, 1925, p. 36.
7. *Ibid.* pp. 59, 64-5.
8. *Ibid.* pp. 79-80.
9. *Ibid.* pp. 86-7, and 81.
10. *Ibid.* p. 103.

11. *Ibid.* p. 79.
12. ʿAlī ʿAbd-ar-Rāziq was declared guilty of heresy by a Court of *ulema* of Al-Az'har, forfeited his status and was suspended from all teaching functions. A Court of Appeal upheld the *ulema*, despite his invocation of freedom of belief and opinion under the Constitution of 1922. He went to live in Paris. A spate of pamphlets and books censured his errors, notably Muḥammad Bakhīṭ, *Ḥaqīqat Islām wa-Uṣūl al-Ḥukm*, Cairo, 1926.
13. This *qiyās* was in fact used in the Report of the Commission on Marriage and Family Laws in Pakistan, 1956. *The Gazette of Pakistan*, No. S.1033, Karachi, June 20, 1956, p. 1209.
14. Legists also sometimes cite 2.143: "We have made you a people in the middle that you may be witnesses to mankind". Its force is somewhat weakened by the sequel: "and that the Apostle may witness against you". For *ijtihād* there is no specific Quranic text, though Iqbal, for example, argues for it from 29.69: "Those who exert themselves in our paths we will surely guide". Sura 2.145 ("... a *qibla* that pleases you") is too inventive a suggestion.
15. *Report of the Court of Inquiry into the Punjab Disturbances of 1953*, Lahore, 1954, p. 211.
16. In Kenneth W. Morgan, editor, *Islam, the Straight Path*, New York, 1958, p. 408. But his view of consensus is quite circumscribed none the less and he declares that a really true *ijmāʿ* has been impossible since the death of ʿUmar, which occurred in A.D. 644.
17. Vols. 22 and 23 (1951). See "Muslims and Taṣwīr", being a translation by H. W. Glidden in *The Muslim World*, Vol. 45, No. 3, July 1955, pp. 250-68.
18. Some effort to illustrate this may be found in the writer's *Sandals at the Mosque*, London, 1959, pp. 49-60.
19. *Report of the Court*, p. 211.
20. *The Gazette of Pakistan*, pp. 1562 f. The pageing is erratic here. The pageing of the *Gazette* is faulty and runs 1565, 1566, 1567, 1568, 1561, 1562, 1563, 1564, 1569, 1570 and on. I have given the page number as in this erratic sequence.
21. "Companion studies" has a happy ambiguity. A big factor in the science of Tradition was the biographical record of the

Companions of the Prophet from whom *Ḥadīth* derived. *Nāsikh* and *mansūkh*, what abrogates and is abrogated, relate to the supersession of one Quranic passage by another. Classically understood they were complex and tedious. On their relation to *ijmā'* see, for example, *Nūr al-Islām*, Cairo, 1930, Vol. 1, No. 1, p. 37, and 1933, Vol. 3, No. 4, pp. 280-6.

22. H. A. R. Gibb, *Modern Trends in Islam*, Chicago, 1945, pp. 10-11.
23. A. A. A. Fyzee, *A Modern Approach to Islam*, Bombay, 1963. He points out that *ulema* very rarely know Western languages and that they have little equipment in Semitic Biblical disciplines, or comparative religion and psychology. Pp. 67-8.
24. *A Vision of History*, Beirut, 1961, p. 160.
25. Iqbal, *Reconstruction*, p. 148.
26. See below in Chapter 6. He wrote a booklet with the title: "Muḥammad and Jesus on the Road Together".
27. Kamel Hussein in *City of Wrong*, Amsterdam, 1959 (translated from the Arabic, Cairo, 1954), draws a perceptive study of the potentiality of communities towards protective self-interest of the worst kind in the name of the collective.

## CHAPTER 6

## MEN AND MINDS

1. Cairo, 1954, pp. 79-80.
2. Cairo, 1929. Vol. I is translated by E. H. Paxton, *An Egyptian Childhood*, London, 1932; and Vol. 2 by H. Wayment, *The Stream of Days*, London, 1948.
3. *Ibid.* Vol. 2, p. 96.
4. Cairo, 1926 and 1927 respectively.
5. *Fī-l-Adab al-Jāhilī*, 4th edit., 1947, pp. 63-4.
6. In *L'Islam et L'Occident*, Paris, Cahiers du Sud, 1947, p. 238. Ṭāhā Ḥusayn's essay has the title: "Tendances religieuses de la Littérature égyptienne d'aujourd'hui" (pp. 235-41).
7. Cairo, 1938.
8. Cairo, 3 vols., 1933. Similar works of his in the same genre are *Al-Wa'd al-Ḥaqq*, Cairo, 1949, and *Ash-Shaykhān*,

Cairo, 1960, a study in the lives of Abū-Bakr and ʿUmar. One might also cite in similar vein Bint-ash-Shāṭi'’s studies in Islamic heroines, e.g. *Banāt an-Nabī*, Cairo, 1959.

9. See *Al-Ḥubb aḍ-Ḍā'iʿ*, Cairo, 1942, and a passage from *As-Siyāsa* cited by C. C. Adams in *Islam and Modernism in Egypt*, London, 1933, p. 258.

10. For an imaginative presentation of Ṭāhā Ḥusayn's championing of liberty against prejudice, as a kind of modern Socrates, and for a vigorous defence of his loyalty to Islam, see Muḥammad ʿAbd-al-Qādir al-Ammāwī, *Muḥākamat az-Zaman*, Cairo, 1942, pp. 149 f. Cf. Pierre Cachia, *Ṭāhā Ḥusayn: his place in the Egyptian Literary Renaissance*, London, 1956.

11. Cairo, 1935 and 1937 respectively. Ṭāhā Ḥusayn, writing in *L'Islam et L'Occident*, p. 239, attests the immense influence throughout the Arab world of Haykal's *Ḥayāt Muḥammad.* See also J. S. Trimingham, *Islam in the Sudan*, London, 1949, p. 259.

12. A vigorous social reformer and disciple of ʿAbduh (1865–1908) whose pioneer works, *Taḥrīr al-Mar'a*, Cairo, 1899, and *Al-Mar'a al-Jadīda*, Cairo, 1901, traced the decay of Muslim principles to ignorance stemming from the neglecting and impeding of women's true role in society and the family.

13. The apportionment of space as a whole is interesting. The Life proper begins at p. 104. The Hijra is reached at p. 206 and Muḥammad's death at p. 486. Three-fifths of the whole are thus devoted to the Medinan years.

14. *Ḥayāt Muḥammad*, Cairo, 1935, p. 154.

15. *Ibid.* pp. 183 f. See also p. 190.

16. *Ibid.* p. 562.

17. *Ibid.* p. 528.

18. His final decision came after a year's vacillation through a talk in English on Budapest radio by a Hungarian Muslim.

19. *Fī-Manzil al-Waḥy*, Cairo, 1937, p. 634.

20. Cairo, 1925. See the first article.

21. *ʿAbqariyyat Muḥammad*, Cairo, 1943, 3rd edit., pp. 260-1.

22. Cairo, 1910, 11th edit., 1952.

23. *An-Naẓarāt*, Vol. 1, Introduction, pp. 18-19.

24. *Ibid.* Vol. 1, pp. 61-9.
25. "The Missing Link", in *Fayḍ al-Khāṭir*, Vol. 1, Cairo, 1938, pp. 24-7.
26. *Ḥayātī*, Cairo, 1950, pp. 143 f. and 212 f.
27. *Fayḍ-al-Khāṭir*, Vol. 1, pp. 89-92, "Mā fa'alat al-ayyām".
28. Cairo, 1950.
29. *Ibid.* pp. 156-7.
30. Sayyid Quṭb's book was published in Cairo in 1945. An English version is J. B. Hardie's translation *Social Justice in Islam*, Washington, 1953. *Min Hunā Na'lam*, Cairo, 1950. Mention may also be made of 'Abd-al-Muta'āl aṣ-Ṣa'īdī's *Min Ayna Nabda'*, Cairo, insisting that we must start where Islam starts, which for the writer is its primitive criteria, avoiding both the "scatterbrain" Khālid and the obtuse Al-Ghazālī. Meanwhile, Jamāl-ad-Dīn al-Afghānī and Muḥammad 'Abduh have found no satisfactory successors in their reform tradition, p. 76.
31. *Min Hunā Na'lam*, p. 15.
32. Cairo, 1946.
33. Baghdad, 1954. His strictures and counsels rather bring to mind the poem of William Plomer:

    "The hypodermic steeple,
    Ever ready to inject
    The opium of the people."

    A minaret, after all, especially the Turkish variety, resembles a needle even more aptly than a steeple.
34. Cairo, 1958.
35. *Le Passé simple*, Paris, 1954, p. 13. See also a passage from the same author's *Les Boucs*, Paris, 1955, quoted by G. E. von Grünebaum, *Modern Islam, the Search for Cultural Identity*, Berkeley, California, 1962, p. 177.
36. *Le Passé simple*, pp. 197-201, and James Baldwin, *The Fire Next Time*, London, 1963. The former says: "My grandfather has posthumously become a saint because he was poor, pious and deranged" (p. 198). The latter remarks: "Your grandfather is dead . . . he was defeated long before he died . . . this is one of the reasons why he became so holy" (p. 15).

37. *Vocation de l'Islam*, Paris, 1954, pp. 163 f. See also Bennabi's *Les Conditions de la Renaissance Algérienne*, Algiers, 1949, pp. 99-100.
38. In the same sense, see also Najm-ad-Dīn Bammate in *Tradition et Innovation: La Querelle des Anciens et Modernes dans le Monde Actuel*, in *Rencontres Internationales de Genève*, *xi*, 1956.
39. Including a bold comparison between the doctrine of the uncreatedness of the Qur'ān and the Incarnation of Christ (*Miḥnatān Mutashābihatān*, pp. 74-84).
40. Cairo, 1954. English translation by the present writer, Amsterdam, 1959.
41. Translated from a paper "The Meaning of Ẓulm in the Qur'ān" read to the Arabic Academy in Cairo in 1956. See *The Muslim World*, Vol. 59, 1959, p. 204.

## CHAPTER 7

## THE MUSLIM BROTHERHOOD

1. Altaf Ḥussein in a Foreword to F. S. Jabri, *The Spirit of Pakistan*, Karachi, 1951.
2. The words are Keith Callard's, in *Pakistan*, p. 216.
3. S. Ghāleb Khān ʿAbbāsī and A. de Zayas ʿAbbāsī, *The Structure of Islamic Polity*, Part 1, Lahore, 1952, p. 36.
4. Albert Hourani, *Arabic Thought in the Liberal Age*, London, 1962, p. 360.
5. See Is'ḥāq Mūsā al-Ḥusaynī, *Al-Ikhwān al-Muslimūn*, Beirut, 1952, chap. 6, "The Brethren and Politics". A translation of this work appeared in 1956, *The Moslem Brethren*, Beirut, by various translators. But it should be used with caution, as the translation is not always competent.
6. See Nadav Safran, "The Abolition of the Sharʿī Courts in Egypt", Parts 1 and 2, *The Muslim World*, Vol. 48, 1958, pp. 20-8 and 125-35.
7. Cairo, 1945. Translated by J. B. Hardie, *Social Justice in Islam*, Washington, 1953.
8. *Ibid.* p. 90.
9. London, 1961.

10. *Ibid.* p. 89.
11. *Ibid.* p. 36.
12. *Ibid.* p. 52.
13. Translated from the Urdu by ʿAbdul Ghanī, Lahore, 1940. His name is anglicised in various ways, such as: Syed Abulala Maudoodi.
14. See a very similar exploration of three levels of Islam in ʿUthmān Yaḥyā, "Man and his Perfection in Muslim Theology", in *The Muslim World*, Vol. 49, 1959, pp. 19-29, being a translation, by this writer, of the original French in *Toumliline, 1, Principes d'Education*, Rabat, 1958, pp. 41-56.
15. *Report of the Court*, p. 211.
16. *An Analysis of the Munir Report*, Jamāʿat-i-Islāmī publication, Karachi, 1956, trans. and edited by Khurshid Ahmad, p. 149. Here it is claimed that the Majlis-i-Shūrā, or Council, gave legal status to Quranic interpretation where the exegesis was in dispute, exercised the power of *qiyās* and *ijtihād* in a corporate way and formulated injunctions having the force of law in matters left to discretion by the *sharīʿa*. The nub here, of course, would be the "Muslim" quality of those comprising the Council.
17. Cf. *ibid.* pp. 26-7.
18. Freeland Abbott in "The Jamāʿat-i-Islāmī of Pakistan", *The Middle East Journal*, Washington, Vol. 11, No. 1, January 1957, p. 45, refers to a stabilised membership of no more than one thousand, though he notes that there is a flux of interested adherents who do not make the grade in probation. It would be a mistake to estimate the *Jamāʿat*'s influence by a statistic of this kind. He notes that between 1952 and 1956 it developed over fifty local dispensaries and in the last of those years aided almost two million patients.
19. Examples are given in *An Analysis*, pp. 73 f. The beard seems to be a symbol of the *Jamāʿat* which its detractors make a butt of ridicule.
20. Wilfred Cantwell Smith, *Modern Islam in India*, Lahore, 1943, p. 55.

CHAPTER 8

## MAWLANA AZAD AND INDIAN ISLAM

1. In *Maulana Abul Kalam Azad: A Memorial Volume*, edited by Humayun Kabir, New Delhi, 1959, p. 47.
2. Ishtiaq Ḥussein Qureshi, in "Foundations of Pakistani Culture", *The Muslim World*, Vol. 44, No. 1, January 1954, p. 8, being a paper read at the Islamic Colloquium, Princeton, in September 1953.
3. For a useful summary, with reflections, see Wilfred Cantwell Smith, *Islam in Modern History*, Princeton, 1957, chap. 6.
4. Edited by Afzal Iqbal, Lahore, 1942. He should be distinguished from the Muhammad Ali who was a main protagonist of the Lahore Aḥmadiyya, and whose English translation of the Qur'ān he keenly welcomed. See *My Life*, p. 164.
5. *Ibid.* p. 124.
6. *Ibid.* p. 127.
7. *Ibid.* p. 217.
8. *Ibid.* pp. 276-7.
9. *Ibid.* p. 226.
10. *Maulana Abu Kalam Azad, Memorial Volume*, pp. 147-8.
11. *Ibid.* p. 82.
12. See the first volume of this series, *Islamic Philosophy and Theology*.
13. *Azad*, *Memorial Volume*, p. 92. For another translation see *The Tarjumān al-Qur'ān*, translated by Syed Abdul Latif, Bombay, 1962, Vol. 1, p. xliii.
14. *Tarjumān*, pp. 47 f.
15. *Ibid.* pp. 185, 186 f.
16. *Azad*, *Memorial Volume*, p. 81.
17. *Tarjumān*, p. xlvi.
18. The phrase is used by S. A. Kamali, in "Abul Kalam Azad's Commentary on the Qur'ān", *The Muslim World*, Vol. 49, No. 1, January 1959, p. 17. He has overstated the issue at stake here in his concluding sentence (p. 18): "What he

(Azad) has done was a dangerous and scandalizing idiosyncrasy before the partition of the country. But it is a precedent of the most vital interest for thirty-five million Muslims living in India today."

19. Bombay, 1963, being a reprint of four papers by Āṣaf 'Alī-Aṣghar Fayḍi previously published.
20. *Ibid.* p. 92.
21. *Ibid.* p. 95; see also p. 54.
22. *Ibid.* p. 107.
23. *Ibid.* p. 100.
24. *Ibid.* pp. 92, 94 and 100.
25. The phrase is Fyzee's. *Ibid.* p. 98.

## CHAPTER 9

## THE SIGNIFICANCE OF TURKEY

1. Christopher Fry, *A Sleep of Prisoners*, London, 1951, p. 3.
2. Thus, for example, Zakī 'Alī, writing in *Islam in the World*, Lahore, 1938, p. 72, insists that "the reinstitution of the Caliphate in its full dignity and power is one of the vital aspirations of the Muslim world". From quite another angle H. A. R. Gibb condemns Ziya Gök-Alp's theory of "customary law" (see below) as "purely subjective". "The setting of customary law on an equal footing with the revealed law, even if it is regarded as the deposit of the historical experience or the character of a given nation, is irreconcilable with the bases of Islamic thought." *Modern Trends in Islam*, p. 92. Yet these two elements in the Turkish transformation, the one practical, the other ideological, were integral to the whole story. On the side of warm approval W. C. Smith, *Islam in Modern History*, may be cited. He writes: "The Turks are far and away the most realistic and self-critical group in present day Islam", p. 200. Or, as a very different witness, one might cite a lyrical Egyptian estimate of Atatürk, in a book of that title by Muḥammad Tawfīq, Cairo, 1936, who hails him as an apostle of Islam through his vigorous championing of state and *umma* (p. 149).

3. This link is clearly stated by Madame Halide Edib, in *Turkey Faces West*, New Haven, 1930, p. 142: "One can safely say that had not the Arabs passed over to the Allies' side it would have proved an impossible task to abolish the Caliphate in Turkey". Arab Muslims by aiding the West had given a *coup de grâce* to the caliphal unity. Atatürk registered a Turkish reaction in kind.
4. The precise date of his "discovery" of Durkheim is not established: some suggest about 1912. Cf. Uriel Heyd, *Foundations of Turkish Nationalism*, London, 1950, p. 32.
5. Heyd, *ibid.* p. 98.
6. *Op. cit.* pp. 120-1. She tells how the notion sprang up that Islam had been from the beginning uncongenial to the Turks. She compares D. H. Lawrence, *The Plumed Serpent*, depicting a similar tendency in Mexico where local reformers discredit Christianity on exactly comparable grounds as the disrupter of the indigenous culture that "nationalism" must recover. Cf., for contemporary Africa, W. Conlon, *The African*, New York, 1961.
7. Ahmed Emin Yalman, *Turkey in my Time*, Norman, Oklahoma, 1956, pp. 34-5. The author, as Editor of *Vatan*, a leading Turkish newspaper, played a powerful role in combating extremist exploitation of the religious issue in the fifties, and resisting encroachments of the state on academic and press freedom.
8. Heyd, *op. cit.* p. 103. He adds, Atatürk and his collaborators were convinced that "Islam and Turkish nationalism were incompatible".
9. The precise length of this period must turn on the criteria by which it is defined. The termination of the Caliphate took place in 1924: the Democratic Party took power after the elections of 1950. University theological study was *non est* from 1933 till 1948: the general educational hiatus dates from 1935 to 1949 totally, with gradual resumptions after 1949 at particular levels. Turkish was compulsorily substituted for Arabic in the *adhān* from 1933 to 1950. Dervish lodges were closed in 1925 and did not begin to reopen until 1950.
10. Albert Hourani, *A Vision of History*, p. 87.

11. Cf. Howard A. Reed, "The Religious Life of Modern Turkish Muslims", in *Islam and the West*, edited Richard N. Frye, 'S Gravenhage, 1957, p. 133. "Youth and the majority of educated people, disdain the *medrese*-trained mentality. The new Faculty of Divinity has found great difficulty in attracting suitable teachers qualified to expound Islamic philosophy and tradition."
12. Mahmut Makal, *A Village in Anatolia*, London, 1954, being a translation, with some adaptation, by Wyndham Deedes, of two Turkish works on village life, published in Istanbul in 1950 and much esteemed for their earthy idiom and realism.
13. H. A. R. Gibb, *Whither Islam?*, London, 1932, p. 345.
14. In K. W. Morgan, *op. cit.* pp. 280-1.
15. Adnan Menderes, particularly after his escape in an air crash in 1959, became a major hero of religious prejudice, or conservatism. Bitter issues of personality and a strife about a reputation, with the need either to prove hypocrisy or establish a "martyr" glory, have complicated and embittered the basic question of secularity *cum* Islam.

## CHAPTER 10

## AḤMADIYYA

1. For example, by Muhammad Ali (see below). The founder, he reported, denied that God ever ceased to "speak" since "speaking" is an attribute of the Divine Being. See *The Founder of the Ahmadiyya Movement*, n.d., p. 66. One may also cite Mirza Ghulam Ahmad himself in *The Teaching of Islam*, Lahore, 1910, p. 78, where he wrote: "No one has ever set a seal upon the lips of God. . . . It is true that the revelation of a perfect Law and necessary rules for the guidance of mankind has put an end to the need for a fresh law to be revealed . . . and apostleship and prophecy have reached their perfection in the holy person of our Lord and Master, the Prophet Muḥammad . . . but still an access to the sacred function of inspiration is not thereby barred."

2. Muhammad Ali, *The Founder*, pp. 83-4. The Al-Az'har Journal, *Nūr al-Islam*, in 1932–33 certainly understood the founder to have claimed prophethood. See Vol. 3, No. 7, pp. 447-63; Vol. 4, No. 1, pp. 5-17; No. 2, pp. 110-20; No. 7, pp. 459-62. The issue was only involved when the third volume of his *Barāhīn Aḥmadiyya* appeared. The early volumes had received a welcome in orthodox circles.
3. *Report of the Court of Inquiry*, p. 189. See further below.
4. Muhammad Ali, *The Holy Qur'ān*, Arabic text with English translation and Commentary, Lahore, 1st edit., 1920. *The Holy Qur'ān*, Arabic text and English translation, Rabwa, 1955, under the auspices of the Second Successor.
5. Examples may be found of the critical resentment of missions, one in a work of scholarship and another in a polemic, namely, A. L. Tibawi, *British Interests in Palestine*, Oxford, 1962, and *At-Tabshīr wa-l-Isti'mār* (Missions and Imperialism) by 'Umar Fārūkh and Muḥammad al-Khālidī, Beirut, 1953.
6. Some effort to do so may be found in the writer's *The Call of the Minaret*, New York, 1956.
7. The most fascinating, recent treatment of the whole issue is M. Kamel Hussein, *Qarya Zālima*, Cairo, 1954; see preface, and cf. Chap. 6 above.
8. Muḥammad Ali, *op. cit.* p. 34. Cf. also Mirza Ghulam Ahmad, *Fat'ḥ-Islam*, p. 17: "I have been sent in the name of the Messiah to shatter in pieces the doctrine of the Cross".
9. Cf. a book of this title, *Ahmadiyyat, or The True Islam*, Qadian, 1924, Washington, 1951. Its author was the second caliph.
10. Cf. K. Callard, *op. cit.* p. 209.
11. *Report*, p. 218.
12. *Ibid.* p. 235. See also p. 239.
13. A notable example is Khwaja Naẓīr Aḥmad, *Jesus in Heaven on Earth*, Lahore and Woking, 1952. This brings together in one large volume the various claims and allegations of numerous Ahmadi tracts. It is full of numerous misprints, misquotations and distortions, though it makes great emphasis on scholarship and evidences. It was banned in Pakistan by government order as "objectionable". When the

author petitioned to have the ban lifted, the Lahore High Court in rejecting his plea declared that its Biblical quotations had been pulled out of context against the sense of the text and that it could not but "breed an intense feeling of hatred" towards its unscrupulous authorship on the part of other communities. (See *The Statesman*, New Delhi, May 27, 1954.)

CHAPTER II

## THE STATUS OF RECURRENT THEMES

1. The best single discussion of the Islamic account of the Qur'ān will be found in Richard Bell, *Introduction to the Qur'ān*, Edinburgh, 1953. A valuable survey of Quranic exegesis in this century is that by J. M. S. Baljon, *Modern Muslim Koran Interpretation*, Leiden, 1961. For the *Manār* school, see J. Jomier, *Le Commentaire Coranique du Manār*, Paris, 1954.
2. This need not, however, be the case always. The English Bible is the most striking example of a translation which lives, a literature in its own right.
3. So, for example, a writer argued in *Nūr al-Islām* (the early name of *Majallat al-Azhar*), Cairo, 1933, Vol. 3, pp. 31 f.
4. *The Meaning of the Glorious Koran*, London, 1930. For the quotation see *Islamic Culture*, Lahore, 1931, Vol. 5, No. 3, p. 431.
5. *Majallat al-Azhar*, 1937, Vol. 7, pp. 77 f.
6. Thus Sūra 42.5: "We have sent it down an Arabic Qur'ān that you might warn the mother of the villages", i.e. Mecca. See also 39.29 and 43.2, for the emphasis on comprehension of the message (*la 'allakum ta'qilūn*) Sūra 41.44: "If We had sent it down in a foreign language, they would have said: 'What! a foreign language and he an Arab!' It is to those who believe a guidance and a healing." Clearly its Arabic form was that it might be intelligible—to Arabs.
7. Cited in Baljon, *op. cit.* p. 99.
8. See, for example, Muḥammad al-Khaḍr Ḥusayn, writing in *Liwā' al-Islām*, Cairo, November 1947, No. 5, p. 8.

9. See, for example, ʿAbd-Rabbāh Muftāḥ and Muḥammad Farīd Wajdī in *Nūr al-Islām* and *Majallat al-Az'har*, e.g. 1935, Vol. 5, p. 67, and frequent articles during Wajdī's editorship of the Journal beginning in 1933 and continuing through two decades.
10. Aḥmad Amīn, Aḥmad az-Zayyāt, ʿAbbās al-ʿAqqād and Badshah Ḥusayn, *inter alia*, might be cited in this connection.
11. Arthur Jeffery, *The Foreign Vocabulary of the Qur'ān*, Baroda, 1938.
12. A point of view upheld in conversation at the Islamic Colloquium at Lahore, 1958, by M. Sakha Ullāh, of the University of Peshawar. As reported by Dr. Daud Rahbar, he said: "By preserving the text in an unchronological arrangement the Divine purpose was to eliminate to the fullest extent the correlation of the temporal and the eternal. If the Qur'ān were preserved in the historical order it would have come to be regarded as a document of temporal nature, which it is not."
13. See Sūra 17.106: "A Qur'ān which We have recited *seriatim* that you might recite it to people at intervals". Also Sūra 20.113 warns Muḥammad not to be impatient for the Recital before it can be completed, and 25.32 explains that it was not sent down to him in one single whole in order that his "heart might be assured". To have done so, according to Sūra 6.7, would have been to invite the disbelievers' comment that a whole parchment from heaven was evident sorcery. Clearly the Qur'ān had to be a cumulative and so environmental thing, mixing itself with successive events.
14. Notably in Daud Rahbar, *God of Justice, A Study of the Ethical Doctrine of the Qur'ān*, Leiden, 1960, and in Muḥammad Kamil Husayn, on *Ẓulm*. See note 41, p. 207 above.
15. See review and discussion in *Islamic Culture*, Hyderabad, 1928, Vol. 2, pp. 146 f.
16. *Al-Hidāya wa-l-ʿIrfān fī Tafsīr al-Qur'ān bi-l-Qur'ān*, Cairo, 1930. Review in English by A. Jeffery in *Der Islam*, Vol. 20, pp. 301-8. For the Az'har reaction, see *Nūr al-Islām*, 1931, Vol. 2, pp. 163-205, and 249-81.
17. Muḥammad Aḥmad Khalafallāh's thesis was finally published, after being twice recast, in 1951.

18. *Op. cit.* Cairo, 1958, p. 131.
19. *Op. cit.* Lahore, 1948, p. 230.
20. *Ibid.* p. 211.
21. Published at Algiers, 1946.
22. *Op. cit.* p. 4.
23. *Op. cit.* pp. 175-6.
24. *Ibid.* p. 177.
25. For example, Ḥusayn ʿAbdallāh Bisalāmah, *Ḥayāt Sayyid al-ʿArab*, 4 vols., Mecca, 1945; Muḥammad Aḥmad al-Mawlā, *Muḥammad al-Mathal al-Kāmil*, Cairo, 1932; ʿAbd-ar-Raḥmān ʿAzzām, *Baṭal al-Abṭāl*, Cairo, 1938; Muḥammad al-Khaḍrī, *Nūr al-Yaqīn fī Sīrat Sayyid al-Mursalīn*, Cairo, 1935; Muḥammad Kidwai, *The Miracle of Muḥammad*, London, 1906; Qāsim ʿAlī Jairazbhai, *Muḥammad, a Mercy to all Nations*, London, 1937; F. K. Khān Durrānī, *The Great Prophet*, Lahore, 1931; K. L. Gauba, *The Prophet of the Desert*, Lahore, 1934; Aḥmad az-Zayyāt, *Waḥy ar-Risālā*, see, for example, Vol. 4, Cairo, 1956, pp. 5-8.
26. *Op. cit.* p. 186.
27. Quoted in Frithjof Schuon, *Comprendre l'Islam*, Paris, 1961, p. 44.
28. *Ḥayatī*, pp. 210-12.
29. See the present writer's *The Dome and the Rock*, London, 1964, pp. 217-18, discussing Sūra 33.53.

## CHAPTER 12

## REFLECTIONS IN PROSPECT

1. Echoing Arnold Toynbee's dictum from the previous chapter.
2. *Op. cit.* p. 194.
3. *Al-Fikr al-Islāmī al-Ḥadīth wa Ṣilatu-hu bi-l-Istiʿmār al-Gharbī*, Cairo, 1957.
4. Toynbee, *op. cit.* pp. 195 and 187.
5. Bernard Lewis, *The Middle East and the West*, London, 1964, p. 96.
6. The basis is in Sūra 2.30, where God sets man as "caliph" in the earth to rule it on His behalf. This is the charter of man's

responsible dignity, his call to mastery linked with the acknowledgement of accountability. All things are under man and he is under God.

7. "It was God", said Ṣāliḥ to the Banū Thamūd, "who made you from the earth and *settled* you therein as life-time occupiers" (Sūra 11.61). The verb in italics yields the noun for "imperialism". See *The Muslim World*, Vol. 49, No. 3, July 1959, pp. 179-82.
8. In *Christianity and History*, London, 1949, and *History and Human Relations*, London, 1951, with their reflection on the tragic in history as the perverse in man.
9. The phrase is *Min dūni 'llāh.*
10. I. H. Qureshi in *The Muslim World*, Vol. 44, No. 1, January 1954, p. 3. Cf. also the remarks of G. Makdisi, commenting on P. J. Vatikiotis, in P. W. Thayer, *Tensions in the Middle East*, Baltimore, 1958.
11. Quoted in *The Muslim World*, Vol. 48, No. 4, October 1958, p. 306, and by M. Halpern in *The Politics of Social Change in the Middle East and North Africa*, Princeton, 1963, p. 127.
12. Grunebaum, *Islam, Essays*, p. 227.
13. *The Fire Next Time*, London, 1963, p. 17. One may cite two examples from *Majallat al-Aẓ'har*, by its General Editor, Aḥmad Ḥasan az-Zayyāt: Vol. 31, 1959, pp. 33-6 and 153-7. The second passage on "Islam tackles Poverty" reviews the familiar *Zakāt*, fair-dealing, etc., and concludes: "If every Muslim observes the right of God in his wealth and follows his kind nature as to give away of his surplus and console the miserable and behave in an altruist manner and if all this finds rulers to administer it in the proper way, it will be easy then to spread love among people. As a result the ill feelings of hatred will calm in the envious, the tears of the miserable will dry, the stomach of the poor will always be in peace and the fears of the rich will cease. Prosperity then will prevail and people will enjoy the happiness of the earth and the blessing of Heaven." This in the highest organ of Islamic theology!
14. Quoted in Halpern, *op. cit.*, from *Majallat al-Aẓ'har*, Vol. 29, December 1957, pp. 481-7: "Our Social Revolution".

15. In T. Kerekes, ed. *The Arab Middle East and Muslim Africa*, London, 1961, pp. 47-61. A Christian writer is F. A. Sayegh, *Arab Unity*, New York, 1958.
16. ʿAbduh in his journal *Al-ʿUrwa al-Wuthqā* and Iqbal in *Lectures*, p. 159, where he questioned whether nationalism was more than a temporary necessity for the eviction of foreign power, after which it ought to give way to Islamic universalism. And see Bernard Lewis, *op. cit.* pp. 96 f.
17. Cairo, 1949.
18. *Yawmiyyāt Nāʾib fī-l-Aryāf*, Cairo, 1937. Trans. by A. S. Eban, as "Maze of Justice", London, 1947.

# SELECT BIBLIOGRAPHY

In some important cases books referred to in the text are noted again here for reasons of comprehension within the Bibliography. The arrangement in relation to Chapters is intended to tie the works cited with the explicit themes of discussion, though inevitably numbers of them belong with a wider reference. By this means it is hoped that they may sufficiently assist the general researcher, despite the general absence of detailed annotation impossible in the space available.

The following abbreviations have been used:

*BSOAS* *Bulletin of the School of Oriental and African Studies*, London.

*EI* *Encyclopaedia of Islam*, new edition, Leyden, London, 1954, etc.

*JWH* *Journal of World History*, Neuchatel; also called *Cahiers d'Histoire Mondiale.*

*MIDEO* *Mélanges de l'Institut Dominicain d'Études Orientales*, Cairo.

*MW* *The Muslim World*, Hartford, Conn.

## CHAPTER 1

J. M. Ahmed: *The Intellectual Origins of Egyptian Nationalism*, London, 1960.

Zakī ʿAlī: *Islam in the World*, Lahore, 1938.

George Antonius: *The Arab Awakening*, London, 1939.

A. J. Arberry and Rom Landau: *Islam Today*, London, 1939.

Edward Atiyah: *An Arab Tells his Story*, London, 1946.

—— *The Arabs*, London, 1955.

Haidar Bammate: *Visages de l'Islam*, Lausanne, 1946.

Ernst Bannerth: *Islam Heute-Morgen*, Austria, 1958.

H. J. Benda: *The Crescent and the Rising Sun*, or *Indonesian Islam under the Japanese Occupation, 1942–45*, The Hague, 1958.

Malek Bennabī: *Vocation de l'Islam*, Paris, 1952.

—— *Les Conditions de la Renaissance Algérienne*, Algiers, 1949.

M. Berger: *Bureaucracy and Society in Modern Egypt*, Princeton, 1957.

M. Berger, ed.: *New Metropolis in the Arab World*, New Delhi, 1963.

Jacques Berque: *The Arabs*, trans. from the French by Jean Stewart, London, 1964.

W. Braune: *Der Islamische Orient zwischen Vergangenheit und Zukunft*, Berne, Munich, 1960.

Raymond Charles: *L'Evolution de l'Islam*, Paris, 1960.

—— *L'Ame Musulmane*, Paris, 1958.

Colloque sur la Sociologie Musulmane, *Actes*, Sept. 1961, Bruxelles, Correspondence d'Orient, No. 5.

C. D. Cremeans: *The Arabs and the World*, London, 1964.

R. D. Ettinghausen, ed.: *Selected and Annotated Bibliography of Books and Periodicals in Western Languages dealing with the Near & Middle East*, Washington, 1952.

N. A. Fāris and M. T. Ḥusayn: *Crescent in Crisis*, Lawrence, Kansas, 1955.

Isma'il R. al-Faruqi: *On Arabism; 'Urubah and Religion*, Amsterdam, 1962.

S. N. Fisher, ed.: *Social Forces in the Middle East*, Ithaca, 1955.

M. F. Frade: *Sectas y Movimientos de Reforma en el Islam*, Tetuan, 1952.

D. S. Franck, ed.: *Islam in the Modern World*, Washington, 1951.

R. N. Frye, ed.: *Islam and the West*, 'S Gravenhage, 1957.

L. Gardet: *Connaître l'Islam*, Paris, 1958.

H. A. R. Gibb: *Modern Trends in Islam*, Chicago, 1947. A most penetrating analysis of Islamic self-direction, its forms and issues.

A. Gouilly: *L'Islam devant le Monde Moderne*, new ed., Paris, 1945.

Douglas Grant: *The Islamic Near East*, Toronto, 1960.

G. E. von Grunebaum: *Modern Islam, the Search for Cultural Identity*, Berkeley, 1962.

—— *Essays in the Nature and Growth of a Cultural Tradition*, Menasha, Wisconsin, 1955.

—— ed.: *Unity and Variety in Muslim Civilization*, Chicago, 1955.

J. E. Heyworth Dunne: *Religious and Political Trends in Modern Egypt*, Washington, 1950.

Arnold Hottinger: *The Arabs, Their History, Culture and Place in the Modern World*, London, 1963. See Parts 2 and 3.
A. Hourani: *A Vision of History*, Beirut, 1961.
—— *Arabic Thought in the Liberal Age, 1798–1939*, London, 1962.
Najla Izzedin: *The Arab World*, Chicago, 1953.
H. L. Kaster: *Islam Ohne Schleier*, Gütersloh, 1963.
J. and S. Lacouture: *Egypt in Transition*, London, 1958.
J. M. Landau: *Parliaments and Parties in Egypt*, New York, 1954.
W. Z. Laqueur: *The Middle East in Transition*, New York, 1958.
—— *Communism and Nationalism in the Middle East*, London, 1956.
D. Lerner: *The Passing of a Traditional Society*, Glencoe, Illinois, 1958.
R. Le Tourneau: *L'Islam Contemporain*, Paris, 1950.
Bernard Lewis: *The Middle East and the West*, London, 1964.
K. W. Morgan, ed.: *Islam, the Straight Path*, London, 1958. A collection of essays by Muslims.
C. A. O. van Nieuwenhuijze: *Aspects of Islam in Post Colonial Indonesia*, The Hague, 1958.
A. Nutting: *The Arabs*, London, 1964. A general history.
Richard H. Nolte, ed.: *The Modern Middle East*, 1964. A volume of essays, in which those by A. Hourani, H. Sharabi and J. Schacht are specially valuable.
H. Nuseibeh : *Ideas of Arab Nationalism*, Ithaca, 1956.
Rudi Paret, ed.: *Die Welt des Islam und Die Gegenwart*, Stuttgart, 1961. A collection of essays.
M. Rifaʿat: *The Awakening of Modern Egypt*, London, 1947. Historical.
P. Rondot: *Destin du Proche Orient*, Paris, 1959.
—— *L'Islam et les Musulmans d'aujourd'hui*, Paris, 1958–60, 2 vols.
Jean Paul Roux: *L'Islam au Proche Orient*, Paris, 1960.
D. A. Rustow: *Politics and Westernization in the Near East*, Princeton, 1956.
N. Safran: *Egypt in Search of Political Community*, Cambridge, Mass., 1961. An analysis of the intellectual and political evolution of Egypt, 1804–1952.
F. Schuon: *Comprendre l'Islam*, Paris, 1961. Eng. edit., trans. by D. M. Matheson, London, 1963.
H. Sharabi: *Government and Politics in the Middle East*, Princeton, 1962.

W. C. Smith: *Islam in Modern History*, Princeton, 1957.

—— *Modern Islam in India*, Lahore, 1943; revised edition, London, 1946.

G. W. F. Stripling: *The Ottoman Turks and the Arabs*, Urbana, Illinois, 1942.

P. W. Thayer, ed.: *Tensions in the Middle East*, Baltimore, 1958.

A. J. Toynbee: *The Islamic World since the Peace Settlement*, London, 1927.

—— *The World and the West*, London, 1953.

—— *Civilisation on Trial*, London, 1948.

Hans E. Tutsch: *From Ankara to Marrakesh*, London, 1964. A competent and up-to-date "foreign correspondent" type account of political and social developments.

T. Cuyler Young, ed.: *Near East Culture and Society*, Princeton, 1951.

Z. N. Zeine: *Arab-Turkish Relations and the Rise of Arab Nationalism*, Beirut, 1958. A useful accompaniment to G. Antonius.

Articles

L. Binder: "Radical Reform Nationalism in Syria and Egypt", *MW*, Vol. 49, 1959, pp. 213-31.

R. Caspar: "Un Aspect de la Pensée Musulmane Moderne: Le Renouveau de Moʿtazilisme", *MIDEO*, Vol. 4, 1957, pp. 141-201.

K. Cragg: "Religious Developments in Islam in the 20th Century", *JWH*, Vol. 3, 1956, pp. 504–24.

Jorg Kraemer: "Der Islamische Modernismus und das Griechische Erbe", *Der Islam*, Vol. 38, 1962, pp. 1-27.

H. Laoust: "Le Réformisme Orthodoxe des Salafiya et les Caractères Généraux de son Orientation Actuelle", *Revue des Études Islamiques*, Vol. 6, 1932, pp. 175-224.

Robert Montagne: "The Modern State in Africa and Asia", *Cambridge Journal*, Vol. 5, 1952, pp. 583-602.

J. Pedersen: "The Criticism of the Islamic Preacher", *Die Welt des Islams*, N.S. Vol. 2, 1952, pp. 215-31.

F. Rahman: "Internal Religious Developments in the Present Century in Islam", *JWH*, Vol. 2, 1954, pp. 862-79.

P. Rondot: "La Pratique Religieuse dans l'Islam d'aujourd'hui", in *Islam* (Studia Missionalia xi), Rome, 1961, pp. 28-50.

N. A. Ziadeh: "Cultural Trends in North Africa", *JWH*, Vol. 9, 1962, pp. 109-33. (Contains large bibliography.)

## CHAPTER 2

Jamīl ad-Dīn Aḥmad, ed.: *Speeches and writing of Mr. Jinnah*, Vol. 1, 5th ed., Lahore, 1952, Vol. 2, Lahore, 1947.
Mushtāq Aḥmad: *Government and Politics in Pakistan*, Karachi, n.d.
A. H. Albiruni: *Makers of Pakistan and Modern Muslim India*, Lahore, 1950.
B. R. Ambedkar: *Pakistan, or the Partition of India*, Bombay, 1946.
L. Binder: *Religion and Politics in Pakistan*, Berkeley, California, 1961.
Lord Birdwood: *A Continent Decides*, London, 1953.
H. Bolitho: *Jinnah, Creator of Pakistan*, London, 1954.
A. K. Brohi: *An Adventure in Self-Expression*, Karachi, 1955.
W. N. Brown: *The United States and India and Pakistan*, Cambridge, Mass., 1953.
Keith Callard: *Pakistan, a Political Study*, London, 1957.
B. M. Chaudhuri: *Muslim Politics in India*, Calcutta, 1946.
F. K. Khan-Durrani: *The Meaning of Pakistan*, Lahore, 1944.
A. R. Ghani: *Pakistan; a Select Bibliography*, Lahore, rev. ed. 1958.
S. M. Ikram, ed.: *Cultural Heritage of Pakistan*, London, 1955. (See pp. 167-83.)
F. S. Jafrī: *Spirit of Pakistan*, Karachi, 1951.
Ivor Jennings: *Constitutional Problems in Pakistan*, London, 1957.
Liaquat Ali Khan: *Pakistan, the Heart of Asia*, Cambridge, Mass., 1951.
E. W. R. Lumby: *The Transfer of Power in India*, London, 1954.
V. P. Menon: *The Transfer of Power in India*, Bombay, 1957.
A. K. Nazmul-Karīm: *Changing Society in India and Pakistan*, Dacca, 1956.
K. J. Newman: *Essays on the Constitution of Pakistan*, Dacca, 1956.
C. H. Philips: *Evolution of India and Pakistan, 1858–1947*, London, 1962.
I. H. Qureshi: *Pakistan, an Islamic Democracy*, Lahore, n.d.
—— *The Pakistani Way of Life*, New York, 1956.
C. Raḥmat Ali: *Pakistan, Fatherland of the Pak Nation*, 3rd ed., Cambridge, 1946.

M. Sadiq: *Urdu Literature in the 20th Century*, Baroda, 1947.
M. H. Saiyid: *Mohammed Ali Jinnah*, Lahore, 2nd ed., 1953.
W. C. Smith: *Pakistan, an Islamic State*, Lahore, 1951.
Percival Spear: *India, Pakistan and the West*, London (1949, 1958).
I. Stephens: *Pakistan*, London, 1963. A historical analysis.
R. Symonds: *The Making of Pakistan*, London, 1950.
M. T. Titus: *Islam in India and Pakistan*, revised ed. Madras, 1959.
R. V. Weekes: *Pakistan, Birth and Growth of a Muslim Nation*, New York, 1964.

On Sayyid Aḥmad Khān

S. M. Abdullah: *Spirit and Substance of Urdu Prose under the influence of Sayyid Ahmad Khan*, Lahore, 1940.
Syed Ahmad: *The Mohamedan Commentary on the Holy Bible*, Ghazipur, 1862.
—— *Series of Essays on the Life of Muhammad*, etc., Vol. 1, London, 1870.
J. M. S. Baljon: *The Reforms and Religious Ideas of Sayyid Ahmad Khan*, Leiden, 1949.
—— article "Aḥmad Khān" in *EI*.
G. F. I. Graham: *Life and Work of Syed Ahmad Khan*, 2nd ed., 1909.
W. W. Hunter: *The Indian Musulmans*, London, 1871.
Mustafa Khan: *An Apology for the New Light*, Allahabad, 1891.
Daud Rahbar: "Sayyid Aḥmad Khān's Principles of Exegesis", *MW*, Vol. 46, 1956, pp. 104-12, 324-35, trans. from *Taḥrīr fī Uṣūl at-Tafsīr*.
H. G. Rawlinson: "Sayyid Aḥmad Khān", *Islamic Culture* (Hyderabad), Vol. 4, 1930, pp. 389-96.

Articles on Pakistan

Aziz Ahmad: "Iqbal et La Théorie du Pakistan", *Orient*, 17, 1961, pp. 81-90.
—— "Sayyid Aḥmad Khān and Jamāl ad-Dīn al-Afghānī and Muslim India", *Studia Islamica*, Vol. 13, 1960, pp. 55-78.
W. Eberhard: "Modern Tendencies in Islam in Pakistan", *Sociologus*, 10, 1960, pp. 139-52.
A. Guimbretière: "Le Réformisme Musulman en Inde", *Orient*, 16, 1960, pp. 15-41. Deals mainly with Ahmad Khan.

Ḥāfiẓ Malik: "Religious Liberalism of Sayyid Aḥmad Khān", *MW*, Vol. 54, 1964, pp. 160-9.

F. Rahman: "Muslim Modernism in the Indo-Pakistan Sub-Continent", *BSOAS*, Vol. 21, 1958, pp. 82-99.

## CHAPTER 3

C. C. Adams: *Islam and Modernism in Egypt*, London, 1933.

Aḥmad Amīn: *Zuʿamāʾ al-Iṣlāḥ fī 'l-ʿAṣr al-Ḥadīth* ("Leaders of Reform in the Modern Age"), Cairo, 1948.

T. Khemiri and G. Kampffmeyer: *Leaders in Contemporary Arabic Literature*, London, 1930.

A. K. Maqdisī: *Background of Modern Arabic Literature*, Cairo, 1939.

Jamāl ad-Dīn al-Afghānī: *Al-ʿUrwa al-Wuthqā* (with Muḥammad ʿAbduh), Beirut, 1910, 2 vols.

—— *Ar-Raddʿalā'd-Dahriyyīn* ("The Refutation of the Materialists"), Cairo, 1903. French trans., Paris, 1942. ʿAbduh translated the original Persian into Arabic.

—— "Pages peu connues de Djamàl ad-Dīn al-Afghānī", *Orient*, 6, 1958, pp. 123-6, advocating national unity based on the Arabic tongue.

—— "Pages Choisies de Djamāl ad-Dīn", *Orient*, 21, 1962, pp. 87-115: 23, 1962, pp. 169-98: 24, 1962, pp. 125-51: and 25, 1963, pp. 141-52. Trans. by Michel Colombe from the travel diary of Jamāl ad-Dīn and well illustrating his dynamic advocacy of a militant Islam, strenuously alert and ethically vigilant.

Muḥammad al-Makhzūmī: *Khāṭirāt Jamāl ad-Dīn al-Afghānī*, Beirut, 1931. The author was his hero's secretary, and writes of his "thoughts".

Muḥammad Salām Madhkūr: *Jamāl ad-Dīn, Bāʿith an-Nahḍa al-Fikriyya fī 'sh-Sharq* ("Author of Intellectual Renewal in the East"), Cairo, 1939.

E. G. Browne: *The Persian Revolution*, London, 1910. A useful account of Al-Afghānī.

Muḥammad ʿAbduh: *Risālat al-Wārida*, Cairo, 1874.

—— *Risālat at-Tawḥīd*, Cairo, 1897, 18th ed. 1961. French trans. with Introduction by Muṣṭafā ʿAbd-ar-Rāziq and B. Michel, Paris, 1925.

—— *Tafsīr al-Qur'ān al-Ḥakīm* (with Rashīd Riḍā) Cairo, 1927–36.

—— *Al-Islām wa-r-Radd 'alā Muntaqidī-hi* ("Islam and its Critics"), Cairo, 1909.

—— *Al-Islām wa-n-Naṣrāniyya ma' al-'Ilm wa-l-Madaniyya* ("Islam and Christianity in relation to Science and Civilization"), Cairo, 1902.

—— *Durūs min al-Qur'ān al-Karīm*, Hilāl series, Cairo, 1959.

Works and articles on 'Abduh

Muḥammad Rashīd Riḍā: *Tārīkh al-Ustādh al-Imām ash-Shaykh Muḥammad 'Abduh*, 3 vols. Vol. 1, 1931 (biography): Vol. 2, 1908 (articles by 'Abduh, etc.): Vol. 3 (tributes and miscellanea), 1910, Cairo.

Muṣṭafā 'Abd-ar-Rāziq: *Muḥammad 'Abduh*, Cairo, 1919, rev. ed. 1946.

Osman Amīn: *Muḥammad 'Abduh, Essai sur ses Idées Philosophiques et Religieuses*, Cairo, 1944, Trans. Washington, 1953. "Muḥammad 'Abduh."

—— *Rā'i al-Fikr al-Miṣrī* ("The Pioneer of Egyptian Thought"), Cairo, 1955.

Muḥammad al-Bahī: *Muḥammad Abduh, Eine Untersuchung seiner Erziehungsmethode zum Nationalbewusstsein und zur Nationalem Erhebung in Aegypten*, Hamburg, 1936.

P. J. Vatikiotis: "Muḥammad 'Abduh and the Quest for a Muslim Humanism", *Arabica*, Vol. 4, 1957, pp. 55-72. See also *Islamic Culture*, Hyderabad, Vol. 31, 1957, pp. 109-26.

Muḥammad Rashīd Riḍā: see under 'Abduh, and

—— *Al-Waḥy al-Muḥammadī* ("Revelation and Muhammad"), Cairo, 1933.

—— *Yusr al-Islām wa-Uṣūl at-Tashrī' al-'Āmm*, Cairo, 1928.

Amīr Shakīb Arslān: *As-Sayyid Rashīd Riḍā*, a Biography, Damascus, 1937.

J. Jomier: *Le Commentaire Coranique du Manār*, Paris, 1954.

H. Laoust: *Le Califat dans la Doctrine de Rashid Rida*, trans. with introd. from Riḍā's *Al-Khilāfa*, Beirut, 1938.

Muṣṭafā 'Abd-ar-Rāziq: *Kitāb at-Tamhīd li-Tārīkh al-Falsafa al-Islāmiyya* ("Introductory History of Islamic Philosophy"), Cairo, 1944.

—— *Ad-Dīn wa-l-Waḥy wa-l-Islām* ("Religion, Revelation and Islam"), Cairo, 1945.

## CHAPTER 4

On Sayyid Ameer Ali, Yusuf Ali and Khuda Bukhsh, see the works discussed in the text and also:

Syed Ameer Ali: *The Ethics of Islam*, Calcutta, 1893.
—— *Personal Law of Muhammadans*, London, 1880.
—— "Memoirs", in *Islamic Culture*, Hyderabad, Vol. 5, 1931, and Vol. 6, 1932. See art. "Amīr ʿAlī" by W. C. Smith, in *EI*.
S. Khuda Bukhsh: *Maxims and Reflections*, London, 1916.
—— *Politics in Islam*, Calcutta, 1920.
—— *Love Offerings*, Calcutta, 1923.
—— *History of the Islamic Peoples*, trans. from A. Mez, Calcutta, 1914.
Abdallah Yusuf Ali: *The Idea of God in Islam*, Lahore, 1937.
—— *The Message of Islam*, London, 1940.
—— *A Cultural History of India during the British Period*, Bombay, 1940.
—— "Muslim Culture and Religious Thought", in L. S. S. O'Malley's *Modern India and the West*, London, 1941.
—— "Religious Polity in Islam", in *Islamic Culture* (Hyderabad), Vol. 7, 1933, pp. 1-21.

The main works of Muhammad Iqbal are:

*The Development of Metaphysics in Persia*, London, 1908.
*The Secrets of the Self* (Asrār-i-Khūdī), trans. with Intro. by R. A. Nicholson, London, 1920, revised edition, Lahore, 1940. See also *Notes*, by A. J. Arberry, Lahore, n.d.
*The Tulip of Sinai*, trans. by A. J. Arberry, London, 1947.
*Poems from Iqbāl*, trans. from Urdu by V. G. Kiernan, Bombay, 1949.
*Javid Namah* ("The Books of Eternity"), a section trans. by ʿAbdul-Hamīd, in *Islamic Culture*, Hyderabad, Vol. 23, 1948, pp. 343-54.
*Ramūz i-Bekhūdī*, 1917; *Payām-i-Mashrik*, 1923; (in Persian): *Bang-i-Dara*, 1924.
*Bāl-i-Jibrīl*, 1935; *Zarb-i-Kamīl*, 1936: (in Urdu).
*Persian Psalms*, trans. by A. J. Arberry, Lahore, 1948. (Zabūr-i-ʿAjam.)
*Complaint and Answer*, trans. by A. Husain, Lahore, 1943.

*The Reconstruction of Religious Thought in Islam*, Lahore, 1930, revised ed. London, 1934.
*Speeches and Statements*, Lahore, 1944.
*Letters to Jinnah*, Lahore, 1943.

There is a large and growing literature on Iqbal, the most useful, immediate introduction being:

Iqbal Singh: *The Ardent Pilgrim*, London, 1951.

and the most sensitive reckoning:

Annemarie Schimmel: *Gabriel's Wing*, Leiden, 1963.

*See also*

Abdul-Ghani and Khwaja Nur Ilahi: *Bibliography of Iqbal*, Lahore, n.d.
Shaikh Ali Akbar: *Iqbal, His Poetry and Message*, Lahore, 1932.
Anwar Beg: *The Poet of the East*, Lahore, 1935.
Bashir Ahmad Dar: *Iqbal's Philosophy of Society, an Exposition of Ramūẓ-i-Bekhūdī*, Lahore, n.d.
Ishrat Hasan Enver: *The Metaphysics of Iqbal*, Lahore, 1944.
K. G. Saiyidain: *Iqbal's Educational Philosophy*, 3rd ed. Lahore, 1945.
—— *Iqbal, the Man and His Message*, Lahore, 1949.
Sachchidananda Sinha: *Iqbal, The Poet and His Message*, Allahabad, 1947.
S. A. Vahid: *Iqbal, his Art and Thought*, Lahore, 1944.
—— *Introduction to Iqbal*, Karachi, n.d.
Various writers: *Aspects of Iqbal* (Iqbal Day Lectures), Lahore, 1938.
—— *Iqbal as a Thinker*, Lahore, 1944.
Muḥammad Ḥasan al-Aʿẓamī and Aṣ-Ṣāwa ʿAlī Shaʿlān: *Falsafat Iqbāl* ("The Philosophy of Iqbal"), Cairo, 1950.

Annemarie Schimmel: "The Idea of Prayer in Iqbāl", *MW*, Vol. 48, 1958, pp. 205-21.

## CHAPTER 5

ʿAlī ʿAbd-ar-Rāziq: *al-Islām wa-Uṣūl al-Ḥukm*, Cairo, 1925. French trans. by L. Bercher in *Revue des Études Islamiques*, Vol. 7, 1933, pp. 353-91, and Vol. 8, 1934, pp. 163-222.

—— *Min athar Muṣṭafā ʿAbd-ar-Rāziq*, Reminiscences and essays, with biography by ʿAlī ʿAbd-ar-Rāziq, and introduction by Ṭāhā Ḥusayn, Cairo, 1957.
—— *Al-Ijmāʿ fī 'sh-Sharīʿa al-Islāmiyya* ("Consensus in Islamic Law"), Cairo, 1947.
Kemal A. Faruki: *Ijmāʿ and the Gate of Ijtihād*, Karachi, 1954.
—— *Islamic Jurisprudence*, Karachi, 1962.
Muḥammad Bakhīt al-Muṭīʿī: *Ḥaqīqat al-Islām wa-Uṣūl al-Ḥukm*, Cairo, 1926. (A reply to ʿAbd-ar-Rāziq's *Uṣūl*.)

Articles

Francis Hours: "A Propos du Jeune du mois de Ramadan en Tunisie", *Orient*, 13, 1960, pp. 43-52. An interesting discussion of a recent initiative claiming, in broad terms, the force of *Ijtihād*.
Henri Laoust: "Le Reformisme Musulman dans la Littérature Arabe Contemporaine", *Orient*, 10, 1959. By an eminent French authority and deals with the main figures from Al-Afghānī to Riḍā and Al-Kawākibī: useful on *Ijtihād*.
Ṣubḥī Maḥmassānī: "Muslims: Decadence and Renaissance", *MW*, Vol. 44, 1954, pp. 186-201. A discussion by a well-known Lebanese lawyer of *Ijmāʿ* and renewal.
D. Rahbar: "Shāh Walī-Ullāh and Ijtihād", *MW*, Vol. 45, 1955, pp. 346-58.

## CHAPTER 6

The most extensive and accessible Bibliography in this field will be found in:

H. A. R. Gibb (ed. S. J. Shaw and W. R. Polk): *Studies in the Civilisation of Islam*, Boston, 1962, pp. 246-319.
S. G. Haim: *Arab Nationalism, an Anthology*, Berkeley, California, 1964.

Other significant studies are:

Amīr Shakīb Arslān: *Li-mādhā Ta'akhkhar al-Muslimūn?* ("Why are Muslims Backward?"), Cairo, 1930.
Muḥammad Kāmil Ḥusayn: *Mutanawwiʿāt*, 2 vols. ("Miscellanies"), Cairo, 1957–60.
ʿAbd-ar-Raḥmān al-Kawākibī: *Umm al-Qurā* ("Mecca, the Metropolis"), Cairo, 1931. A call to Islamic revival, reproaching

both despotism and *taqlīd* and deploring the accretions of a superstitious Ṣūfism.

Muḥammad Kurd ʿAlī: *Al-Islām wa-l-Ḥaḍāra al-ʿArabiyya* ("Islam and Arab civilisation"), 2 vols., Cairo, 1934–6.

—— *Kunūz al-Ajdād* ("Treasures of our Forbears"), Damascus, 1950. An energetic vindication of Islamic institutions and a call to the postures of renewal, by the historian of Damascus.

A. M. H. Mazyad: *Aḥmad Amīn, Advocate of Social and Literary Reform in Egypt*, Leiden, 1963. (On Amin *see also* art. "Aḥmad Amīn" by H. A. R. Gibb in *EI*.)

Muḥammad al-Muwayliḥī: *Ḥadīth ʿIsā Ibn-Hishām*, Cairo, 1907. A satire on the social life of Egypt.

Salāma Mūsā: *Tarbiyat Salāma Mūsā*, Cairo, 1947. A lively biography modelled on *The Education of Henry Adams*, and reflecting the mental and social movement of a secular humanism in the life of an Egyptian Copt. The Eng. trans. by L. D. Schuman (Leiden, 1961) has many infelicities and has to be used with caution.

ʿAbd-al-Mutaʿāl aṣ-Ṣaʿīdī: *Tārīkh al-Iṣlāḥ fī 'l-Az'har* ("The History of Reform in Al-Az'har"), Cairo, 1943.

Fā'iz Ṣayigh: *Risālat al-Mufakkir al-ʿArabī* ("The Arab Thinker's Message"), Beirut, 1955.

Maḥmūd Shaltūt: *Al-Islām, ʿAqīda wa Sharīʿa* ("Islam, Creed and Law"), Cairo, 1960. By the late Rector of Al-Az'har, this work is the first of a series of basic works planned for general translation. The title recalls Goldziher. For analysis see *Orient*, 19, 1961, pp. 27-42.

Muḥammad Farīd Wajdī: *Al-Madaniyya wa-l-Islām* ("Civilisation and Islam"), by the long-time editor of the Az'har *Journal*.

ʿAlī al-Wardī: *Usṭūrāt al-Adab ar-Rafīʿ* ("Literary Illusions"), Baghdad, 1957. A sharply radical criticism of Arab assumptions and attitudes.

Aḥmad Ḥasan az-Zayyāt: *Waḥy ar-Risāla*, 4 vols., Cairo, 1940–1956. A collection of essays on literary and social themes from *ar-Risāla*.

The main works of Ṭāhā Ḥusayn are:

*Fī 'l-Adab al-Jāhilī*, Cairo, 1927. Revision of *Fī'sh-Shiʿr al-Jāhilī*, Cairo, 1926. (See text.)

*Al-Ayyām*, Cairo, 1929. 2 vols. (See note.)

*ʿAlā Hāmish as-Sīra*, 3 vols. Cairo, 1933.

*Mustaqbal ath-Thaqāfa fī Miṣr*, Cairo, 1938. Eng. trans. by

S. Glazer: "The Future of Culture in Egypt", Washington, 1954.

*Al-Muʿadhdhabūn fī 'l-Arḍ* ("The Earth's Oppressed"), Cairo, 1949.

*Mirʾāt al-Islām* ("The Mirror of Islam"), Cairo, 1959.

*Al-Fitna al-Kubrā* ("The Great Revolt"), Cairo, 1947.

*Mirʾāt aḍ-Ḍamīr al-Ḥadīth* ("The Mirror of the Modern Conscience"), Beirut, 1949.

*Bayna Bayna* ("Here and There"), Beirut, 1954.

*See also*

P. Cachia: *Ṭāhā Ḥusayn, his place in the Egyptian Literary Renaissance*, London, 1956.

ʿAbd-ar-Raḥmān Badawī, ed.: *Li-Ṭāhā Ḥusayn*, Cairo, 1962. Essays in Honour of his 70th Birthday.

Sāmī al-Kayyālī: *Al-Fikr al-ʿArabī bayn Māḍī-hi wa Ḥāḍiri-hi* ("Arabic Thought in Transition"), with an Intro. by Ṭāhā Ḥusayn, Cairo, n.d.

—— *Maʿ Ṭāhā Ḥusayn*, Cairo, n.d. An appreciation of his literary work.

Muḥammad ʿAbd al-Qādir al-ʿImmāwī: *Muḥākamat az-Zamn, aw Ṭāhā Ḥusayn* ("Trial of the Time"), Cairo, 1942.

ʿAbbās Maḥmūd al-ʿAqqād: *Muṭālaʿāt fi-l-Kutub* ("Musings and Perusings"), Cairo, 1924.

—— *Dīwān al-ʿAqqād* ("Poems"), Cairo, 1928.

—— *ʿAbqariyyat Muḥammad* ("The Genius of Muhammad"), Cairo, 1943.

—— *ʿAbqariyyat ʿUmar*, Cairo, 1943.

—— *ʿAbqariyyat Khālid*, Cairo, 1944.

—— *Allāh: Kitāb fī-nashʾat al-ʿAqīda al-Ilāhiyya* ("God, a Study in the Development of the Doctrine of God"), Cairo, 1960.

—— *Ḥaqāʾiq al-Islām wa-Abāṭīl khuṣūmi-hi* ("The Truths of Islam and the Errors of its Opponents"), Cairo, 1962.

—— *Lā Shuyūʿiyya wa lā Istiʿmār* ("Neither Communism nor Imperialism"), Cairo, 1957.

—— *Afyūn ash-Shaʿb* ("The Opium of the People"), Cairo, 1960.

—— *al-Islām fī 'l-Qarn al-ʿIshrīn* ("Islam in the 20th Century"), Cairo, 1954.

—— *Al-Insān fī 'l-Qur'ān al-Karīm* ("Man in the Qur'ān"), Cairo, 1960.
—— *Al-Falsafa al-Qur'āniyya* ("Quranic Philosophy"), Cairo, 1947.
Muṣṭafā Luṭfī al-Manfalūṭī: *An-Naẓarāt* ("Essays"), 3 vols., 5th ed. Cairo, 1925–6.
Aḥmad Amīn: *Fayḍ al-Khāṭir* ("The Welling of Thought"), 8 vols., Cairo, from 1938.
—— *Ash-Sharq wa-l-Gharb* ("East and West"), Cairo, 1955.
—— *Zu'amā' al-Iṣlāḥ* ("Leaders of Reform"), Cairo, 1948.
—— *Ḥayātī* (Autobiography), Cairo, 1950.
Khālid Muḥammad Khālid: *Ad-Dīn fī Khidmat ash-Sha'b* ("Religion in the Service of the People"), Cairo, 1953.
—— *Hādhā aw aṭ-Ṭūfān* ("This or the Deluge"), Cairo, 1954.
—— *Ma'an 'alā 'ṭ-Ṭarīq: Muḥammad wa-l-Masīḥ*, ("Muḥammad and Christ, on the Road together"), Cairo, 1958.
—— *Muwātinūn lā Ra'āya* (Sociological Essays), Cairo, 1959.
—— *Lillāhi wa-l-Ḥurriyya* ("For God and Freedom"), Political and Economic essays, Cairo, 1958.
—— *Kamā Taḥaddath al-Qur'ān* ("The Voice of the Qur'ān"), Cairo, 1962.
—— *Afkār fī 'l-Qimma* ("Summit Thoughts"), Cairo, 1959.
—— *Ma' aḍ-Ḍamīr al-Insānī fī masīri-hi wa-maṣīri-hi* ("The Human Conscience: Ways and Ends"), Cairo, 1959.

Articles

'Abd-at-Tafāhum: "A Cairo Debate on Islam", *MW*, Vol. 44, 1954, pp. 236-52.
K. Cragg: "Then and Now in Egypt: The Reflections of Aḥmad Amīn", *Middle East Journal*, Vol. 9, 1955, pp. 28-40.
M. Ferīd-Ghāzī: "La Littérature Tunisienne Contemporaine", *Orient*, 12, 1959, pp. 131-97.
A. K. Germanus: "Trends of Contemporary Arabic Literature", *Islamic Quarterly*, London, Vol. 3, 1956, pp. 88-108, and Vol. 4, 1957, pp. 29-42, 114-39.
Muḥammad Kāmil Ḥusayn: "Modern Egyptian Literature", *Indo-Asian Culture*, Vol. 6, 1957, pp. 49-59.
Ṭāhā Ḥusayn: "Tendances Religieuses de la Littérature Egyptienne d'aujourd'hui", *L'Islam et L'Occident* (Cahiers du sud), Paris, 1946, pp. 235-41.
I. M. Ḥusayni: "Modern Arabic Literature", *JWH*, Vol. 3, 1957.

## CHAPTER 7

Muḥammad Ḥasan Aḥmad: *Al-Ikhwān al-Muslimūn fī 'l-Mīzān* ("The Muslim Brethren in the Scales"), Cairo, n.d.

Ḥasan al-Bannā': *Mudhakkirāt ad-Daʿwa wa-d-Dāʿiya* ("Notes on our Mission and its Service"), Cairo, n.d.

—— *Ar-Rasā'il ath-Thalāth* ("The Three Manifestos"), Cairo, n.d. See French trans. "Vers la Lumière", *Orient*, 4, 1957, pp. 37-62.

—— *Min Khuṭab Ḥasan al-Bannā'*, Damascus, from 1938.

Muḥammad al-Ghazālī: *Laysa min al-Islām* ("Islam is not thus"), Cairo, n.d.

—— *Naẓarāt fī 'l-Qur'ān* ("Readings in the Qur'ān"), Cairo, 1958.

—— *Fī-Mawkib ad-Daʿwa* ("In the Path of the Mission"), Cairo, n.d.

—— *Ẓalām min al-Gharb* ("Shadows from the West"), Cairo, n.d.

—— *Kayfa Nafham al-Islām* ("Our Understanding of Islam"), Cairo, n.d.

Ishāq M. al-Ḥusaynī: *Al-Ikhwān al-Muslimūn*, Beirut, 1952. Eng. trans. *The Moslem Brethren*, Beirut, 1956.

Ṭāhā Ḥusayn and others: *Hā'ulā' Hum al-Ikhwān* ("These are the Brethren"), Cairo, n.d.

Sayyid Quṭb: *Al-ʿAdāla al-Ijtimāʿiyya fī 'l-Islām*, Cairo, 1945. Eng. trans. *Social Justice in Islam*, Washington, 1953.

—— *At-Taṣwīr al-Fannī li-l-Qur'ān*, Cairo, 1945.

Francis Bertier: "L'Idéologie Politique des Frères Musulmans", *Orient*, Vol. 8, 1958, pp. 43-57.

Muṣṭafā as-Sibāʿī: "Islam as a State Religion, A Muslim Brotherhood View in Syria", trans. by R. B. Winder, *MW*, Vol. 44, 1954, pp. 215-26.

The newspaper of the *Ikhwān* was *Al-Ikhwān al-Muslimūn*, and among their magazines *Ad-Daʿwa*, *Ash-Shihāb* and *Al-Muslimūn*.

K. Ahmad: *An Analysis of the Munir Report*, Karachi, 1956.

Jamaʿat-i-Islami: *Trial of Mawdudi*, Karachi, 2nd ed., 1951.

—— *Statement of Mawdudi before the Punjab Disturbances Court of Inquiry*, Karachi, n.d.

Sayyid Abū-l-ʿAlā al-Mawdūdī: *Towards Understanding Islam*, trans. from Urdu by Abdul-Ghani, Lahore, 1940.
—— *The Islamic Concept of State*, Aligarh, 1940.
—— *Islamic Law and Constitution*, Karachi, 1955.
—— *Nationalism and India*, Pathankot, 1947.
—— *The Qadiani Problem*, Karachi, 1953.
—— *The Process of Islamic Revolution*, Lahore, 1955.

F. K. Abbott: "Maulana Maududi and Quranic Interpretation", *MW*, Vol. 48, 1958, pp. 6-19.
—— "The Jama ʿat-i-Islami of Pakistan", *Middle East Journal*, Vol. 11, 1957, pp. 37-51.

## CHAPTER 8

Syed Abdul Latif: *Towards a Re-orientation of Islamic Thought*, Hyderabad, 1954.
(Mawlana) Abul Kalam Azad: *The Tarjumān al-Qur'ān*, Vol. 1, Sūrat-al-Fātiḥa; ed. and trans. from Urdu to English by Syed. Abdul Latif, London, 1962.
—— *Speeches of Mawlana Azad, 1947–55*, Delhi, 1956.
—— *Maẓāmin-i-Abū l-Kalām Āẓād*, Essays, in Urdu, Karachi, 1960.
Aziz Ahmad: *Studies in Islamic Culture in the Indian Environment*, Oxford, 1964. Part 1, Chap. iv, on Pan-Islamism and Modernism, outlines Azād's thought, with summary discussion of Aḥmad Khān and Iqbāl also.
Mahadev Desai: *Mawlānā Abū l-Kalām Āẓād*, London, 1941. The author was Mahatma Gandhi's secretary.
A. A. A. Fyzee: *A Modern Approach to Islam*, Bombay, 1963.
—— *Conférences sur l'Islam*, Paris, 1956.
Humayun Kabir: *Science, Democracy and Islam*, London, 1955. Essays by a well-known figure in Indian Islam.
—— "Indian Muslims", *JWH*, Vol. 2, 1954–5, pp. 476-84.
D. E. Smith: *India as a Secular State*, London, 1963. A study of the theory and practice of secular government in the Hindu ethos and a multi-religious population.

A. Guimbretière: "Le Réformisme Musulman en Inde", *Orient*, 18, 1961, a continuation of the earlier study on Aḥmad Khān dealing with Iqbāl and Āzād.

S. A. Kamālī: "Abū-l-Kalām Āzād's Commentary on the Qur'ān", *MW*, Vol. 49, 1959, pp. 5-18.

Ḥāfiẓ Malik: "Abū-l-Kalām Āzād's Theory of Nationalism", *MW*, Vol. 53, 1963, pp. 33-40.

## CHAPTER 9

H. E. Allen: *The Turkish Transformation*, Chicago, 1935.

N. Berkes: *Development of Secularism in Modern Turkey.*

—— *Turkish Nationalism and Western Civilization*, trans. of selected Essays of Ziya Gökalp, London, 1959.

J. K. Birge: *Guide to Turkish Area Study*, Washington, 1949.

E. Bisbee: *The New Turks*, Philadelphia, 1915.

Nuri Eren: *Turkey Today and Tomorrow*, London, 1964.

Ziyaeddin Fahri: *Ziya Gök Alp, Sa Vie et Sa Sociologie*, Paris, 1936.

M. Halpern: *The Politics of Social Change in the Middle East and North Africa*, Princeton, 1963.

Uriel Heyd: *Foundations of Turkish Nationalism*, London, 1950.

G. Jäschke: *Der Islam in der Neuen Türkei*, Leiden, 1954.

—— *Die Türkei in den Jahren 1942–51*, Wiesbaden, 1955.

K. H. Karpat: *Turkey's Politics, the Transition to a Multi-Party System*, Princeton, 1959.

Lord Kinross: *Ataturk*, London, 1964.

Karl Krüger: *Die Neue Türkei*, Berlin, 1963. (Chaps. 11, 12 and 13.)

Bernard Lewis: *The Emergence of Modern Turkey*, London, 1961.

Geoffrey Lewis: *Turkey*, London, 1955.

H. C. Luke: *The Making of Modern Turkey*, London, 1936.

I. Orga: *Portrait of a Turkish Family*, London, 1947.

Leon Ostrorog: *The Angora Reform*, London, 1927.

R. D. Robinson: *The First Turkish Republic*, Cambridge, Mass., 1963.

D. E. Webster: *The Turkey of Ataturk*, Philadelphia, 1939.

N. Berkes: "Ziya Gökalp, His Contribution to Turkish Nationalism", *Middle East Journal*, 8, 1954, pp. 379-90.

Bernard Lewis: "Islamic Revival in Turkey", *International Affairs*, 28, 1952, pp. 38-48.

H. A. Reed: "Revival of Islam in Secular Turkey", *Middle East Journal*, Vol. 8, 1954, pp. 267-72. "The Faculty of Divinity at

Ankara", *MW*, Vol. 46, 1946, pp. 6-23, and Vol. 47, 1957, pp. 22-35. Two perceptive articles: see also Reed's "Religious life of Modern Turkish Muslims" in *Islam and the West*, R. N. Frye ed., pp. 108-48.

L. V. Thomas: "Recent Developments in Turkish Islam", *Middle East Journal*, Vol. 6, 1952, pp. 22-40.

A. L. Tibawi: "Islam and Secularism in Turkey Today", *Quarterly Review*, 609, 1956, pp. 325-37.

## CHAPTER 10

The pamphlet literature of the Ahmadiyya Movements is very considerable and is hardly susceptible of effective bibliographical treatment here. The main sources are the journals, *Review of Religions* (Qadian), *Light* (Lahore), and *Islamic Review* (Woking, England).

The two complete Quranic Commentaries are:

*The Holy Quran, Arabic Text with English Translation and Commentary*, Lahore, 1917, and numerous editions. Translator: Maulvi Muhammad Ali. Over 50,000 copies of this work have been circulated.

*The Holy Quran, Arabic Text and English Translation*, Rabwah, 1955. Translator: Maulāwī Sher ʿAlī, under the auspices of Hazrat Mirzā Bashīr ad-Dīn Maḥmūd Aḥmad, Second Successor.

Both Commentaries have extensive Prefaces.

Mirza Bashir ad-Din Ahmad: *Aḥmadiyya, or the True Islam*, Qadian, 1924, 3rd ed. Washington, 1951.

—— *The Aḥmadiyya Movement*, London, 1924.

—— *Invitation to Aḥmadiyyat*, Urdu edit. Qadian, 1926: Eng. trans. Washington, 1961.

Mīrza Ghulam Ahmad: *The Teachings of Islam*, London, 1910.

—— *Barāhīn-i-Aḥmadiyya* (in Urdu) from 1880.

—— *The Philosophy of the Teachings of Islam*, Washington, 1953.

And voluminous writings in Persian, Urdu and Arabic.

Nazir Ahmad: *Jesus in Heaven on Earth*, Lahore and Woking, 1952.

Muḥammad ʿAlī: *The Aḥmadiyya Doctrines*, Lahore, 1932.

—— *The Religion of Islam*, Lahore, 1936.

—— *A Manual of Hadith*, Lahore, n.d.

—— *The Living Thoughts of the Prophet Muḥammad*, London, 1947.

—— *The Founder of the Aḥmadiyya Movement*, Lahore, n.d.

Kamāl ad-Dīn: *The Ideal Prophet*, London, 1925.

H. J. Fisher: *Ahmadiyyah, A Study in Contemporary Islam on the West African Coast*, London, 1963. A careful and revealing enquiry into the shape of Aḥmadiyya mission in Africa.

Muḥammad Iqbāl: *Islam and Aḥmadism*, Lahore, 1936.

Muḥammad Zafrullāh Khān: *Islam, its Meaning for Modern Man*, London, 1962.

W. C. Smith: Art. "Aḥmadiyya" in *EI*, Leiden, 1954.

H. A. Walter: *The Aḥmadiyya Movement*, London, 1918.

J. T. Addison: "Aḥmadiyya Movement and its Western Propaganda", *Harvard Theological Review*, Vol. 22, 1929, pp. 1-32.

S. A. Brush: "Aḥmadiyyah in Pakistan", *MW*, Vol. 45, 1955, pp. 145-71.

H. Fisher: "Concept of Evolution in Aḥmadiyyah Thought", *MW*, Vol. 49, 1959, pp. 275-86.

## CHAPTERS 11 AND 12

K. Abdul Hakim: *Islamic Ideology*, Lahore, 1951.

Muhammad Asad: *Islam at the Crossroads*, Lahore, 1934.

—— *The Road to Mecca*, New York, 1954.

ʿAbd-ar-Raḥmān ʿAzzām: *The Eternal Message of Muḥammad*, trans. from Arabic by C. E. Farah, New York, 1964.

J. M. S. Baljon: *Modern Muslim Koran Interpretation, 1880–1960*, Leyden, 1961.

Malek Bennabi: *Le Phénomène Coranique*, Algiers, 1946.

M. Chailly et autres: *Notes et Études sur l'Islam en Afrique Noire*, Paris, 1962.

Muḥammad Ḥamīdullāh: *Le Prophète de l'Islam, I. Sa Vie et II. Son Œuvre*, Paris, 1959.

M. M. Ḥusayn: *Islam and Socialism*, Lahore, 1947.

Ṭanṭāwī Jawharī: *Al-Jawāhir fī Tafsīr al-Qur'ān al-Karīm*, Cairo, 1920.

Nizamat Jung: *Approach to the Study of the Qur'ān*, Lahore, 1947.

Tibor Kerekes, ed.: *The Arab Middle East and Muslim Africa*, London, 1961.

Muḥammad Aḥmad Khalafallāh: *Al-Fann al-Qaṣaṣī fī 'l-Qur'ān al-Karīm*, Cairo, 1950–1.
Muḥammad Yūsuf Mūsā: *Al-Qur'ān wa-l-Falsafa*, Cairo, 1959.
Sayyid Quṭb: *Fī Ẓilāl al-Qur'ān*, ("In the shade of the Qur'ān"), Cairo, 1945.
Fat'ḥī Raḍwān: *Muḥammad ath-Thā'ir al A'ẓam* ("Muḥammad the Great Revolutionary"), Cairo, 1954.
Daud Rahbar: *God of Justice, Ethical Doctrine of the Qur'ān*, Leyden, 1960.
M. R. Sharif: *Islamic Social Framework*, Lahore, 1954, rev. ed. 1963.
Ḥāfiẓ Ghulām Sarwar: *The Philosophy of the Qur'ān*, Lahore, 1938.
—— *Life of the Holy Prophet*, Lahore, 1937.
Mazheruddin Siddiqi: *Marxism or Islam*, Hyderabad, 1951.
Muḥammad Abū-Zayd: *Al-Hidāya wa-l-'Irfān fī Tafsīr al-Qur'ān bi-l-Qur'ān*, Cairo, 1930.

Muḥammad Ferīd-Ghāzī: "La Littérature Tunisienne Contemporaine", *Orient*, 12, 1959, pp. 131-55, followed by selections, pp. 157-97.
J. Jomier: "Quelques positions actuelles de l'exégèse coranique en Egypte révélées par une polémique récente (1947–51)", *MIDEO*, Cairo, Vol. 1, 1954, pp. 39-72.
Charles Malik: "The Near East, the Search for Truth", *Foreign Affairs*, Washington, Vol. 30, 1952, pp. 231-64.
A. Hourani: "Near Eastern Nationalism Yesterday and Today", *Foreign Affairs*, Vol. 42, 1963, pp. 123-36.
M. Lelong: "*Aspects de la Pensée Tunisienne Contemporaine*", *IBLA* (Revue de l'Institut des Belles Lettres Arabes, Tunis), 23, 1960, pp. 453-62.
D. Rahbar: "The Challenge of Modern Ideas and Social Values to Muslim Society", *MW*, Vol. 48, 1958, pp. 274-85. A paper at the Islamic Colloquium, Lahore, 1958.

# INDEX

(The Arabic article *al-*, with its variants such as *an-*, *ash-*, etc., is neglected in the alphabetical arrangement.)

# INDEX